The Criminal's Handbook

The Criminal's Handbook

A Practical Guide to Surviving Arrest and Incarceration in Canada

C.W. Michael

INSOMNIAC PRESS

Library and Archives Canada Cataloguing in Publication

Michael, C. W., 1960-
The criminal's handbook : a practical guide to surviving arrest and incarceration in Canada / C.W. Michael.

ISBN 978-1-55483-082-4

1. Criminal justice, Administration of--Canada. 2. Criminal law--Canada. 3. Prisoners--Legal status, laws, etc.--Canada. 4. Prisoners--Civil rights--Canada. I. Title.

HV9960.C2M53 2012 364.971 C2012-905399-6

The publisher gratefully acknowledges the support of the Department of Canadian Heritage through the Canada Book Fund.

Printed and bound in Canada

Insomniac Press
520 Princess Avenue, London, Ontario, Canada, N6B 2B8
www.insomniacpress.com

NOTE: This book is for information purposes only, not legal advice about your case or situation. If you need more information or an explanation of how the law may apply to your situation, consult a lawyer.

Canada

Contents

Foreword

From a Convict's Eyes: Criminology from the Street

Matthew G. Yeager, Ph.D., Department of Sociology
King's University College at the University of Western Ontario

C.W. Michael isn't this convict's legal name; instead, it is his pen name. Michael writes better than the vast majority of convicts in the Canadian penal system, and he knows that system up front and personal. Indeed, he is presently serving a twelve-year sentence for manslaughter, care of Her Majesty the Queen.[1] Like a lot of "rounders" or career criminals, he started in his early teens. First, he was a ward of the court as a neglected or runaway child; later, he was sent to group homes for juvenile delinquents at the tender age of thirteen. He would graduate to a stint in reform school (a youth detention facility) by age sixteen.

Michael grew up on the east side of Hamilton, Ontario. He was the product of a single-headed household: just him, an older brother, and his mother. His biological father had been to prison when he was conceived, and the family later broke up in California. His mother subsequently returned to Hamilton with her two children. While Michael did well in school—evidence of a latent writing aptitude—he was also subject to little supervision at home. Indeed, he had a

1 At the request of both the publisher and this convict, details of his offence have been excised—in part, to protect this convict's safety in prison.

bad habit of running away after arguments with his mother. So, he roamed the streets of Hamilton and developed "sticky fingers." More important, he also "hung out" with other delinquents, a key feature of youthful criminality.

Michael is currently serving a sentence for manslaughter. Why privilege the views of such a convict in this book? The discipline of criminology has traditionally neglected the standpoint of convicts. Crime is supposed to be studied by only academics, wardens, commissioners of corrections, legislators, and Department of Justice operatives.

Yet, there is a rich history of writing on crime and prisons by convicts and others who sometimes share the same perspective, often as a result of criminal or political imprisonment. One immediately thinks of great works by Aleksandr Solzhenitsyn (1974, 1975, 1976), Alfred Dreyfus (1901), Jean Genet (1964), Henri Charrière (1970) or Fyodor Dostoyevsky's *Crime and Punishment* (1914). Out of the sociological tradition, there is Clifford Shaw's *Jack-Roller* (1940) and, of course, Chic Conwell in Edwin Sutherland's classic treatise *The Professional Thief* (1937).

Noteworthy have been a number of scholarly studies of the prison and convicts by academic researchers such as Gresham Sykes (1958), Donald Clemmer (1940), and James Jacobs (1977). However, actual convicts have written a good portion of this literature, including the acclaimed author Edward Bunker (2000: 258), who said:

> Many books are written about criminals, but the writer is always observing them and the world from society's perspective. I was trying to make the reader see the world through the criminal's perspective, what he saw, what he thought, what he felt—and why.

In this rich vein, we have Roger Caron's *Go-Boy!* (1978);

Jimmy A. Lerner's recent *You Got Nothing Coming* (2002); Bruce Jackson's *In the Life* (1972); Mansfield B. Frazier's *From Behind the Wall* (1995); Caryl Chessman's *Cell 2455, Death Row* (1954); Luise Rinser's reminisces in *A Woman's Prison Journal: Germany, 1944* (1987); L. Wayne Carlson's *Breakfast with the Devil* (2001); Eva Evelyn Hanks's *Test of Faith* (2000); Julius Melnitzer's *Maximum, Minimum, Medium* (1995); Jean Harris's *They Always Call Us Ladies* (1988); Jack Olsen's biography of Geronimo Pratt, *Last Man Standing* (2000); Jennifer Gonnerman's *Life on the Outside: The Prison Odyssey of Elaine Bartlett* (2004); and Luis J. Rodriguez's *Always Running* (1993), among others.

This approach to criminology falls within an interpretive framework, examining official designations and the reactions to those deviant labels from a discourse often purposefully excluded in debates about crime and justice in society (Davis, 1975; Thomas, 1993; Kirby and McKenna, 1989). What makes this "convict" perspective unique is that it is often quite at odds with those in control of the criminal justice system. Even the solutions to crime are often quite different. Listen to a black ex-convict describe re-entry into society (Dailey, 2001: 255): "I am convinced that the prospects for post-release success depend critically on the personal resources and expectations of the parolee. If he believes that the criminal justice system will help him to re-enter society successfully, he is predestined for failure." Examine some dialogue between a free-world person and a state-raised convict in the California prison known as Folsom:

> FREE PERSON: I've heard so many people, free and convict alike, knock the justice system, but I have yet to see a comprehensive *constructive* suggestion as to how the system *should* work; what actual changes should be made?
> JOE CON: You mean a *real* system of justice?
> FP: Yes!
> JOE CON: Man, you're talking about a whole lot of change!

> FP: That bad?
>
> JC: Worse! You're talking about changing the complete concept of thinking of a whole nation. There are over two hundred million people out there that have had their thinking warped by *centuries* of propaganda put out by "public relations" departments...of hundreds of bureaucracies whose only goal is to justify their own existence and to perpetuate and guarantee their own jobs. You're also talking about doing away with, or greatly reducing the size of, many of these bureaucracies. This last is a formidable task.
>
> (*Folsom Prison Convicts*, 1976: 81-82)

On the question of poverty and class, the analysis is sometimes highly politicized, such as in the work of Randall G. Shelden (2001) and Jon Marc Taylor (1995). Jimmy Lerner colourfully summarizes it (2002: 145) as he surveyed the denizens of a Nevada state maximum-security penitentiary:

> These dawgs here are the people who are never invited to focus groups to share their views about the relative attributes of cellular versus PCS technologies. They are the castoffs, the undesirables of the Old Economy and the wretched dwellers in the crevice of the New Economy. They are the sunken-cheeked shadow people, the ungreat unwashed who silently seethe with a thousand ineffable resentments until, fueled by drink and drugs, they lash out blindly at their imagined oppressors, who often turn out to be their girlfriends or "common law."

Historically, both the natural and social sciences have pursued "methods" designed to reduce or eliminate the researcher's social values. These values are presupposed to introduce "bias" into the methodology and thus render the results less valid. Sandra Harding (1987) argues that this epistemology has always been a facade. Culture-wide, androcentric prejudices have permeated scientific inquiry, and it is false to assume otherwise. Indeed, both convict criminology and feminist epistemology reject "the notion of objectivity, neutrality, and value-freedom in the research process and instead emphasize the production of knowledge from 'below'" (Ballinger, 2003: 220).

Here, convict criminology represents a claim to particular truths not usually espoused by members of the correctional industry. In one sense, it may be even more objective, to quote Sandra Harding (1998: 153), because it provides another window of data and its interpretation to enter the social equation:

> Empiricism tried to purify science of all such bad politics by adherence to what it takes to be rigorous methods for the testing of hypotheses.... Thought that begins from the lives of the marginalized has no chance to get its critical questions voiced or heard within such an empiricist conception of the way to produce knowledge....

This is not to claim that only convict criminology can capture this knowledge or that only convicts can perform such research. This perspective, however, can transform traditional penal policies and pose a serious challenge to the dominant state discourse on dangerousness.

Among academic criminologists (i.e., those with Ph.D.s) who are also ex-convicts, this has created a small but new movement called "convict criminology." One of its chief proponents in North America was the late John Irwin (1970, 2005), and it benefited from a recent anthology by Jeffrey Ian Ross and Stephen Richards entitled *Convict Criminology* (2003).

Not only is the "inside" perspective deemed essential for proper theorizing about criminality, but ethnography also becomes central as a process to obtain this standpoint. "How do the views of ex-con academics differ from those without insider status?" (Richards and Ross, 2001: 183). The prevailing critique is that much managerial criminology, especially highly statistical number crunching, "masquerades as objective science [and] obscures the truth and supports the functions of managerial elites" (Richards and Ross, 2001: 185, 182 below):

> The problem...is that all good efforts to build reform systems seem inevitably to disadvantage the offender. This is because, despite the best intentions, reform systems were never intended to help convicts. Reformers rarely even bothered to ask the convicts what reforms they desired.

And while it hasn't received as much attention as "convict criminology," the *Journal of Prisoners on Prisons* has published a highly politicized form of convict discourse since 1988. Criminologist Robert Gaucher (1991), the former editor of the journal, has written eloquently about how National Prison Justice Day came into being as a result of the struggles for human rights by prisoner groups within Canadian penitentiaries. Lifer Victor Hassine (1995: 10) has described the reality of prisons in Pennsylvania, highlighting the caustic testimony of a former Commissioner of Corrections who was fired and then testified to "incident after incident of corruption, violence, drug dealing, and incompetence by his former DOC bosses, co-workers, and subordinates." Finally, ex-convict and academic criminologist Brian D. MacLean (1991:113-114) describes his firing at the University of British Columbia, related largely to his "master status" as a potentially violent convict. Notice that discussions of individual pathology (i.e., Italian positivism) are not prominent in this discourse.

As such, convict criminology requires "entering prisons, spending time with convicts, and learning to understand their concerns" (Richards and Ross, 2001: 185). This brings us full circle to the contribution made in *The Criminal's Handbook: A Practical Guide to Surviving Arrest and Incarceration in Canada.* Michael has spent time in solitary confinement ("the hole"), has done time in maximum security, and has been through the system as a "rounder," more than once. Along with his addition to the literature, he is still serving a long sentence and will be on high-intensity supervision for another ten years even after being released from custody. The terms of that supervision are quite strict. Any violation of a technical condition of his supervision can result in suspension and a new indictable charge carrying up to an additional ten years in penitentiary.

This work can also be read as a cautionary tale to both the public and lawbreakers. What Michael describes is hardly a "soft on crime" justice system. Indeed, one message is that "any other career [besides lawbreaking] would have been a wiser choice." But for those unfortunate souls caught up in delinquency and crime, Michael puts forth the nitty-gritty of lawyers, courtrooms, police interrogations, arrests, and the lockup side of criminal justice. And he is not averse to concluding with a little convict criminology:

> What most of the public knows about prison and the justice system is what they want to believe. They want to believe it's not cruel and unusual punishment, or at least not too cruel. The public wants to believe they are compassionate and that the system is no longer barbaric and inhumane.[…]
>
> The grey existence of being accused and found guilty of a crime and then locked in a cage fosters a personality fit for darkness. What better way can the system continue to portray to the public that it's just and true than by locking up and silencing the very people who would claim otherwise?

Introduction

The public wishes to believe the legal system and prison industry are guided by reason and fairness. Unfortunately, people on the receiving end are often restricted in contesting such a concept of model-dependent reality. As Julius Caesar so eloquently said two millennia ago, "Men freely believe that which they desire."

This handbook, born of frustration, is to assist the novice caught in the system and inform those who care. Not every reader will agree or accept what follows, especially if they have never endured a negative brush with the law or felt the helplessness and despair of prison, where time, the devourer of all things, takes its toll upon the soul.

With criminal inclination, fear of arrest is absent to most people, but courtrooms and prisons are filled with people who never imagined it could happen to them. For this reason alone, it is strongly recommended to pay close attention in reading Chapters 1 to 4, if only to avoid experiencing first-hand the turmoil of what is written in later chapters.

Unexpected troubles fall into every life. A family member, a friend, or a co-worker could be arrested, and this guide can supply information to pass along to such a friend in need—who may be trapped in a space barely twice the width of a coffin as their sanity and strength become more and more depleted by the cold stone and steel that is their crypt tonight.

The late Dr. Liz Elliott, a champion of restorative justice, taught her students at Simon Fraser University to imagine the monotony of prison life like that of the movie *Groundhog Day*, where Bill Murray's character wakens each morning, repeating the same day over and over. Elliott was a bit off in comparing a comedy to the tragedy of prison. While movies often have happy endings, people leaving the no-touch torture of prison may come out broken further, rehabilitated, or simply reloaded.

A plethora of TV crime shows and media marketing of mayhem makes it seem as if crime is rising when in fact it has been falling for decades. Sin-spinning fear merchants carefully craft such terms as *road map*, *tackling crime*, *truth in sentencing*, and *accountability* to cull billions from taxpayers. Under the rule of law, public servants have a duty to act fairly, but in the siren call to be tough on crime, more and more laws are written and, as poet Oliver Goldsmith would say, ruled by the rich to grind upon the poor.

Chapters 5 to 10 are about trying to survive prison. The words may incite some readers' anger, curiosity, confusion, open minds, or closed hearts. Humanitarian readers may think it criminally negligent that as crime rates continue falling punishment increases to keep the keepers employed. Fear too easily trumps rationality as moral hazard becomes lost in the shadows of penal power. Hard time hardens prisoners. A recent report by Francis T. Cullen et al. entitled "Prisons Do Not Reduce Recidivism" published in *The Prison Journal* states that prisoners "reenter society harboring an intensified, if not overpowering, propensity to offend." This truth of the tough-on-crime mindset will lead to more crime and a bigger deficit as reflected by Paula Mallea, research associate at the Canadian Centre for Policy Alternatives and author of *Fearmonger: Stephen Harper's Tough-on-Crime Agenda*. One can remain distrustful of my cageling's cant or a politician's rant but must continue questioning fallacies too often made true by repetition.

The final two chapters offer points of reintegration but lack suggestions for positive change. That is left to others and you, the reader. It is difficult to use words such as *release* and *offender*, knowing people may leave court or prison remaining chained to the system, have reputations stained or destroyed, or be haunted by the pillory label of offender. A prisoner is someone oppressed, but an offender is someone to disfavour—even decades later. The recent passing of the omnibus crime bill C-10 has in it the denial of pardons to certain Canadians, with future revisions likely to deny more claimants.

The anonymous Latin maxim "the people's safety is the highest law" is an obligation still exploited to control the masses at great expense. Without knowledge to enlighten us, those with power will always rule and oppress those lacking knowledge, finances, and freedom, for as William Pitt wrote a century ago, "Necessity is the plea for every infringement of human freedom. It is the argument of tyrants; it is the creed of slaves."

Being arrested is a humiliating experience, and being trapped in prison can be a helpless and horrible existence. This book will help illuminate the realities too often unrealized until it's too late. It is my hope that it will inform readers that things are not always as they seem.

C.W. Michael, July 2012

Chapter 1

Busted

My lifelong venture into crime began as a teenager. Had I known then what I know now, as the old saying goes, any other career would have been a wiser choice. "You have the right to remain silent. Anything you say can and will be used against you…!" These are the words of warning (Miranda rights in the U.S.) you will hear upon arrest, and you must pay close attention to the auxiliary verbs *can* and *will.* In simpler terms, shut up! Don't say another word until you speak to a lawyer. In fact, the first thing a lawyer will ask you is, "Did you say anything?"

The Arrest

When arrested and handcuffed, your survival instincts will trigger a "fight or flight" response, which will leave you helplessly high on full alert. In such a state of trepidation, being physically restrained, anxious, and in fear, your mind will race to find a way to escape. Those who are foolish or who become pathetically submissive will expend their energies vocally while trying to bargain their way back to freedom. Once arrested, don't try talking your way out of anything with the police. Keep quiet! Lawyer up!

The first experience of being arrested as a juvenile, or even an adult, will be memorable and likely traumatic. For the lucky ones, it only happens once. They are released on bail and later found not guilty or the charges will be tossed out. The word *lucky* can apply to anyone, guilty or innocent. If guilty, you're lucky to walk. If innocent, you're lucky you don't spend months, or years, waiting to be found innocent, because a judge can only give time to serve, not give it back. As for the financial costs, you may have to pay to be found innocent—oh well, your loss. All too often, people who have never had the displeasure of being busted can only relate their knowledge to movies, television, print, or what they have heard from others. We roll down life's highway not expecting it to happen, but as sure as death and taxes are inevitable, so too is the unexpected.

The Crime

You think it can't happen to you? Think again. As quick and easy as running a red light, you could go bumpity-bump over someone's grandmother. You could be sitting in the park, chilling with a friend who's testing a new herb. You could unwittingly have purchased stolen property. Maybe you'll be driving home, just once, after having had one too many drinks, and get that sad sick feeling in your stomach when you see those flashing lights in your rear-view mirror. You could be arrested because of a mistaken identity, false accusations, or simply being in the wrong place at the wrong time. Of course, if you knowingly break the law, already have a criminal record, or hang out with others who do, your odds of being arrested will be much higher. Still, it can happen to anyone, including the innocent. Never having broken any law—that you know of or would admit to—or having no fear of ever being arrested is no guarantee it couldn't happen. Yes, the odds are far lower for those with no criminal intentions, but, unlike the lottery, you don't have to buy a ticket to lose.

As any cop or lawyer will profess, ignorance of the law is no excuse. You can be charged for breaking a law even if that law was unknown to you. If it's a minor charge or the evidence is weak and you have no prior arrests, you likely won't even be charged. On the other hand, if the police know you have a criminal past, it's likely you will be targeted for what they call selective incapacitation and charged. Then there are offenders who knowingly break one law only to find they are later being charged with several extra, unexpected, or unheard of charges as well.

Not long ago, if someone robbed a bank, they were charged with bank robbery, tried, and off they went to prison. Now when someone robs a bank, they can also be charged with possession of a dangerous weapon, concealing a weapon, no permit for a weapon, dangerous use of a firearm, attempted murder, possession of stolen goods, car theft, endangering, conspiracy, wearing a disguise, resisting arrest, etc., and off the perp goes to prison.

On the minor end of the offender scale, if, in a fit of anger during an argument, you spit and it lands on the person with whom you are arguing, that's assault! If the spitter is female, charges are highly unlikely. If the spitter is male onto a female, charges are possible. If the spitter is male with any kind of a criminal past, charges are very likely even if the act was accidental. I'm speaking from an actual event I witnessed. Any malefactor who commits breaking and entering (a B and E) can additionally be charged for burglary with intent. The offender may have had no idea there was someone inside the house. However, if the police think the offender may have been breaking in to also assault the person inside, they will add the extra designation of intent, which is a more serious charge.

The charge of threatening has become a ridiculously abused law in today's "bitch and moan" society. I've not yet had the displeasure of this charge, but I've heard some sorry stories from others. I even know someone who did thirty days for threatening a dog. Threatening, attempted burglary, attempted fraud, attempted theft, attempted anything, conspiracy to commit, aiding and abetting, and other such charges can often be unfairly laid. If you say to anyone, even in jest, that you are going to rob a bank, kill someone, or do something illegal, you could be charged and convicted. In today's society, you can be arrested for thinking about a crime out loud. Also, if you hear someone else say something of this nature and don't rat them out, you can be arrested for not notifying the police. Oddly, if someone is dying in front of you, you're not legally bound to help (except in Quebec), but you must call the police if they talk about breaking the law!

Warrants

Police often execute arrest/search warrants at the crack of dawn. This way you are more likely to be home asleep and incoherent in bed when they rush in after kicking down your door. The only way they are legally allowed on private property without a warrant is if they are in pursuit of a fugitive or a fleeing suspect or are assisting someone they think needs immediate help. If they knock on your door, don't invite them inside. You could try being courteously hospitable, as well as foolish, if you make the mistake of inviting them inside. Maybe you just won't want your neighbours observing you being arrested or having police on your doorstep. Allowing them inside gives them full control as soon as they arrest you, and they can stay inside after you are taken away. Once inside without a warrant, they are getting a free "look around." Information given to them may not be enough to obtain a search warrant or grounds to arrest you. Once inside, they may see evidence they want or consider suspicious. It could be evidence needed to make an arrest and/or they could detain you while another cop returns with a warrant. In the U.S., any property or evidence obtained without a proper search warrant, or without permission to enter from the occupant, will not be allowed at trial. These rules are far more lax in Canadian courts.

The police may arrive only to ask questions. After questioning, they may say you are under arrest without even telling you what the charge is and then start searching. Everyone should know that the police must produce a search warrant if they come to search your home or business. The warrant must state the time of its execution and specify what area is to be searched. A judge or justice of the peace (JP) will have issued a search warrant after the police have given them the appropriate information. They, in turn, will have learned about your alleged actions from informants, witnesses, co-workers, next-door neighbours, or possibly someone you thought was a friend.

If the police knock on your door and ask to come in, first ask what it's about. They may have timed their arrival with your absence, hoping to be invited inside by your roomie or a family member. Hopefully, that person will be wise enough not to let them in. What if they come asking about your child's friend who may have stolen a bike only to see it in the hallway once they come in? Good luck trying to explain to your possibly innocent child later why they were hauled away.

If a search is carried out and evidence is found, you, or a roomie or family member, are in trouble. If the police find nothing, you may, although rarely, be able to sue for damages. One thing everyone should know is to ask a lawyer for a list of any seized items after the police have searched a residence, car, or workplace. If you don't, and you remain in custody for more than several months, you won't know what they took and you'll likely never get your property back. The exception is cash, which they are supposed to notify you to pick up. Unclaimed property is eventually destroyed or sent to a public auction. If you are stuck in jail not knowing what or if anything is being held by the police, you will lose it. If you are aware of any seized property, have someone claim it on your behalf. The authorities don't notify you to retrieve seized property, so your property could be long gone by the time you are finally released from custody.

Regardless of whether the police arrive with a warrant or just show up to ask questions, keep in mind that they likely have prepared and rehearsed their line of questioning.

Questioning

It's odd how most people would never invite a total stranger into their homes but are quite willing to do so when that stranger has a gun and a badge. We submit to authority far too easily, assuming the police must be upstanding, decent, and moral just because they have a uniform. If their investigation has nothing to do with you, family, or a friend, then it's your duty to assist them. Be aware that their questioning you is to gain information not to give any to you. This technique helps them maintain control over the investigation. They also don't go around gathering information and evidence to prove someone is innocent or set them free. They gather facts to produce a suspect or to narrow a list of suspects. Once they tunnel their vision, they don't want information that exonerates a target.

Police questioning at home can make anyone nervous. If they ask you to come down to the station, why go? Should you use your time for their convenience? You don't have to go if you're not under arrest. They may even threaten to arrest you if you don't co-operate. Such a ploy often works, and they know it will be easy to intimidate and record you at the station. They also know you will be far more nervous and fearful having them stand over you in your bedroom as you lay handcuffed on the floor. In such a state of awe, don't say anything. Stay quiet until you speak to a lawyer. They will try to get you to talk even when you're not under arrest. Remember that they have the experience you lack. Keep quiet! On the other hand, you can choose to cooperate if they arrive peacefully to speak with you about a crime done to you, family, or a friend. Be careful about volunteering unnecessary or unrelated information for their records if you value your privacy.

Where and when the police question you can give them an emotional advantage. It's oppressively dominating for them to accost you within your own personal sanctuary and it's embarrassing at work with co-workers watching. Just slapping cuffs on someone even if there's no intention of arresting them may be all that's needed to make them talk. The fear of jail time is enough to make most people want to say anything! Fear can make people say and do things they will later regret. Feelings of having one's freedom violated—of feeling vulnerable to the powerful wrath of the law—can later be followed by feeling stupid for incriminating oneself, or a friend, from something said. Any lawyer will confirm this.

The police will only give you tidbits of information they think will get you to cooperate, win you over, or steer the interview where they want it to go. If necessary, they will say terrible things about a suspect, whether true or not, with the hope that you will too. Although it's one thing to give the police info about an incident, it's quite another to give up a friend. When talking with the police about a friend, one should heed the words of E. M. Forster: "I hate the idea of causes, and if I had to choose between betraying my country and betraying my friend, I hope I should have the guts to betray my country."

Giving information to the police should be thought of as giving your life savings to an unknown charity. Any information you give, correct or slightly incorrect, could be used as well as abused later. Police can easily distort information to another witness or to the prosecuting attorney, who then distort it further in front of a judge. Faulty information will be used against the accused for years to come through prison staff and parole officers.

Some witnesses, such as informants and ex-lovers, transcend themselves and/or get a thrill from giving information to the police in order to get someone busted. For the real twisted ones who thrive on manipulating power, getting away with sending someone to jail, regardless of the truth, may be their biggest thrill of all in their boring powerless lives. You can easily be blamed for more than what was actually done and suspected of much more. If there are others who played any part in your downfall, they can focus and point all the blame on you.

During questioning, the police will likely pull the "good cop/bad cop" routine like they do on TV. Police prefer to pull this tactic on their own turf rather than yours, since it's more controllable at the station. They may interrogate you with the intent of arresting someone else based on the information they hope to obtain. They may spend hours in the course of captious questioning trying to break you down and make you say what they want to hear, regardless of the truth. In psychological terms, this is called general adaptation syndrome, i.e., alarm, resistance, exhaustion. You'll be alarmed arriving at the station; you may resist squealing or confessing; and the police will try to exhaust you into breaking down. Sadly, it's during this process that friends justify blaming you, squealing on you, or absolving themselves from guilt after ratting you out by convincing themselves that you were not really a good close friend anyway.

The police can only interrogate you for several hours before they must either charge you or let you go. They may repeatedly contact you to question you. They will try to break you as soon as possible. If they fail to do so, they may even lay a bogus charge on you to justify their actions. They can also lay one charge to hold you and upset you, hoping to elicit a response or action, while not telling you right away about other pending charges. They may pull such a move when they don't have enough info to arrest you or a friend, or they may simply be looking to strengthen their case. They may leave you alone in an interview room or cell for hours. Trapped in a barren cell, staring at a brick wall for hours, you may be willing to say anything to get out. Anything!

Pampering is another effective approach. The police may "compassionately" listen to your problems and offer words of advice or concern. They may truly seem to care, offering you coffee, a tissue for your tears, and a comforting pat. To get you to talk, they will claim you had been conned and used by someone, and then they can use you. They'll offer you smokes, jokes, and compliments and will try to make you as comfortable as possible. They'll say how important your help is to their investigation and that you should have nothing to hide if you, or someone you know, have done nothing wrong. They may even say, "We know he's your friend, but you have to tell.... It's the right thing to do."

During questioning, the police may surround and confuse their prey. This is an old Neanderthal hunting skill. It works quite well. You could say things out of defence, anger, stupidity, or confusion and then have to deal with the consequences later in court, in jail, or years later when the person you squealed on gets out of jail and bumps into you on the street one night.

The police can pressure or pamper any witness right up until the trial. Then it's all over, and if it's not you or an old friend they just convicted, they may use that person again at another time. Those who testify even get paid for testifying and sending a friend away. The police don't care about any friendships or family ties ripped apart when they turn people against each other. This is where police powers can run rampant and undetected. Their priority is to catch criminals. Some cops don't personally care if this involves ruining relationships. In fact, anything done to damage and weaken a criminal's ties to helping family and friends is a bonus to them. United we stand, divided we fall.

Abuse of power is possible in any job situation. It happens with the smiling mechanic who charges you double for a shady tuneup, the innocent babysitter who leaves the baby wallowing in wetness until only moments before you arrive home, or the respected doctor who errs only to bury the evidence six feet underground. We don't want to believe we live in a culture of deception. Demosthenes, an Athenian orator from the fourth century BCE, said it best by saying, "A man is his own easiest dupe, for what he wishes to be true he generally believes to be true." If we repeatedly tell ourselves something that was faulty from the start, replaying it with errors can burn it deeper into memory.

The police will try to influence your opinion about someone. They will start rumours and say things to shock, anger, or offend a potential witness, all in the name or law and order—*to serve and protect*. They expect that you'll accept, without question, inferences about an individual who they imply is a villain and that you'll help catch them. They can say things to news reporters, your employer, neighbours, or friends, things that are not fully true but with just enough spin to make others keep an eye on you and start talking to create suspicion. Rumours have brought down kings and nations for eons. Once you're arrested and in jail, the police can also influence any friends not to visit, write, or even accept your calls. It's all part of their way of weakening the enemy in order to win. Divide and conquer!

Cops

Many law-abiding citizens don't view the police as heroes. In this respect, police are unlike altruistic role models such as overworked medical people, daring firefighters, underpaid teachers, and volunteers who give tirelessly. Those who see the police as heroic and think they should have more powers are lambs who think they have never suffered directly from police abuse. More laws and police means less freedom. Arresting people unfairly and treating them like animals can make them angry and violent for their return to society. Many people don't want to believe the extent to which police powers are abused. Ultimately, in an unseen way, all of society suffers.

There are several kinds of police forces. The Royal Canadian Mounted Police (RCMP) monitors Northern Ontario and other provinces and maintains the Canadian Security Intelligence Service (CSIS)/Canadian Police Information Centre (CPIC) databases. In Ontario, there are city police forces as well as the Ontario Provincial Police (OPP), who monitor all rural areas, highways, and some small towns or any area of fewer than five thousand inhabitants. Quebec also has the Quebec Provincial Police (QPP). In the U.S., there are city police and state troopers to monitor rural roads, interstates, and freeways. Smaller American towns have sheriffs and deputies. Then there is the United States Marshals Service (USMS) and other U.S. agencies such as the Federal Bureau of Investigation (FBI); Central Intelligence Agency (CIA); Drug Enforcement Agency (DEA); Immigration and Naturalization Service (INS); Bureau of Alcohol, Tobacco, Firearms, and Explosives (ATF); Naval Criminal Investigative Service (NCIS); Federal Bureau of Prisons (FBOP); and the fastest growing one since 9/11, the Department of Homeland Security (DHS).

Police officers were once easily hired and would carry a gun after a minimal amount of training. Job training and education requirements have increased, as have salaries. With the authority to rule over everyone, they can put chains on anyone they choose with no compassion required. Police can use fear, intimidation, deception, physical force, massive amounts of tax dollars, and, if necessary, a bullet to achieve their goal. Their job involves catching criminals, especially really bad ones, but the prices paid and methods used are rarely fully known to the public. Limitless are the public servants who possess the desire to govern others. Police, politicians, prosecutors, victim rights groups, retributivists, etc., all hunger for power and stiffer sentencing. Such an endless hunger and throw-away-the-key attitude has dire consequences for all of society. With so many more laws called for and enforced, public freedom is slowly eroded as the police continue to be a growing force.

The public wants to believe police are basically good, criminals basically bad, and that the justice system is fair. Not all cops are good or all criminals bad, and the system is not always fair. Even the word *belief*, from the Anglo-Saxon root *lief*, means "to wish." Our perception, primarily the modification of our anticipation, is an active process conditioned by our expectations, and we adapt it to various situations.

No cop, prosecutor, judge, guard, or parole officer who make up and support the system can truly know how unfair it is without ever being on the receiving end. They may tour the jail but have never spent a single day in custody. They are on the farthest end of the justice spectrum: doling it out and harping on about it to everyone, yet never being on the other side. Many claim that faults and unfairness in the system affecting the guilty will help deter them and others from ever breaking the law again. Unfortunately, this will not deter everyone. Furthermore, the most embittered ones will be far more likely not only to commit another crime, but a harsher crime.

Rookie cops with high hopes and honest intentions may try to be decently fair and by the book but will later fall short of their ideals because of human frailty. Veteran cops, exposed to years of horrendous crimes and losing hard-worked cases, can bend their values and, if need be, the rules if it means the difference between winning and losing a case. They can excuse away any guilt by filing it under noble cause corruption, and, as in every type of career, there are veterans who wrongfully influence fellow workers, if only slightly. However, this kind of misconduct can have a profound effect on the accused. Such drastic results may not be seen or known by anyone other than the accused. For the police, busting or interrogating any first-timer is an easy target for them to attack, scare, manipulate, and groom. Their job gives them training and lots of experience on how to extract information or a confession from a witness or perp. Details of an incident can be impaired and subject to manipulation when imprinted into one's memory. Strong emotions can blur the source of memory.[i] Even witnesses to a crime that choose to speak with police can still make fatal errors.

Verisimilitude

Human passion exalts itself by reaching for the divine. We long to know the truth, to know all, and when we don't, we often profess that we do. To name is to know; to know is to control.[ii] To *know* placates the ego and lifts us above those who don't know. In talking to the police, many people feel confident about retelling an incident or recalling information about someone. Unfortunately, confidence has no relation to accuracy or nebulous recollections. Telling a story is not an act of reproduction but of recreation. Within the accretion process of memory recall, or recreating, missing bits and pieces are automatically filled in. These bits and pieces can be incorrect, influenced, or supplied incorrectly by others who add their own version. Add to this people exaggerating, lying, imagining, being afraid, or simply erring without ever knowing, or willing, to admit it later. We would all prefer to be correct and righteous rather than being wrong or admit possessing a transient memory. Even later, if we learn our own words were incorrect and have caused another person damage, we can and often diffuse our responsibility for it and/or deflect blame to others.

People who are angry, sad, confused, medicated, or intoxicated often say things they don't mean or later regret. They may also convince themselves that their verity is of value when the police are gathering information. Many people can feel important and lofty when speaking down to condemn others. We've been casting stones long before we ever even learned to speak. For centuries, people loved a good hanging. To this day, we love to watch two men get into a ring and beat each other into unconsciousness. We'll even pay the best fighters millions to do this. However, the greatest sin still around is bearing false witness.

Two thousand years ago, false witness and the wielders of justice unfairly nailed thousands of many wrongfully accused on crosses to die. Four hundred years ago, false witness, "prickers," and judges burned witches. Four decades ago, false witness of the effects of homosexuality put men in prison indefinitely. Some wielders of the law, supported by the false witness of puritans, wanted Elvis Presley arrested because of the way he moved his hips. False witness helped ignite the Iraq War. Are the witnesses who make up and support and enforce these laws always correct? *To protect society!* Over the years, millions have suffered unfairly and wrongfully because of false witness and false testimony against them. Many accusers of yesterday, not their victims, would be seen as the guilty ones today. Guilty of ignorance and false witness, we prefer to believe, today, that we are far more civilized, knowledgeable, and advanced with...*justice.*

If Grandma lends her grandson's bicycle to the paperboy and forgets to tell him, who in turn reports it stolen, the outcome can vary greatly. If the paperboy was charged before and beat the case in court, guilty or not, the police will want him more the second time around. They will ignore the fact that Grandma has a touch of Alzheimer's or the boy's claims of innocence. Months later, when he's dodging shanks in juvie, Grandma may suddenly remember that she did lend the bike out to someone, except now time has passed and the boy is long gone. It's easier to do nothing and forget the error, and errors can turn into tragedies when we refuse to correct them. It's not really classed as an error if the police say he did it before and got away with it. So everything will have worked out all right. The police *must* be correct. They wouldn't lie or deceive a helpless old woman or lock up anyone who didn't deserve it, would they?

Anything less than the truth, the whole truth, and nothing but the truth can be especially damaging in cases of domestic disputes. A fundamental attribution error is an act of self-preservation. It's when we deflect blame from ourselves onto others rather than admit we could be partly to blame, slightly wrong, or definitely mistaken. Once a suspect is charged, they become the focus of guilt. Of course, criminals cry louder than anyone about mistakes, false accusations, and the unfairness of the system, except their voices are muffled behind steel and concrete. The truth is humans blame humans because humanity is at fault.

The police may not say you, or a friend, are suspects or are about to be arrested. They prefer to have you talk first or at least try explaining yourself out of a situation. You'll only end up implicating yourself or a friend more and then get arrested anyway. The police know it's easy to get ex-business partners or ex- or jealous friends to give negative statements about you. Such statements can easily contain exaggerations and lies fuelled by hidden underlying resentments. People can avenge angst of the past by slandering you in the present. They may later be asked to repeat any statement in court and will then likely be even less willing to admit they exaggerated or lied the first time around.

The police may imply or outright lie about facts in the interview or interrogation process. When a witness or informant tells them a stretched fact or outright lie, the police will want to roll with it. Like gold fever, the police hope big tips are true. Getting one makes their job far easier. It also pampers their ego to catch a "really bad" criminal rather than just a criminal. It's the same with journalists who can alter a few choice words to make a story sensational and sell more newspapers. The worse criminals are portrayed, the better the police appear for catching them and the more support and sympathy they win from the public. Crown attorneys (a.k.a. Crowns) and judges do the same thing. If you buy a crappy pound of leafy homegrown for a few hundred dollars, the police will often claim it had a street value of several thousand. That might be true if you sold it one joint at a time to as many idiots. Victims of crime can also exaggerate their peril in order to gain more support and sympathy from the police, courts, friends, and public. Unfortunately, ulterior motives such as child custody rights, financial gains, publicity, venting frustrations, or revenge affect perception and cause destruction. It is frightening on a far grander scale trying to imagine, much less estimate, why being slightly wrong can be so damaging to the guilty. But who cares? They're guilty!

It's a known fact that innocent people get busted and carted off to prison because of faulty information. We all want to believe that even fewer, if any, actually lose their lives from such errors. Those who die or are never exonerated are lost to history, and the only thing new is the history we don't know. A tragedy that's difficult to measure, much less expose, is not just the innocent sometimes later being cleared by an appeal or a new trial, but the guilty who are painted to be far worse than they really are. In our current throwaway society, too many people still get a vicarious sense of pleasure in screaming for blood. Few can admit there is evil in the heart of each and every one of us from birth. Our vanity and hope leads us to dream that good *always* triumphs over evil. The protagonist of almost every movie and novel is a heroic figure that trumps evil in the end. In reality, if we think the guilty always get what they deserve and that truth is always brought to light in the honourable courtroom, we may be fooled and beaten by the deviant brilliance of evil itself.

Rats

Squealing on a friend or partner may get you a lighter sentence or even off entirely. Such betrayals happen often. If you are a first-timer who puts it on someone else with a record, even if you are more to blame, the police will most likely go after the prior offender. The police know inexperienced first-timers are the easiest to squeeze to make confess or turn against others. Unfortunately, when the charges are something for which you never would have gone to jail, or evidence so weak that you wouldn't even have been charged, you could be squeezed and tricked to roll on yourself and others. Fear is a crucial tool in any cop's, Crown's, or news reporter's arsenal. A lawyer can tell you the police have nothing, charges are weak, or that you'll only get probation. If you blab, you may then end up doing time or receiving a criminal record. With a more serious crime, you may be unable to avoid jail. Negotiate this later with a lawyer, not the police. It will be up to a judge to convict and sentence you. Talking to the police only tightens their grip on suspects.

Small-time criminals, first-timers, informants, witnesses, or suspects don't always get deceived into talking. People say things they forget, and then not realize it helped the police bust someone. You could say something to a snitch at a club, party, over the phone, or in a holding cell. A couple hours of interrogation and you won't likely remember where you slipped up. You'll want to believe you or one of your friends never told the police anything incriminating. After several run-ins with the law, you will see things differently and will learn to keep quiet.

Repeat offenders who always refuse to talk when detained may not even be questioned if the police know they always "lawyer up." The police and Crowns will be less likely to charge a known offender with a weak charge if they know the accused always fights it out in court. As for those offenders who the police and Crowns know usually end up pleading guilty, they are more likely to be charged. It's best to say nothing, but many people hauled in can't stop talking. They often say anything to save themselves. Some would turn in their own grandmothers. The police will often say, "Your partner has already confessed," "Your friend said you did it," "We have evidence that proves you did it," or, "Only the guilty need to call a lawyer." Gullible people fold under stress when police use the Roman strategy of divide and conquer. Police will say your neighbour, boss, wife, partner, best friend, or even the paperboy swears you did it. The police will try guessing and tossing scenarios at you, or even insult you, hoping you will react and say something in return.

Even if you lawyer up, refusing to say a single word, the police will record your expressions and posture to possibly use against you later. If they think you flinched or looked worried when asked a certain question, it will be recorded in their words to be used in court. They may say your mate was unfaithful or involved in a serious crime and stretch any rumours to win you over so you will confess, cooperate, protest, or abandon a friendship. If the police can make you dislike someone who was once a friend, then it will also clear your own conscious in ratting them out. If they're not after you or a friend, you can choose to talk freely. You may never know how the information you gave is used or misused to destroy another person. Then again, if it's used against someone who's not a friend or unknown to you, why should you care? Or should you care?

When several people are questioned in relation to a crime, the police will always focus on the weakest link: the first-timer. The inexperienced person knows the least about how the police work to manipulate emotions, trick someone into confessing, or force and coerce people into cooperating. The police will often say, "We can't promise you any thing right now," or, "It will look better in front of the judge that you cooperated." If you hear such words, respond with, "Can I call my lawyer first?" Then see how they avoid letting you call one while they continue pressing you for answers. Many people later regret cooperating with the police only to drag family and friends down. Jails are full of prisoners who have taken their fear and anger out on others for dragging them down with them. If you let anyone know some illegal act you committed or trusted them to join you on a crime, that's your mistake. There are also many selfish, jealous, and stupid people who simply refuse to go down alone. They often dig their own grave and pull others in with them to share the blame.

Statements As Evidence

In being questioned or interrogated, a smart person/suspect will refuse to give up much, if any, information. They may try to manipulate facts by putting blame onto someone else. Informants, witnesses, suspects, or victims may willingly talk to the police not because they are good people but because they want a catharsis from their boring life. It can feel exciting and powerful to help the police catch someone and help condemn them. Witnesses and people labelled victims are made to feel special and bestowed with a sense of importance in their heroic journey to help the police and Crown condemn the accused.

People rarely know that the defence attorney and the accused can later view information that was given in a statement to the police. Some accused don't even realize they are entitled to see everything their lawyer sees. It's called full disclosure and means a prosecutor is supposed to allow the defence attorney to see all evidence related to the case. The prosecuting Crown is duty bound to come forth with any exculpatory evidence. If they don't, it could be grounds for an appeal—that is, if your lawyer can discover missing facts. Unfortunately, lawyers don't like to share anything. Some defence lawyers are very tight with letting their client see evidence. The accused should always ask, if not demand, to see the transcript evidence if only to learn who said what to the authorities. What a friend tells you they said and what you read may differ considerably.

Police must now be more cautious when obtaining statements through video interviews that get transcribed. Transcripts don't show body language or what was said to any witness before they make a video statement. Having a brief chat before any interview helps win over a witness or determine what questions to ask. Inserting a few thoughts into someone's mind before any interview helps guide it too. Such subtle contamination is common and rarely detected later. With written statements, the police always wrote while someone spoke, or they would write it out later. The witness would then be asked to read and sign such facilitated statements. After a few stressful hours in the police station, then being asked to decipher some police officer's sloppy handwriting, people may just sign it to get the hell out of there, regardless of any errors. Voice recorded statements are also liable to error when transcribed to print. These don't express countenance, posture, nods of denial, eye contact, nor police intimidation and prior grooming chats. Video statements are now considered the most accurate—that is, if the truth is accurately told and not influenced beforehand by others. The prosecutor will coach Crown witnesses and show them the video before trial.

Information given to the police, courts, or doctors can go public. Unlike confessing to a priest or telling your deepest thoughts to a shrink and having that confidence protected by law, such protection may not apply to one in custody. Words you spill may even make headlines. A doctor's testimony or report may not help convict you, but it can easily hurt you down the road. After being busted, your privacy will be shattered and personal information put on paper will be read not only by the police but others in the system. Knowledge is power. Even when information is wrong, it can still be a powerful tool to use against someone. Any advantage to win is not just to "know thy opponent" but know all you can to use against them. The more private information the police or government can gather on anyone, the more power they gain. Computers allow massive storage and massive control. Police, government agencies, and parole boards now hold far more data on offenders than ever before. When info is gathered, erroneous or not, it is added to their files for later use.

When questioning witnesses, police will often empathize, toss in the occasional condolence, and compliment or offer suggestions. They will often ask test questions to check honesty. They have more psychology training than ever to use, and any first-timer can be scared, prepped, and fooled easily. Even if you think you can stick up for a friend and not say anything negative, you're still giving them information to use. The best thing you can say of any friend, if you must, is "I don't know" or "I can't remember." Unless you are supplying an alibi, it's best you don't say anything. It's also not against the law to have a terrible memory or remember an incident differently later on in court. If you can't recall parts of any original statement you gave to the police because you were under stress at the time, it's not a crime to recant. Some people simply have terrible memories, but it can later save a friend from impending judicial doom.

If you're gullible and think all police are honourable and decent and would never use excessive force, break the law, alter facts, or lie, I suggest you stop reading this book and chuck it over your shoulder. Maybe the next person to pick this up won't be so naive. Rodney King experienced police brutality, but lies can be more damaging than an act of violence. Criminals can lie, bend the truth, or use deception to attain their goal but so too can the police and witnesses. Since many believe a criminal is more likely to lie than any other person, a suspect targeted by the police is already at a disadvantage. People deceive others to get what they want or to project a wanted image. This does not mean that all police lie or that some always lie, nor does it mean all witnesses lie in court, although some do and do it very well.

Lying in a court of law is supposed to be a criminal offence. Criminal offences are supposed to be prosecuted by the police and Crown. But when they are the ones lying, what then? It is rare for a police officer or Crown to go to jail for it or even lose their job. They protect their own, if only to give the public a good image of honour. A lie on the stand, if ever caught, is quickly spun into a mistake or error by the overworked stressed-out police officer or Crown witness. Rarely are charges brought against anyone on the Crown's side for deviating from the truth on any level. An untruthful defence witness, however, might be charged. As for the police, they don't like to risk losing their job or righteous reputation by lying on the stand. They, as well as the Crown, know that such antics have the potential of undermining public confidence in the administration of justice. If caught, they simply turn it into a mistake of memory or say they misquoted their recollection rather than admit to an outright lie. The police know that if it's their word against a known criminal's, theirs will be believed. If it's several law officers' words against a criminal's—usually just bending or distorting the truth a little—it's all that is necessary to tip the scales of justice. A witness can easily do the same.

Most people don't even know the police are officially allowed to lie during any interrogation process. This makes their job easier in turning people against one another, or against you. They are careful not to get caught deceiving a helpful witness for two reasons: 1) they may need willing cooperation from that person at a later date in court or on a future matter, and 2) they don't want the public to think any less of them for using deceptive tactics. Police must maintain an image of integrity at all costs.

The police may not need to pressure, groom, or coerce anyone when gathering evidence or statements of witnesses. A guilty person may want to confess anyway. If this is not the case and the police keep asking the same questions repeatedly, they may not simply be checking to hear whether you missed any details. They may be testing the definition of insanity: "doing the same thing over and over again and expecting different results." They could be making you strengthen a story by helping you repeat it as they give you an occasional "tweak" in all the right places. After arresting a suspect and having the newspapers and gossipmongers spread their version, the police may then want a second statement from the negatively influenced witnesses.

When being interviewed or interrogated, if you have done nothing wrong, you won't have anything to worry about, right? Wrong! It can mean someone else has implicated you or a friend, and the police are looking for more info. If they seem elusive, be extra suspicious. You can try explaining yourself and talking your way out of a situation if you are sure you are absolutely innocent or can deflect blame…and still be charged!

Science

With the completion of the Human Genome Project (genetic mapping) several years ago, the forensics of genetics has become a booming industry for criminal investigators. The cost and time needed to decipher one's genetic fingerprint has plummeted. Technology will soon bring the costs down further, providing more data from a pinprick of blood at the touch of a fingertip. Unfortunately, such information is more often used to convict rather than exonerate the accused. The funds for the majority of such sciences are for the police and prosecutors to manipulate and use. Once your DNA has been left, found, or planted at the scene of a crime, you're a prime suspect and easier to be convicted in a court of law. This means officers who think they could find evidence as simple as a fallen eyelash somewhere may get a warrant from any judge to search. DNA evidence can help exonerate the accused, but it's the Crown who has unlimited finances and resources behind them, not the accused. A Crown can spend lots of taxpayer money on forensic expertise, but a legal aid lawyer will be very limited financially. The Crown can also outlast defence lawyers with motions and actions that quickly deplete a defendant's funds. The first act is getting a suspect to put up as much cash bail as possible so they will have less to use in hiring a defence attorney or others to help. Professional experts are more often consulted, retained, and used to testify for the Crown because Crowns have virtually unlimited funds.

Databanks

The police will charge, even wrongfully, more people with assault or sexual assault to obtain genetic samples for their growing databanks. The psychiatric industry, fuelled by creating as many clients as it can, also has quite a vested interest in supporting such databanks. Databanks on criminals (over 3.3 million Canadians) along with databanks on their DNA (over 322,000 profiles) are growing fast.[iii]

Bloodstains, fingerprints, hair samples, saliva, and semen can all be collected from crime scenes. Even footprints and earprints are now being collected by some police forces. There will eventually be collections of scents, airborne DNA, and body odours left at a crime scene. The police will begin using genetic samples to generate profiles of gender, age, eye and hair colour, ethnicity, etc., and possibly even habits of the accused before they are even apprehended.

You may not fear having your DNA taken, believing you have nothing to hide, but the premise of justice in a democratic society is that we are innocent until proven guilty. No one should have to defend oneself before even being accused of a crime. Such data is used to judge individuals in court as well as sentence them, with parole "risk" profiling already a much-abused reality. A police officer, anyone in the government, or anyone willing to pay a fee could soon know intimate information about you, even if you're not a convicted criminal. You only need to be arrested once.

The DNA Identification Act became law in June 2005, and all criminals now convicted of any murder, manslaughter, serious assault, or sexual assault must submit a DNA sample for the federal registry. Revisions to the act made this law retroactive for anyone still sentenced. More revisions in 2007 added additional crimes to the list, with more to follow. Other countries even take DNA samples of anyone accused of a traffic offence. The police can threaten sex charges to pressure you into squealing, confessing to other charges, or offering a DNA sample since no one wants to be labelled a sexual predator.

Since DNA can be left at the scene of a burglary, assault, or any other crime, upcoming laws will make all criminals and even suspects submit a DNA sample. If anyone even wrongfully says you threatened them, you can be charged and a sample will be taken. The police would surely prefer every Canadian, criminal or not, be in the

DNA bank to make their job easier. Face and gait recognition by cameras in public areas will be able to spot and track anyone who has ever been involved with the police or government. This can also be done with a picture on a driver's license. With a full genetic/personal profile available to them, those in power could watch you walk down the street and know you are due to drop from a coronary long before you do. Such a system will help perpetuate officially sanctioned stigmatization of anyone ever arrested or investigated by the police. Freedom and privacy are slipping away with Orwellian realities creeping in. Everyone's DNA, like barcodes, will exist to serve the controlling elite. Analyzing credit card and cell phone usage is mere child's play compared to DNA tracking.

Agencies that gather data, such as Equifax, LexisNexis, Acxiom, and ChoicePoint, alone with twenty billion files from the Cub Scouts to the CIA, sell data to banks, insurance companies, police forces, and almost anyone who pays. Some of these agencies are now amassing genetic samples. The DNA fingerprint, with its battery of fifteen gene markers, is a sort of barcode used for matching a crime scene sample to a suspect. Assessed individuals can be turned down for jobs, insurance, adoption, healthcare, and other social services based on their DNA profile. Genetic diseases, heritage, and criminal traits will be someone's subjective idea of a genetic flaw, as was the global oppression once hungrily pursued by Nazi Germany.

The collection of DNA has some positive aspects. It helps discover what handicaps or diseases one is to expect and prepare for. However, these results should be kept confidential like other private medical issues between patient and doctor. Collecting samples from violent criminals is a helpful tool for the police provided they don't abuse this new science. However, what is a violent criminal? There needs to be a clear definition. It would appear that the present definition of *violent* is any physical contact without the express permission of the person being touched regardless of the extent of contact, or a threat—direct or implied—of any potential harm to another person. Since the extent of contact necessary for application of a "violent" label may be nothing more than a push, a gentle touch, or even a verbal assault, this can leads to the abuse of this designation. The misuse of the "violent" label aids in the collection and analysis of forensic evidence, which has leapt ahead in the last two decades, assisting many prosecutors in courtroom battles.

Hair, fingerprint, and bullet lead samples along with other evidence tested by new scientific methods have been supported by the testimony of lab experts. The problem is that many of these so-called experts need nothing more than a lab coat and a business card to set up shop. Unregulated forensic labs have popped up all over North America. As of this writing, there is serious debate on the validity of their findings. Two of the ongoing debates currently raging in the U.S. have to do with hair comparison (without DNA) and ballistic metallurgy.

Neuropsychological and genetic profilers will be the justice soothsayers of this century. They, in their new ignorance, can use genetic discrimination and will condemn people to suffer for crimes not yet committed. This is already happening when offenders are evaluated and assessed for recidivism. If brain scanning were cheaper, as it will be eventually, people will be judged for the quality and amount of mirror neuron and spindle cells recently linked to empathy, the prelude to compassion. And as the "predictable" odds of reoffending increase, so too does the punishment. Offenders may be sent to higher security prisons, turned down for parole, gated, or put on a tighter leash after release all because someone "guesstimates" they will likely reoffend. (For more on gating, please see Chapter 11.)

There will be some positive support from science to aid the justice system in catching criminals as well as help reforming some of them. Such sciences will be destructive too, but this will not be as easily seen. Profilers, behaviourists, the police, Crowns, parole officers, etc., will not only view one's past but also try interpreting other potential genetic predispositions. Genes even linked to violence will help "guess" the future. Will such psychic soothsayers be much more accurate than the oracle was at Delphi? How much of the science will be faulty in the beginning? Who will suffer the most for the mistakes? Past supporters of burning witches, bloodletting, phrenology, and electroshock therapy preached the diagnostic values and power of science. As always, the greatest sorrow of the world is fuelled by the ignorance of those who hold such power over others.

As science and technology grows faster than ever, our population is also exploding. Religious rule is fading, while government rule continues to grow. So too are the laws that govern and ultimately restrict freedom by posing long-term threats to individual privacy, the primary value in a free society. How can one ever know true freedom and autonomy if so many restrictive laws are passed? There are many ridiculous laws in Canada today. In Thompson, Manitoba, for example, it is illegal to throw a snowball, and repeat offenders can get up to thirty days in jail.

Protagonists

Villain versus victim is always prime fodder to entertain and incite the public. Most people are quickly swayed to support the alleged victim and condemn the alleged villain. The villain is usually male, and it's usually the males who resort to violence, though women sometimes do ignite violent acts. Claims of child and spousal abuse are recorded and can later be used to secure sympathy, security, finances, and support from friends, counsellors, police, and the courts. However, any deceptive acts may undermine the efficacy of victim rights groups, criminal injuries boards, and other associations who are there to help those truly in need.

Some women will be advised to abandon their mates and charge them lest the mate "repeat this abuse again on the next woman." Is locking away these less-than-perfect mates the simple solution to this potential family situation? Childcare workers may also threaten to remove children from a home if a mate does not take action against the other. A woman may find herself stuck between several threatening authorities and give in. Unlike the U.S., where a victim must be willing to proceed with charging someone, Canadian law permits police to charge any person with assault even without the other's complaint or cooperation.

If people give statements about their version of an event, it helps the police determine if a law was broken. Arrests show the police are doing their job, just as convictions show prosecutors are doing theirs. The police get a collar, Crowns get a conviction, defence lawyers get a fee, and the accused gets jail time. And today's tough-on-crime advocates want even harsher and longer sentences.

Enforcement

If a "badge-heavy" cop has it in for someone, one can bet such a cop will try hard to turn others against the individual. If you are a pawn or a suspect, and the police threaten you with "unless you cooperate," why tell them anything? You can blab to save yourself at the cost of losing a friend. In our society, if you threaten anyone with harm or anything to cause fear, you can end up in jail. So why should the police be allowed to terrify people so easily?

I would prefer to get a beating from the police rather than go to jail. The threat of being struck by an officer is less fearful than being caged in prison with many violent criminals. There will be continuing violence in prison too. Even the police know there's always a "cowboy cop" who pushes his authority too far. If I were to threaten to lock my girlfriend in the basement for several days unless she admitted to her affair with the neighbour, I would be breaking the law. She may even lie just to avoid punishment or to protect him. Why are the police, the enforcers of these laws, allowed to use such acts? Threatening a suspect, a witness, or anyone with physical confinement in a cage is meant to instill fear just as raising a fist would. If the police are mean or desperate enough and think you're gullible, they would say they were going into the next room to take a rubber hose to your crying grandmother if they think it would make you tell them where your stash is hidden in her house. The police surely have many laughable memories of the ways in which they frightened and tricked people into talking, squealing, confessing, and saying things the authorities want to hear.

Overzealous police are the ones most likely to corrupt justice. There are many such officers who, once they think a perp is bad, will always try to make them look bad. Such officers will continually go out of their way to harass and arrest an individual for anything, no matter how weak the evidence or testimony is against them. If you have a previous criminal record, you will be targeted first with selective incapacitation. If they arrest and lay charges on you, bogus or not, your only hope may be a good lawyer, although weak evidence and a weak lawyer are a bad combination.

Relevance

If someone commits a terrible crime and suffers horribly for it, that may seem fair. In jurisprudence, the Latin term referred to is *lex talionis,* originating from the *Code of Hammurabi* (eighteenth century BCE), "an eye for an eye," the law of retaliation. Such a law requires the infliction of the same injury caused to another upon the wrongdoer. Such levels of inflicted hardship are often never equal. In our society, you cannot take the life of someone's child simply because they took the life of yours. If someone physically confines an individual for a day, is it fair to confine that person for years for such a crime? I've met a few prisoners inside who seemed to have been dealt a blow far more damaging than the crime they committed. Then again, I have met some heinous prisoners who got off with light sentences with whom I would never associate on the outside. Then there are people on the outside who have never broken any laws but are very cruel by nature. I suspect the greatest and most evil ones of all are the ones about whom we never know.

You may be treated fairly if you're busted on minor charges and no "cowboy cop" has a vendetta to get you or force you to inform on someone else. If you're a first-timer and/or the charges are more serious, violent, or involve others, guilty or not, expect the unexpected. If a friend says bad things about you, squeals, or tries blaming you, at least it will be a learning experience, albeit a costly one. It will hurt to discover that someone you once liked has turned on you, even if it were only minor. Aside from the pain of learning which friends are real, the worst may turn out to be learning that the truth was distorted or that outright lies were told, and you are helpless to prove these allegations false. Such untruths, exaggerations, and simplest of lies can condemn you for years to a long cold prison existence.

I have repeatedly altered the roles and scenarios between informants, witnesses, and suspects. I have also intentionally repeated information in different ways. There's a good reason for such tiring tautology. If one day you find yourself or a friend in any similar situation, you may find yourself in another role on another day. These may all play a part in the infamous experience of being busted.

Getting busted may only be the start of a nightmare slide. Being busted, strip-searched, and tossed into a cell is the "exercise of power of consent over another person."[iv] Remaining in prison may then make your troubles worse, and what may haunt you will be much of what you've just read. Shit happens! Your bad dream cannot only rise from a false witness, betrayal, or the judicial torture of an unfair system but all three regardless of innocence. Even a crime of which you are guilty and for which you deserve penal punishment can have very unexpected results. Don't expect a horrendous crime to ever be downplayed, but know that a lesser crime will often be exaggerated.

Witnesses unknown to you who talk to the police about you are just doing their civic duty. Most would never believe how damaging their words can be or bother to learn of the unseen damage done to prisoners by the system. The system is complex and esoteric at best, and as Protagoras said, "Justice, goodness, beauty, even truth—all are relative and transitory, for being man-made, they change as man changes."

Those who break the law play for high stakes. The prices paid are often much higher than they expected. If your fall from grace begins because of slight alterations in the truth, justice can falter with devastating consequences. We want to believe that justice is fair and true, but rarely is it always so. Justice is an ideal, a hopeful illusion, like expecting the sun to rise tomorrow when it's really the earth we stand upon that spins.

Chapter 2

Bail

After being told you are under arrest and what for, the police must then take you in front of a judge or justice of the peace (JP) within twenty-four hours for bail. The police know this, which is why they often detain you for hours, stalling as they gather more information from interrogations and interviews before actually charging you. If they think that you used the paperboy as fertilizer or that you're a missing Manson family member, a terrorist, or extremely violent, they'll portray you as such via the Crown's protests. Chances for bail may become slim.

Character assassination is a common practice in the courts. The police and Crown will compile a document known as an order to show cause for the judge. Unfortunately, unlike a trial, where facts are supposed to be proven, the rules are more lax at a bail hearing. You may be inaccurately portrayed in the document, but a good bail lawyer can refute most overblown claims. Even with serious charges, you may still obtain bail provided that you or someone else has not confessed to a heinous crime or if evidence is weak.

Whatever the charges are, they fall into two categories: 1) summary, or 2) indictable. A summary offence is the lesser of two evils. Charges of shoplifting, trespassing, theft under $5,000, and other misdemeanours are summary, while charges such as burglary, robbery, or murder are indictable. With minor charges, you may be released from the police station on the spot or a few hours later by signing a recognizance, i.e., a promise to appear for court. Some police stations have a JP show up with paperwork to sign for your release. In such cases, you likely won't need a lawyer to be set free. Signing your own recognizance is the quickest and easiest form of release, while a bail/surety contract (bond in the U.S.) is not as simple. Your lawyer negotiates your bail with the prosecuting Crown attorney and then puts it before a JP or judge in the courtroom. A surety may also be called to speak on your behalf and then sign a surety paper for your release.

If you are arrested on more serious felony charges, inform someone you know to contact a family member or friend for legal assistance. This can save time while sitting helpless in a cell. At the police station, after being interrogated or repeatedly refusing to talk, you will eventually be allowed to use a phone. This may mean one short call or, if you're lucky, a couple of calls. Beware: the police will record any number you call. Conversations can also be monitored. If you don't know a lawyer, call someone dependable to contact one for you. Any lawyer will usually refer you to or call another one for you, but then you're passing the ball to them. A friend outside can keep calling lawyers, trying to learn who is more experienced.

If you have no one to call, the police will provide you with a phone book or a lawyer referral number. A referral service will simply give you three random numbers from the phone book. You may have trouble locating an appropriate lawyer depending on the time you're offered use of the phone. An answering service is not much help, and not all lawyers forward their office number to their home or list their home numbers. If you don't reach a lawyer for help, the police may allow you to try again or they may take you to jail. You may spend a night in the police station, sleeping on a cold steel cell bench. In the morning, you should be taken directly to court. You may also spend a weekend at the station or in jail before going for a bail hearing. There likely won't be a phone to use at court. Phone access at the jail may be limited and calls again monitored. Be extra careful talking to prisoners about your offence, as they may be snitches or undercover cops.

If you refuse to confess or spill the beans on someone else at the police station, the police may threaten you by saying they won't allow you out on bail. This is just another tactic to make you talk. Though they can make getting bail more difficult in serious cases, claiming you're dangerous and/or a flight risk, it's really up to the JP or judge to grant bail. The type of person you are and the type of charges you have are also important. Are you a real threat to the community? Have you missed court before? Will you skip town? Do you have ties in the community, a job, a family, a home, etc.? It helps to have someone you know show up to verify facts, produce any needed documents, and offer to post bail.

If bail is granted, you and whoever bails you out then sign papers stating conditions. Cash may also have to be posted or the signed surety paper itself may work as a promissory note. If bail is broken, then 10 percent or up to the full amount may be kept or later demanded by the courts. In the U.S., bail is often executed using a bail bondsman. A bondsman accepts a deed to your house or other assets as collateral and then signs for bail at court. You often pay the bail bondsman 10 percent of the full bail, and they cover the rest. If you fail to show for court, they may use a bounty hunter to find you, because they are liable to lose money if the police can't find you. Bail bondsmen and bounty hunters are currently illegal in Canada.

Hearings

At bail hearings, lawyers hope you will continue to retain them, but you don't have to keep the same lawyer. If one hasn't come running to defend you by the time you reach the courthouse, a duty counsel lawyer will be appointed for free. Duty counsel lawyers are like the day's house lawyers and are similar to the U.S. public defenders. They may be a student lawyer or any random lawyer called upon for judicial services. They are adequate to use if your charges are not too serious and you think you will get bail. Don't let wanting bail confuse your reality. If obtaining bail seems difficult, it may be worth waiting a day or two in jail before trying. The duty counsel will give you free advice and can inquire about your status with the Crown. If a friend has arrived to help bail you out and the duty counsel says the Crown is not opposing bail, then you should get bail. The duty counsel can also call anyone you may need to show up for bail or contact a lawyer for you. If you dread spending another night in jail and can't get a lawyer right away but wish to use duty counsel, hopefully you'll get bail.

It may also help to have more than one person appear for support at your bail hearing. Your lawyer will then have the choice of who to use or, if necessary, put on the stand. It is important to have the right people appear, such as a spouse, relative, employer, friend, or neighbour. Almost anyone, except the paperboy, is better than no one, and they may only need to sign a piece of paper to bail you out. If they take the stand, they *must* assure the judge they will keep an eye on you and inform the authorities if you don't follow any conditions set by the courts. If you own a home or business, are employed, have a family to support, and are well known to the community, your chances for bail are better. You're considered stable!

A lawyer you already know, preferably a criminal lawyer and not a distant cousin's real-estate lawyer, can be better informed to tell the courts who you are. If possible, ask around about lawyers in jail or the bullpen (the prisoner holding area in court). You could ask the police, but I wouldn't. The bailiffs at court or guards at jail can also advise you of popular lawyers, but fellow prisoners will be much better informed. They have the experience to recognize which lawyers are currently good, bad, or unknown. If you hear several people say that one lawyer is good, you should be confident in using that lawyer. Be cautious of only one person's referral.

You can tell your lawyer you are homeless and jobless, but never tell the police you have nowhere to live unless you don't want bail. It's better to say you have a job even if you must stretch the truth a little. It's not as if the Crown or the judge is going to run to the phone to verify your address, employment history, or bank portfolio. A little bit of bull to make you look better, stable, and responsible can really help, but don't overdo it. If you shovel your neighbours' driveways in the winter, you can say you're a snow removal contractor. If you sell gift baskets online, you can say you're a web entrepreneur. It will also help if you have an employer who is willing to show up to bail you out. A close friend will often suffice, preferably one without a criminal record, since they could be questioned if put on the stand. Regardless of how badly you or your charges are made to look in front of a judge, you must quickly find a good bail lawyer and sureties to help you look trustworthy.

A bail hearing may last several minutes, several hours, or an entire day. It's usually less than an hour since the lawyers often haggle before you or the judge even enters the courtroom. It also depends on how many people take the stand to speak on your behalf. One or two will usually suffice. In most cases, it is better to go for bail ASAP. A Crown may not have yet prepared your case or have all your records available at your first court appearance. This also applies to out-of-town courts and/or if the police have not yet laid more charges. If you quickly get bail and the police later wish to add more charges, provided they are not more serious ones, you're already free, so your bail is often only appended, not revoked. Sometimes a Crown hopes you postpone your bail hearing, as they can't ask for a delay. This is so they can gather more information or charges against you to stop you from obtaining bail. Your lawyer may ask for a delay as well to better prepare your case, change venue, or return on another day to face a different judge they'd prefer to use.

If you lose a bail hearing, you may appeal the decision. A new hearing can take thirty days or more, but you will have to remain in custody. There is no guarantee you will get bail the next time either, but you will have had more time to prepare and possibly have a charge or two tossed out as well. Conversely, if more charges are laid while you're still in custody, obtaining bail becomes more difficult.

Charges

When your charges are serious, as long you don't have a prior history of failing to appear (FTA), breaches, failing to comply, or escape charges, your chances for getting bail can still be good. A trustworthy character, stability, and ties to your community help. What hurts is when a spouse, victim, or witness, truthfully or not, tells the police they are terrified you will come after them. Some people are afraid of the friendliest dog that passes them. Especially in cases of assault, the police will relay concerns to the Crown, who then informs the judge. Exaggerated facts or concerns from citizens, cops, or the Crown easily ruin chances for bail.

People can exaggerate an incident or their fears, which will help send you and keep you in jail. Be aware they may have ulterior motives. If an alleged victim or witness knows they are exaggerating or have lied, they may also realize you could be the only one aware of it. The fact that they had you charged and arrested can make them even more fearful of you and determined that you don't get bail. The police may never know the whole truth (they rarely do) but will inform the Crown of the slimmest chance of danger in releasing you. They may inform the Crown that there is an ongoing investigation and more charges forthcoming. Again, the police, via the Crown's cry, will inform the judge about any worried victims, witnesses, spouses, or friends, making bail higher and harder to obtain.

Once the police are called and someone points a finger, the officers try to gain full control of the situation. Even a spouse who verbally tells the police they were "struck or threatened" cannot later have the charges dropped. Years ago, it was possible for a spouse to forgive and later refuse to proceed with court action. Not anymore! If the next day they regret having played a part in someone being charged, they may not be able to stop the rolling wheels of justice.

Location

If you have a checkered past or lengthy criminal record, you can still be granted bail, although location can make a difference. Court data of bail decisions in 2000-2001 showed that 89 percent of those requesting bail succeeded, but the percentages across Ontario vary greatly. Of those arrested in Windsor, 96 percent were granted bail, while 50 percent in Kitchener and only 34 percent in Belleville were granted bail.[v] If arrested far away from home, as in another province, state, or country, your bail will be much higher and harder to obtain if the courts feel you won't return. The reality is that after getting arrested in another country on anything less than a charge of murder, if granted bail, you may never return to that country if you don't want to go on trial. Countries have various rules for extradition and enforcement does not usually apply on any charges less than murder or serious conspiracy or fraud offences. If it's another province, the charge itself may not necessitate a countrywide warrant. The police in Nova Scotia don't care if the paperboy flees to B.C. from a minor charge of bicycle theft. They will be glad he's gone and won't want to extradite his return. The radius of warrants for lesser crimes may not exceed a few hundred kilometres, although more serious charges will have a far greater reach.

Costs

Never tell a lawyer you have lots of cash. If you imply that you have or can raise any needed amount for bail, why should they do any work? If it's possible to be released on a $1,000 bail or a signature, why admit that you have $10,000 available in the bank?

The lawyer's job of dealing and haggling with the Crown for your release would be made easier if they offer $10,000 from the beginning. Your money does the job for them without their doing much work. Also, if you're on bail for a year or two, you won't collect any interest, and you could lose more money later if you break bail. If your lawyer doesn't know that you have access to so much money, or that your parents have money to burn, then they will have to work to get you a lower bail.

Letting a lawyer know you have plenty of cash will often make them drool and calculate ways to get more from you later. If they know you can easily pay for six appearances of court remands rather than two or they can bill you for extra unnecessary consultation time, they will bill you for more hours and services. Conversely, Crowns also prefer you to be depleted of funds and represented by a lowly paid legal aid lawyer rather than a highly paid successful one. A weaker opponent means an easier victory. The Crown can first try to weaken any defendant mentally by denying bail. Failing that, the Crown can weaken them financially by asking for a high cash bail and forcing extra court appearances and other procedures they know will increase the defendant's legal fees.

A bail hearing can cost anywhere from a few hundred dollars to several thousand, depending on the charges and lawyer. You can ask about expected costs, but no lawyers give written estimates. Most lawyers, except the highest priced ones, won't make you pay up front for a bail hearing but will expect a retainer before they do anything more. Lawyers don't go to trial without being paid in advance. If a lawyer gets you out on bail, you'll be more willing to give them money to keep you out too.

Not all lawyers accept legal aid, especially high-profile lawyers, unless it's a high-profile case to garner them publicity. Why should they accept legal aid when they can charge much higher rates to cash-paying customers? Still, some firms will send a rookie mouthpiece to bail court or may take on the occasional legal aid case. If you do retain a good lawyer to take legal aid, you may be lucky in being poor and never have to spend a dime. If you have assets, savings, or a job, the provincial legal aid organization will expect partial payment later. You could spend years paying it all back.

Reality

Do you really want bail? This sounds like a dumb question, but not everyone does. Some people don't have a nice home, a job, family, or friends to return to on the outside. I hate to agree with an old common jail saying, but some people are "not arrested but rescued." They may not have much of a life, or it could be spiralling downhill quickly because of drugs, alcohol, health, or some traumatic event. They may have come upon some difficult times and have nobody to help them or nowhere to live. Going to jail may not be the best option available; it may be the only one.

For some people, going to jail for a couple of months may be a welcomed respite from a cold hungry street life. There are more homeless and nearly homeless people in larger cities than most people realize. Not everyone seen walking down the street has a home to walk to, at least not always a decent, happy, safe, and comfortable one. Some would prefer to spend a few approaching winter months in jail. If you are arrested in the fall and get bail, you may not get a trial until the following spring. Then you could spend all summer in jail serving a sentence. Instead, if you refuse bail and gather some dead time before trial, you could be free the following summer. Seasonal employment may also be a factor in deciding if someone wants bail.

Sadly, staying in jail as a better alternative to being free on the streets is a cruel reality for some in an uncaring society. Even worse is keeping someone in jail for six months or longer, waiting for a trial that may garner a shorter sentence—but only if they're guilty! The police and Crown know that you are much more likely to plead guilty if you don't get bail. Pleading not guilty can mean serving more dead time than what you might eventually be sentenced to anyway. Stopping you from obtaining bail can be a victory for the police and Crown, as it helps force you to plead guilty even if you considered going to trial. It is easy for anyone who has never been charged and caged to say they would never plead guilty to something they didn't do, but if you can't obtain bail on a charge for which you may only receive a short sentence, why serve time and pay the price of a longer sentence before your trial even arrives? It's a difficult choice to make when caged, but it does happen.

Having a criminal record from pleading guilty also means less to someone who already has one. For most repeat offenders, doing the least amount of time becomes more important than having a record. The police and Crown are aware of this and will try to stop you from getting bail in the hope you will then plead guilty. They also often add extra weak charges. This is another way of manipulating the scales of justice. Both they and many repeat offenders know that laying extra charges, no matter how weak or impossible to prove, makes bail more difficult and gives the Crown more bargaining power for cutting deals. Some offenders even prefer not to get bail in order to gather up some dead time. Until recently, judges had the discretion to accept two-for-one dead time credit into account on sentencing. If you spent six months in custody, you could get a one-year sentence from the judge, who then reduces it to "time served" and you're released. In 2011, the tough-on-crime Conservative government abolished two-for-one sentencing.

Conditions

The local police usually know most of their own repeat offenders and those with whom they associate, including other criminals. Bail conditions often prohibit association with the co-accused or anyone with a criminal record. It can seem an unfair condition if your closest friends have a record. If any cop sees you with such friends in a public place or pulls you over, your bail is revoked and you are charged with a breach or failure to comply. It's not only that repeat offenders are more likely to screw up on bail; they are also easier targets for the police.

Stipulations imposed on bail can be few or many—usually a few for first-timers and many for repeat offenders. Common conditions include: keep the peace; non-association with criminals, co-accused, or victims; no drinking, no drugs; curfews; a radius of limitation on travel; and signing in regularly at the local police station. For responsible people, most bail conditions are all easy to follow, but most repeat offenders are not all that responsible. When trying for bail, many people will easily agree to any conditions at court to be set free only to regret it later. Many who are granted bail only to have it revoked wish they had never obtained it in the first place. A good option is to obtain bail first and then have your lawyer apply for a bail review a month or two later. This can be done to lessen, alter, or even remove restrictions if you can justify it. Anyone who acts as your surety can also contact the courts to revoke your bail. You will then be taken back into custody at your next court appearance, when signing in at the police station, or at any time.

Delays

If you have no one to bail you out, you can waive your hearing from the start. This allows you to request a faster trial date because you are in custody, and you can still try for bail later. Months later at a pretrial, a witness may fail to appear, evidence might seem weaker, or some charges might even be withdrawn. Bail will then be much easier to obtain. You will then have a bit of dead time to barter if you plead or are found guilty. With minor charges, if you can't sign your own recognizance or find a surety, there are agencies that may help. The Salvation Army, the John Howard Society of Canada, or the Elizabeth Fry Societies for women may offer assistance in a few cases. If they already know you, they may send someone to speak at your hearing, offer counselling, provide a place to stay, or even sign your bail. They can also help with personal and family matters.

If you are too worried about losing your job by staying in jail a few days, you may not want to put off the hearing. For some people, waiting a few extra days may mean getting a better lawyer, sureties, money, and a better chance to get bail. Even if you get bail, you may have to stay in jail while you wait for someone to sign papers or raise the amount of cash needed as set by the judge. Sometimes, it's best to have a person right there in the courtroom with cash in hand. The judge then knows your sureties are solid and the granting of bail is not a waste of time and paper on someone who says they have funds but can't raise the cash.

In some cases, before giving bail or before sentencing, the judge may order a community assessment report (CA), especially for young or new offenders. The Crown or your own lawyer may also request this if they think it will help judge you. If an assessment is required, you will have to remain in custody for approximately thirty days. A probation/parole officer (PO) will arrive to visit and interview you, then possibly your family and spouse as well. The PO will ask questions about your past, but they are not allowed to ask questions about your charges if you have not yet gone to trial. They will ask about your work history, family, and any prior convictions. They will also ask about your juvenile record, if one exists. It's your legal right to refuse them access to records such as family or children's aid reports. You will be asked to sign a release allowing those records to be viewed. Why allow them access? Once you give them consent, those records will follow you, open to the justice system, for the rest of your life. A CA can be positive or negative. It can play a minor or major role when trying for bail, or it can be totally ignored. It can and likely will be used later in sentencing, classification, or parole. Be careful what you say to the

PO. What you or any family members say to them can cause bias or come out differently, negatively, or incorrectly in the report. The report will also remain an official unchangeable document.

In trying for bail, you may want it for some charges and then plead or fight other charges. You should discuss this with a bail lawyer as well as the lawyer you plan to use for any trial. This can allow for your release at a later date. If you end up serving time on some charges, you can still be released when that time is up if you have bail on any remaining charges. When applying for parole, the board prefers that you have no outstanding charges. You can still try for parole, but if you have remaining charges without bail on them, you will automatically be denied.

Release

Your first night in jail will likely be a restless one. You may feel as if your free will has been violated. The feeling of helplessness, reminiscent of early childhood, becomes crucially painful because you can't fight from a caged crib without getting bail. If you are lucky to be released and have lots of support from friends and family, you should survive better, although you may wish to conceal your situation from many people. Being out on bail is not a proud existence, and you may live a cloistered life until your trial date arrives.

Being out on bail means limited freedom. In a way, you may feel as if you are being punished before ever going to trial. If you don't screw up on bail, it may help in receiving a lighter sentence if the charges are not too serious. You could have extra time added to any sentence if you forgot to sign in at the police station or breached any conditions. Out on bail means the police will target you for anything. If you pick up any more criminal charges, you can also be in breach for being re-charged! The judge may also not be as lenient in learning that you have screwed up while out on bail. First-timers rarely know that charges from screwing up any bail can also haunt them down the road. It will decrease the chances of being classified to a lower security prison, and parole and future attempts at bail will be more difficult. For a breach, you could be sentenced to thirty days, six months, or more and have further problems when facing a judge and the system years later.

If you are out on bail, not being allowed to drink, travel, stay out late, etc., can really suck. It will be a ghostly existence. You won't feel like a normal person while your freedom is limited and your future is in jeopardy. You'll feel as if you have lost control of your bearings and future. The feeling of helplessness can push you to the edge. You may worry or start to become paranoid, and paranoia can cost you your freedom. You may worry about being watched, forgetting to sign in on time, the police arresting you for something else, or your surety cancelling your bail. All these fears may cause you to run and hide, and then there really will be a warrant out for your arrest.

If you have settled down and been out on bail for a long time, it may or may not mean much to a judge upon sentencing. If you are attending Alcoholics Anonymous (AA), Narcotics Anonymous (NA), or counselling; remain a productive problem-free member of society while out on bail; and continue to have support from your community, you will look and fare better in court. None of this, however, can occur without first being released on bail.

Chapter 3

Lawyers

There are often three sides to every story in a court of law: 1) the version a prosecuting lawyer portrays and wants everyone to believe, 2) the version a defence lawyer portrays and wants everyone to believe, and 3) the truth. As a result of lawyers' hemming and hawing, many people, myself included, have nothing positive to say about them. Many even find the word *lawyer* and *liar* synonymous. A common joke is: How can you tell when a lawyer is lying? When their lips are moving. Quite seriously, if lying were a criminal offence easy to prove, there would be little need for lawyers. In fact, there would be few lawyers around since most would be incarcerated—provided capital punishment were not reinstated to hang all liars.

Regardless of the strength of any evidence used, if your lawyer is not as good or better than the opposing lawyer, justice may not be served upon you. Knowledge of the law, court procedures, grooming skills, manipulation of words, showmanship, putting the spin on sin, or just telling little lies that count win in the courtroom. Even the guilty can only receive their just deserts if the truth, and only the truth, is told. Unfortunately, this can't always happen, since absolute truth and honesty is only utopian idealism. In real life, the cost of winning often turns verity into a lie with the deceptive hiss from the lips of lawyers, preferably by yours, to win.

This may seem a harsh indictment of the law profession, but in the performance of their services, lawyers don't care much about the truth. Winning is their number one goal. Second to this is commanding power and/or the financial gain that comes with it. Masking this is what's best for the public and fair to one's client. Does all this amount to justice for the accused? Hardly, for the adversaries deliberate in a court of law not of justice. Before the Renaissance, people were greatly ruled and governed by cardinals, bishops, and priests. Today, it's cops, barristers, and politicians. Canada today has more than sixty-nine thousand cops and one hundred thousand lawyers.[vi]

In a civil matter such as a lawsuit, divorce, or any litigation, why should two lawyers quickly resolve a matter? Even to win, why resolve a case in an hour or a day only to gain a paltry paycheque if it can instead be dragged on for weeks or months for bigger bucks? Lawyers work for profit—as much as they can grab. True, your case may take time to resolve, but even if your chances of winning are slight or zero, no lawyer will tell you that if money can be made. They will up your odds, increasing your hope, so that you will up some fees. Their reputation is important to maintain to garner more money and clients, but if they feel they have any chance of winning, they will gamble. After all, it's not their money or freedom at stake, it's yours.

Retaining

When searching for a lawyer there are many factors to consider. In criminal matters, retaining the wrong lawyer can be a financial terror and may tip your chance of going to prison. You could lose little or big here. Even if you are guilty and considering pleading guilty, some lawyers are also better than others at making deals. Of course, that won't be listed in any lawyer directory. Choose well and remember you hired them to work for you, not the other way around. You must direct them as well as supply needed facts. It may also help to prepare your own version of events on paper. Make sure it is as accurate as possible. Tell them all you know and discuss your options and possibilities. Tell them what you want, expect, and hope for. Ask questions, demand answers, and don't accept elusive replies.

If you're a first-timer, choose a good lawyer as early as possible after several referrals. Lawyers who refer you to other lawyers may also just be referring you to their friends, former schoolmates, or distant partners. Such referrals can be worthy but should be taken with kickback cautions. There are good lawyers out there who work hard and truly care about their client getting a fair day in court, but finding one is not always easy.

In searching for a lawyer, you will find many listed in the *Yellow Pages* with ads to make them seem experienced. There's corporate law, family law, criminal law, civil law, etc. Each area of law involves using differently trained lawyers, and some lawyers dabble in more than one field to help make ends meet. On phoning any lawyer, one may claim to be a criminal lawyer even if they have never done a trial or defended anyone in criminal court for years, if ever. How would you know? Just because their ad says so or they say it themselves does not mean it's true. If you ask them, they could say they just attended the courthouse yesterday concerning a legal matter. For all you know this could mean they went there to pay a speeding ticket, so they didn't actually lie.

Don't hesitate to ask a question twice if you don't get a straight answer. Lawyers are often vague in answering questions so that they can't be held accountable later. This is why politicians are lawyers first—to master the skill of ambiguous rhetoric. If a lawyer seems elusive to any of your queries, you can interpret this in two ways: 1) they are not hearing your question properly and can't answer it, or 2) they are well practised in the art of deception and are avoiding a solid answer. If you think they aren't very convincing, don't expect them to be very persuasive in front of a judge or jury either.

Be sure to ask how long they have been in practice—criminal law practice. A new lawyer, who could be young or in their forties, may be inexperienced but hungry for work and have more desire to fight for a win. One who works in a firm may charge twice as much simply to cover overhead expenses, such as a prestigious address, administrative assistants, walls of books, and fake Picassos. Some lawyers may pool their resources and share the same office and administrative staff. These may lower or raise the fees they charge you. Many lawyers in firms will use underlings to prepare cases as well. On their own, a lawyer may be cheaper but have fewer assistants and advisors. Ask about their latest trials. Ask about the types of cases, both past and current, and about recent outcomes. Be careful, however, as they will likely exaggerate any victories and understate any losses.

Ask what they think of this or that lawyer or trial. Definitely ask how many cases like yours they have done. You may even want to get specifics before you tell them exactly what your charges are. Doing this over the phone is easy, and you could even take notes. It's best to call around 4:00 or 5:00 p.m. to catch them out of court and in their office. You often need to leave a message or speak with a receptionist. You may be told they are in court (tennis, perhaps) and will return your call later. This will be difficult if you are in custody, although the guards may relay an incoming phone message from your lawyer asking you to call them back. When trying to reach a lawyer, if they are too busy to call you back or they forget to, do you really want such a lawyer? Try calling several lawyers before deciding which one you want.

Your best source of referrals will come from other clients. Hearing several prisoners tell you which lawyers are the most popular and in demand will be more valuable than what your grandma says she read in the *Yellow Pages*. Even if you get a name or two from other prisoners, there is still further concern. Many prisoners exaggerate and blame the lawyer for losing a case or will exaggerate and claim their lawyer is the best. Some prisoners try to get more clients for their lawyer, hoping the lawyer will appreciate it and work harder for them in return. Some prisoners may not even want to refer you to their own lawyer because they don't want them to be overworked. Prisoners may even worry the blame may come back to them if they refer you to a lawyer and you lose.

When you first speak with a lawyer, if they think you're a potential client, they will give you their legal opinion and sales pitch, tossing in lines to instill confidence that they will be able to save you. If you have a previous conviction from using another lawyer they don't know or like, they may imply that you should not have been found guilty or at least should have received a lesser sentence. They will say this to make you regret not using them previously. However, lawyers don't usually badmouth other lawyers. It's a professional courtesy of sharks not to bite each other. Just remember that they are very skilled in bending the truth to suit their own needs first. They are much like the police or Crown in manipulating words and facts.

If you are paying cash, it's likely the only service where you will be asked to pay in full in advance. Nobody wants to pay a lawyer if they lose. If a lawyer charges more, it may not mean they are better than those who charge less. They may simply have kids to feed, alimony payments, gambling debts, a cocaine habit, or a new golf club membership up for renewal. They may charge more because they are better than most other lawyers are, and they may act like it too. They may simply be a better salesperson. If you're paying cash and later feel you are getting little in return for your money, don't expect much, if any, of your retainer to be returned after firing any lawyer. If you feel a lawyer has done something morally, financially, or criminally wrong, you can report it to your provincial law society.

Dump Trucks

The term *dump truck* is popular among the prisoners' fraternity. It can be used for different reasons when referring to a lawyer. It can refer to a lawyer who takes your case and says your chances are good only to later dump you over to the mercy of the court. It may be used suspiciously when a lawyer gets one client off on a deal with the Crown in exchange for letting another one (you) fall. How would you ever know? A lawyer may seem to be trying hard, and then you suddenly feel dumped at the foot of the judge to be found guilty and filleted.

A lawyer may take on your case and not like you personally, or your crime, and then put less and less effort into defending you. Again, how would you ever know? They won't say it to your face, and if they talk a good talk, you may get screwed! Lawyers may wrongfully be called a dump truck. This possibly happens when a client expected a miracle or felt they were unfairly punished. One can continue claiming their innocence, true or not, by blaming their legal counsel. If several prisoners refer to a specific lawyer as a dump truck, take the advice.

It does happen that a lawyer on their way to becoming a very good one, with a solid reputation and high demand, decides to "cash in." Lawyers can begin their career working hard for little pay. Years can pass as they win many cases and build a list of happy clients. They then can start charging much more money but also take on far too many clients. Their gained experience may help them work faster in resolving cases, but they may also not put forth their full energy overall. They can easily pick and choose clients or cases they know they're more likely to win, thereby upholding their success rate and reputation while sloughing off most other cases.

Once they are popular and in demand, they can take on extra cases, only to end up advising you they did their best while you go off to prison. A lawyer also gains experience in losing cases. They learn to fault witnesses, the police, judges, or you in the hope that you don't think they were the one who failed. If a lawyer plans on cashing out, retiring soon, moving, or starting another profession, financial gain will mean more to them than any reputation. They will know from experience how to pacify grieving clients, thereby extending any profit plans. Their reputation as a "good lawyer" that may have taken a decade or more to build can keep carrying them over many years while not being as good. More and more of their clients may be carted away to prison, but too many losses should eventually label them a real dump truck.

One simple example of possible deception I noticed in my younger days involves how offenders take a lawyer's words as gospel. Since they are your only possible saviour, you really want to believe in them. In many bullpens and cell-to-cell talks, prisoners talk of how their lawyer got them a good deal. Prisoners will say something like, "The Crown wanted three years, but my lawyer got it down to sixteen months." The prisoner then believes, "Hey, my lawyer really saved my ass!" Yet, if the prisoner was not actually there to hear the Crown's words, how could he know it's true? Maybe the Crown said sixteen months, and the lawyer baited the client with the possibility of a much higher sentence. By prepping you with the Crown wanting two or three years, you will be grateful and happy for your lawyer's work in getting you sixteen months. Anything less than what the Crown wants and you think you saved time in prison!

You often wait in the bullpen or outside a courtroom for your lawyer to come back after haggling with the Crown about your case and possibly over whose turn it is to buy lunch. When your lawyer gives you the details about pleading guilty, it's not written in stone. As in many business deals, the first offer can often be turned down for a better one. It's not always absolute, but almost every time my lawyer told me what the Crown offered, I would say no unless a little more time was shaved off. Don't always take the first deal a lawyer tells you. Don't act happy to accept it, unless you really are. Just like making a lawyer work a little harder for a lower bail, tell them to try getting a better deal. It often worked for me.

On a cautionary note: once you plead guilty, the judge occasionally may not agree with any joint submission of a sentence by the defence and prosecutor. In some cases, if you are guilty, it's best to just plead guilty quickly with almost any lawyer you can grab. This can be similar to trying for bail quickly before the Crown learns more about you and other possible victims and files more charges. In such a situation, you won't need a good trial lawyer, just a good quick deal for pleading guilty.

Legal Aid

The majority of prisoners use legal aid, so lawyers need a certificate in order to get paid for their services. The more clients they process, the more certificates they are issued. The certificate allows a specific amount of time for certain cases. A number of study hours to prepare and a number of court appearances are allowed, plus limited time to travel and speak with any out-of-town clients in custody. If your lawyer asks, legal aid may consider paying extra for a private investigator to obtain information or provide some fees needed for laboratory work or medical assessments. Most clients have little idea of how the billing system works, but even new lawyers quickly learn how to milk the system to the max.

Across Canada, there are three models in which legal aid systems are based. The first is the judicare model, a fee-for-service system where clients can retain a private-sector lawyer of their choosing who's willing to accept legal aid and its low-paying certificates. This system exists in Ontario, New Brunswick, and Alberta. The second system is the staff system used in Newfoundland, Labrador, Prince Edward Island, Nova Scotia, and Saskatchewan. This system uses a team of lawyers employed specifically for legal aid services. Occasionally, extra outside private lawyers may be called in as well. Finally, there is the mixed model in Quebec, Manitoba, British Columbia, Yukon, Northwest Territories, and Nunavut using private and staff lawyers in combination. Excluding New Brunswick and Prince Edward Island, a total of $762 million was spent on legal aid services in Canada in 2009-2010.[vii]

Legal aid fees were fixed or frozen from 1987 to 2002, remaining at about $67 per working hour. Negotiations conducted in 2003 raised the base rate 5 percent, far from the 33 to 35 percent raise Crowns and judges have received over that same period.[viii] If you're stuck with legal aid, once you pick a lawyer, you will have to stick with your choice. A few years ago, if you felt a legal aid lawyer was not being straight with you or doing a good job, you just fired them and got another one. Legal aid no longer allows this, except in rare cases. Some lawyers may take many legal aid cases while others take only a few, when they need or want to. Big time lawyers usually don't. If they do, they often turn the case over to a student lawyer underling in their firm, unless it's a sure win with lots of publicity.

In many cases, it's better if you don't have a job, car, home, or assets when hiring a lawyer. Applying for legal aid is easy then. You just go to their office. If you are in custody, they visit you or interview you on a video monitor. If you have a job, money in the bank, or even in your jail account, they will want it. They can place liens against your home or assets and/or make you sign a payment plan before issuing a certificate. Legal aid may also allow an open certificate in case legal proceedings are extended. If you are penniless and jobless, you get a free lawyer without ever having to pay back a cent. Win or lose, they still get paid.

Times Are a Changin'

In the last decade, the number of female lawyers, judges, and cops has grown rapidly. With the majority of offenders being male, most prefer having a male lawyer, but there are females who do better than male lawyers in negotiations and the courtroom. With many new female lawyers needing work, they may be more inclined to become Crowns, and after the required ten years of practice, many become judges. One might wonder if females do better in a profession where resorting to subterfuge and deception annihilates any male's chauvinistic advantage of resorting to violence? Female lawyers may also have the added skill of feminine charisma to lace with their legal forked tongue. Crowns, male or female, will have virtually unlimited resources and hunger for power as public protectors condemning you as best they can. The worse they can portray the accused, the better they look as prosecutors and protectors of the public.

In any case, unless you know them personally, lawyers are not your friends. They may act friendly, and you will want to believe they're your friends if you are trapped alone in a cage. You must confide and depend on them, but remember they are being paid. They come across as friendly and concerned for professional reasons. Don't expect a Christmas card from them after you've been carted off to prison. They are hired to defend you in court and may or may not do it well. Lawyers are skilled in handling clients, win or lose. It's also harder to blame them for screwing up if you think they are your friends and tried hard, even if you catch their mistakes. If you think your lawyer goofed, it may haunt you for years while you have a criminal record or sit regretfully many years in a prison cell. Guilty or not, you can be wrongly accused and convicted—wrongfully sentenced as well. The cycle can repeat itself again on appeal or at a later parole hearing. Even winning may simply be the result of timing, chance, or getting the right judge, rather than a lawyer's skill or lack of it.

In the end, the only true friend may end up being Lady Luck….

Chapter 4

Remands and Dead Time

Arrival

Clang! Clang! You know that hollow sound you hear if you kick an empty steel garbage can? Well, that's what prison sounds like, except your head is inside the can. I've often wondered if that is why one of the slang terms for jail is *the can*. Others may say it's where the garbage of society is tossed away to rot. With any dump-truck lawyer, remand after remand, court can be delayed for months or years. (For more on dump trucks, please see Chapter 3.) A competent lawyer can delay one even longer. Unfortunately, without bail, you will stay in custody, serving dead time. There you will taste the sensory deprivation, monotony, and despair of jail.

Upon arrival at any provincial jail's admitting and discharge (A&D) area, you will again be fingerprinted, photographed, and degradingly strip-searched. You'll be told to stand naked, open your mouth, stick out your tongue, run your fingers through your hair, and lift your scrotum. You will be asked to turn around, show the bottoms of your feet, and finally to bend over and spread the cheeks of your ass. This status degradation ceremony is repeated every time you return from court or during cell searches. You'll be given a blanket, a toothbrush, a towel, maybe some sheets, a pair of coveralls (a.k.a. pumpkin suit), and hopefully fresh socks and underwear biweekly. Then you will be taken to a range, pod, or cellblock where you will live 24/7 with many unhappy people.

The Range

This is where you'll spend your entire day when not in court. The cells are made entirely of concrete and steel. Even the sinks and the new seatless toilets are stainless steel, as old porcelain ones break into shanks. When flushed, toilets are very loud and have the strength to swallow a small puppy. Prisoners have strict rules about flushing late at night. If you wake someone up in your cell or an adjoining cell, fists may follow. Double-bunking saves money—another on the floor saves even more. Money overrides the fact that crowding and double-bunking causes dramatic increases in the rates of violence, medical illnesses, psychological breakdown, and suicide attempts.

With no more smoking allowed in provincial detention centres (DCs), also called remand centres, no one needs to worry anymore about unhealthy second-hand smoke or ashes ending up in beds. Except now, caged smokers recently cut off from their habit make the tight quarters in the netherworld of prison more stressful. Contraband tobacco is nearly as valuable as illegal drugs. Wherever you end up, if you do get stuck sleeping on the floor, avoid sleeping close to the toilet, if possible. *Tinkle! Tinkle!*

Years ago, there were many small luxuries such as toilet seats, wooden chairs, free tobacco, canteen allowances, cell radios, and pillows. Sadly, those comforts are now virtually non-existent. The advancing civil penal lords in their sagacious powers have changed prisons to make them harder, safer, and more cost efficient. There are no open visits, which curtails the flow of drugs and weapons. There are no weapons to protect yourself from bigger prisoners. There are no more cell radios to help you relax and remind you there is still a world outside. There are no more pillows for smothering other cellmates. Okay, maybe they took away the pillows just so prisoners can't sleep comfortably. You will have a thirty-inch-wide mattress on which to sleep. These are six inches thick for a few days when new, but you're not likely to get a new one. You will likely get a flattened, two-inch, dirty, stained mattress to sleep on the cell floor. Cost-cutting hurts prisoners but won't affect prison staff salaries.

The first time you awaken in jail, you'll feel emotionally disoriented. It will be difficult to realize where you are at first. A nightmare has become a "daymare," and you will close your eyes and wish it all away. Others will begin to awaken and start cleaning or getting breakfast. Someone will fill you in on what to do or expect. After cleaning your cell, you will then be locked out of it and put onto the range. There will be a TV to watch, but you'll likely not hear it well. In the hollow environment of stone and steel, and possibly a wall of Plexiglas, twenty to forty other prisoners have nowhere else to go and neither does the sound.

The newer DCs and superjails are the worst, with nothing to absorb the noise. Every sound echoes and is very discomforting. All day long, prisoners will be talking, playing cards, working out, pacing, trying to listen to TV, talking on phones, tapping a beat, or singing. It's often a narcissistic brother who sings solo in vain. Don't expect silence! Bigger city jails will have younger prisoners on one range, older ones on another, or a mix. The composition continually changes. A troublemaker quickly raises stress levels. The younger prisoners are usually the noisiest, but the higher-security prisoners or hardened older prisoners often keep the younger ones quiet and in line. It may take only one or two to change the range's atmosphere, making it more quiet and peaceful or entertainingly wilder and dangerous.

The sound of someone whistling is a big no-no in jail. Even the guards know this. I've heard the occasional guard do it, even in the middle of the night while walking their rounds. There are various explanations for this: 1) people are not supposed to be happy in prison, 2) whistling was the only sound heard when a condemned person was escorted to their execution, 3) the sound of whistling travels irritatingly throughout the house of pain, 4) whistling is offensive to some people's spiritual beliefs, 5) a free bird whistles, etc.

It has been said that prisoners are treated like garbage but counted like diamonds, and most places have a count-up yelled out twice daily by a guard.

The clanging of steel doors and bars, the jingle of keys, laughing, yelling, or banging can be easily heard, especially at night. Fire alarms going off daily; PA system announcements for code blue (fighting), red (fire), or yellow (hospital); harsh lighting; and cruel prisoners and guards all inside cold stone make prison a tough reality. Getting busted can throw your life out of sync, but staying in custody can make your life feel both out of sync and flushed away.

Remands and dead time can be especially hard on a first-timer trapped in prison. For them, as well as for others, seeing a new movie on TV or hearing a newly released song will be remembered forever. Years later, in seeing or hearing it again in the land of the living, it will bring back the memory of a trip to the bucket. If you are a first-timer, especially if you are young, the stress and boredom of being trapped in a cage, waiting for bail court, or doing a short sentence will seem like an eternity. The very young have a different perception partly because they have little experience. On the other end of the time scale, an older person can find it difficult for other reasons. They have less time on earth left to waste. Time will be more precious to them, and the harshness of prison will be harder to take, especially if they are unhealthy.

Telephones

There will likely be a phone on the range, possibly even two or three. A phone call may be the only peephole to the outside world. There may also be one or more phone bugs—prisoners who stay on the phone for hours every day. Many fights begin over the use of phones. With all the noise, you likely won't hear well while using the phone.

These phones are similar to payphones except there won't be a coin slot or phone book attached. Your call will be by automated operator and possibly even recorded. You won't be able to speak to a human operator much less use directory assistance. In the new out-of-town superjails, calling long-distance collect is expensive. Friends and family may get their phones cut off for unpaid bills. Fewer prisoners call friends and stay in contact with the outside world. In the early eighties, before phones were installed on ranges, guards had to take written requests from prisoners to call and relay messages to lawyers and others. This was a burden on guards and made it impossible for prisoners to speak directly and privately to their lawyers. Installing collect-call phones on the ranges solved the problem. Ma Bell was happy too.

If you're new to jail and desperately need to call someone but a phone bug who's bigger than you won't get off...you can wait! Some prisoners will claim they need to call their lawyer when they really only want to call a girlfriend. Local calls are $0.75 with no time limit. Some newer phone systems now work on a timer and cut off calls within fifteen or twenty minutes. Placing the call again is rebilled, even at the higher rate for that initial long-distance minute. Phone companies were quick to cash in on prisoners' loss of freedom. Then again, many prisoners don't pay the phone bill, thus adding stress to the friendship of whomever they called.

Medical

Larger jails often have a medical range, but getting onto one is difficult unless it's for a few days to heal from stitches or for other medical observations. Staying on a medical range is unlikely if you're not seriously injured or ill. Getting to see a medical specialist is also difficult unless you have serious or visible symptoms. Colds and the flu are rampant in such tight quarters. When infected prisoners arrive, germs and viruses spread fast. It's best to practice washing your hands as often as possible and learn to avoid touching any of your cranial orifices. Federal prisoners are thirty-nine times more likely to be infected with hepatitis C and fifteen times more likely to be infected with HIV compared to the population as a whole.[ix]

General practitioners visit daily at larger jails and weekly at smaller ones. The doctor, nurse, and dentist you see won't be the ones who graduated in the top half of their class. Most jail staff workers are under contract. Such proposed contracts get submitted yearly with the lowest bid accepted. You'll see the doctor upon arrival. After that, any complaint will be assessed and likely rejected by a roving nurse. Nurses will pass by daily, accompanied by a guard, to dole out medication—the *meds*. You can complain to them, usually wasting your breath, or send a request to the doctor, usually a waste of paper. A few nurses may be decent about any requests, whereas some can be rude and colder than the prisoners. Most nurses will act like doctors in response to your request. They must do so in order to weed through all the whining worthless complaints of other prisoners.

Don't expect any privacy to your requests. The guard to whom you hand it can read a written request about hemorrhoids, a burning sensation when urinating, or the runs. If the complaint is voiced while talking to a nurse at the bars, the prisoners in the line can hear you. Unless you are actually in pain and can prove it, you likely won't get any attention for it. If you have severe headaches or muscle pain, all you will likely get is a non-prescription Tylenol or Bufferin. Canadian jails may be rated among the best ones in the world compared to Third World nations, but they are the worst places in Canada to expect any decent medical attention. Services are limited, and you don't get to choose the medical personnel. The place to which you get transferred later could be slightly better and may have programs that you can attend, but it all depends on where you go.

Having a sudden toothache in jail is a bad thing indeed. The killing pain of a toothache needs fast relief. I know from experience. Twice I have used pliers to pull an infected tooth from someone waiting for release from the pain. If a cavity becomes infected or root canal work is suddenly needed, you will in all probability have to wait days or even weeks to see a dentist. By the time you finally see one, you may be happy to accept the simple offer of just pulling the tooth. It may only be a cavity that needs filling, but for the dentist, it could be quicker just to pull it. The dentist will also probably be working under contract not as a Beverly Hills professional. Maybe the lower-skilled dentists are more inclined to pull a tooth quickly rather than take the time and the effort needed to fill a cavity. Maybe some just have personalities tainted by a crime-and-punishment streak.

You may need to see a psychiatrist for reasons of stress, anxiety, or hearing voices in your head—or maybe you think you keep seeing the paperboy peaking around corners. Shrinks can be seen on a weekly basis if necessary. Don't expect to see a good doctor, as they are also under contract. One you want or have seen on the outside won't be coming to help. Again, you don't get to choose. You'll be stuck with the jail shrink. Still, a couple visits to express your demons or worries may get you some zombie pills to help time pass in a blur. There will often be more than one person on a range taking methadone, uppers, or several other types of medication to placate them. Some prisoners make up maladies to get meds for getting a buzz, to save up to sell to others, or in order to sleep more. If you feel you need to speak to a shrink, be careful in spilling your guts to one. Jail doctors are not employed to help you so much as evaluate you. They gather information from speaking with you in order to build a file for prison officials to use later, and any faulty or negative information gathered will influence other reports that follow. These reports will be used as evidence in court and later on when classifying you and during parole hearings. Reports are added to your jail records for all future staff, parole officials, the police, or Crowns to read. Years later, these reports can again be used against you.

Those who work in the "just us" system—the police, Crowns, doctors, guards, and POs—all make mistakes, which are ignored or played down later if ever exposed. Many of these mistakes add up and can have devastating effects on the accused down the road. The mistakes public employees make and the resulting information compiled, some gleaned from a "reliable source" (a.k.a. a rat), are now done in massive ways thanks to greater storage systems. In such a system, once errors are recorded, a prisoner has no way to correct them. Using forms provided by a prison library, prisoners can try requesting records under the Access to Information Act. What they will likely discover is that there will be nothing they can do to correct anything without proof.

When a staff member incorrectly writes down something you said, there are no sufficient grounds to correct it. I once wrote a request for my records. After they arrived, I was angry to notice many errors. Information I said to a PO was written differently from what I said. I filed an application to make corrections but was surprised to be told I had to prove it. Anything you say to anyone in prison can easily be spun to a listener's version, and there is nothing you can do about it. Most important, you should never joke or vent while communicating on record.

If you're depressed and try hurting yourself or seem suicidal, you can be taken to the hole, stripped naked, given padded clothing (a.k.a. baby dolls), and then left alone in a cell. This deprivation should help you feel less depressed! Prisoners are seven times more likely to commit suicide than people in the general population.[x] Some guards won't care and just don't want you dying or getting hurt, because paperwork is tedious. The jail doesn't want to incur blame for not delivering you to court, the court wants it's day to serve justice upon you, and a lawyer won't get paid if you die before trial. It would upset management's projected image of control over everyone inside, and it would negatively affect public opinion. Jail is supposed to deprive you of your free will, ensuring that you cannot die by your own hand until your day in court. To die would deprive a contemptuous society of satisfaction. The final act would be one of choice—yours.

When you become the caged cargo of any prison, there can also be unseen suicides such as prisoners who intentionally overdose or knowingly challenge a violent prisoner or armed guards. Such self-destructive acts of defiance may seem like the only way of escape to troubled prisoners. A short stay in jail may be all that it takes to help you decide to never want to return. For others stuck there for months or years, waiting for a trial with a lack of medical attention and the continuing struggle to endure not knowing if they will ever prevail, the physical and mental deterioration continues.

Exercise

The only physical outlet for releasing stress, other than pacing, doing pushups, or fighting, will be the gym or yard. Depending on where you're stuck and staff availability and willingness, you're supposed to get gym/yard access regularly. Twenty minutes a day is the written rule, but that rarely happens. Days may pass, or during lock downs, weeks. Yard may be offered so guards can search cells. Expect "yard-up" to be offered on the ugliest of days as well, since guards know prisoners are more likely to say no in inclement weather, and then at least they can state it had been offered. Job done!

The type of yard, gym, and equipment once popular and used by prisoners has since vanished. It is said that a healthy body contribute to a healthy mind and lifestyle. Studies of endorphin release during exercise suggest at least one reason. Exercise was once seen and promoted as a positive rehabilitative factor for prisoners. Many jails had good exercise equipment and well-maintained yards. That has now all changed. Saving money takes priority over a prisoner's health. Recreation staff have mostly disappeared from provincial facilities. Currently, exercise yards have little or no equipment and are enclosed with more razor wire and netting tarps. Is this precaution to protect sensitive skin? No! It's to stop drugs from being tossed over the wall and to make escape attempts more of a bloody workout.

It's possible to stay fit in jail, just more difficult. Inside on a range, it's harder, and in solitary, it's the hardest. With no more weights or gym, and with smaller yards, working out becomes very tedious. It's difficult to continue any workout regime with only sit-ups, push-ups, and pacing. Getting out to the yard to run or simply get some fresh air and sun is a daily need when caged. You may be able to use a broom for chin-ups in some places or bags of water for weights, but there are only so many exercises one can do without proper space and equipment.

Food Rations

Jail food is not as bad as I once remember it to be. Bean cake was a popular but horrible food served as a punitive meal to those in solitary. Happily, it's gone! Different jails vary in the quality and quantity of food doled out. Some provincial governments have now consolidated the food programs. If you're hooked to dining on Mom's fine cuisine or eating in good restaurants, you won't be happy with jail grub. If you are one of the less fortunate who don't normally eat well and considers a great meal to be a Big Mac, three squares a day in jail may be a welcome change. The meals served will be borderline nutritionally adequate—even the juice is often just flavoured water. You won't get to choose your meal, only what part you don't want to eat. If the meat serving is liver and you don't like it, there goes your meat intake. If the vegetable is cabbage, which you hate, there goes your vegetable intake. If you are seen throwing out food that others want, you will likely be told about it. If you give any part of your food away, expect the person to whom you give it to keep returning for more. The best reply you can give anyone asking for anything is to say, "Sorry, I can't help you out." It's better than giving in or just saying no. And *never, ever*, reach over someone else's food for any reason. It's disrespectful and may instantly start a fight.

You may start to like many foods you hated before coming to jail. However, once you return to the free world, you will hate them again even more. The food in the federal system can be slightly better, and you can even prepare some foods yourself and purchase provisions from the larger canteen stores. In the provincial CCs and DCs, your canteen selection is very limited. Your best creative culinary skills may only be getting hooked on french-fry sandwiches. Special diets such as vegetarian, kosher, halal, diabetic, etc., may be a better welfare-like meal depending on where you are. Good luck!

Boredom

While killing time trying to keep the workouts up and the food down, playing cards can be your biggest event in conquering boredom. Though working out is a positive activity, you can't do it endlessly. You can passively play cards non-stop. It is the easiest, most worthless way to waste away time in jail. This is why for years I have never played. I still wonder if allowing cards in jail is truly for leisure or, in someone's conspiratorial paranoid schizophrenic mindset, a clandestine form of mental punishment and decay. This is the mental equivalent of giving out free tobacco to young teens for their health! Playing cards for hours, day after day, month after month, year after year, is an easy trap in which to fall. Spending hundreds of hours honing your card skills may have prepared you for release in the days of riverboat gambling, but today it's useless. What skills will you have gained for your release? Experience in taking on Grandma at cribbage or finally being able to beat her and her friends at strip poker? It's as valuable as card tricks to impress the paperboy!

An hour of working out in addition to hours reading, writing, drawing, or watching something worthwhile on TV will make you look and feel better. Being a card junkie truly makes you serve dead time because you may as well be brain dead upon your release. As any neuroscientist will say, not using your mind will cause it to atrophy just as muscles do. Playing cards in jail is addictive. It's also the source of arguments leading to fights. Gambling on cards is common, as is cheating. Also popular is betting on sporting events.

Many prisoners don't deal well with their emotional problems. That's why many of them ended up in jail in the first place, so when the stress builds and anger flares in a card game, look out! I have observed the sly table talk and the dumbest cheater's moves. I've known partners who break up only to team up with unsuspecting players, intentionally losing and later splitting the won goods. There are many ugly losers. Some can't always find a partner to blame after losing. Whenever I was asked to play, I always said, "No, I hate playing cards." Such a response also prevents them from offering to teach me. I like playing cards, just not in prison. By not playing at all, I avoid wasting time. I also avoid turning new friends into new enemies.

Watching the idiot box all day is the next major entertainment event. Although watching television is more passive than cards, you may at least learn something if you watch informative programs. Don't get hooked on soap operas or on a regular program unless others have the same tastes. What gets watched repeatedly may come from the majority, the muscle, or both. Fights start here as well, just as they do over cards, gambling, phone use, and drugs. If a sporting event is being watched on TV, don't try having a nap on the floor, as loud shouts and roars will awaken you. Watching sports isn't educational, but many people long to watch them for escapism, entertainment, social reasons, and living vicariously through them. The same goes for gossip and storytelling, which can often be more popular than cards or TV. For many prisoners, all they own are memories to tell and retell. Anyone arriving at an open DC range will likely see a couple of prisoners pacing, several more playing cards, and the rest watching TV. Many will spend their entire day watching TV in a vegetative state.

Data from Educational Kinesiology (Edu-K) reveals that everyone has dominant and non-dominant body parts—a dominant eye, arm, testicle, etc. This also applies to the two halves of the human brain, which is designed to be either bilaterally integrated (two-sided) or homolaterally specialized (one-sided). Certain actions such as watching TV is a right-sided action, and the left side of the brain can become lazy because of excessive visual stimulus, a two-dimensional activity. Excessive sitting, which is common in a DC environment, means learning is acquired under stress; the lateralized brain recalls only the one-sided (low-gear) aspect of that learning. Depth perception and the ability to actively move around is limited as well; therefore, any physical activity becomes all that more important.[xi] There is also the Brain Gym program, which includes simple exercises for the brain. It can help, but that's another book altogether. Play some chess!

Although removed from society to watch TV, play cards, or tell tales all day, being caged with many others is still stressfully boring. Many feel helplessly alone, but there is no privacy or space where one can be alone. If you're lucky, you may occasionally spend a night alone in a cell. However, a new cellmate will arrive quickly, and you'll soon be double- or triple-bunked once again! Hopefully, you will get compatible cellmates.

"Do Your Own Time"

This is an old saying often heard in the prison environment. It is usually spoken as a weapon against others and wielded unfairly by many. It's supposed to be used when disrespectful prisoners make others around them feel stressed, used, or irritated. Staring at another prisoner or looking into their cell, whistling, yelling, filthy habits, and spreading gossip are all considered disrespectful. Not wiping the sink or toilet seat and butting in on others' conversations are also unwelcome in such close quarters. The word *respect* is another popular word barked by many prisoners who have none, yet bitch and blame others for doing the same! This is used when a prisoner is dirty, nosy, or noisy. Many things can irritate others, such as singing, slamming down cards, gossiping, hogging the phone or TV, borrowing stuff, or turning up music someone else may not want to hear—the list is endless. Some things can't be helped, such as snoring or an obnoxious laugh, but consideration and respect for the space you live in, and for others in it, is important for survival.

Many prisoners fall somewhere between sociopath and psychopath. Some are ignorant, uneducated, unsympathetic, violent, or all of these, and locked in the Stygian perdition of a cage. How can anyone ever do their own time? To try would be like reading or writing a letter, then someone coming and sitting down to see what you're up to! You can't read or write for very long before someone interrupts you. When you're trying to write a letter or read a book, it's amazing how someone will start a conversation and will keep talking to you even though you appear preoccupied with something else. The best way to "do your own time" is in solitary confinement.

The Hole

The maximum punishment a prisoner once received for misbehaving in jail was thirty days in the hole with a loss of all privileges (LOAP). In the sixties, Kingston Pen had a prisoner count of a thousand, but only a few at one time were ever placed in solitary and only for a few days. Such a form of "no-touch torture" was deemed damaging to the psyche. There have been many studies conducted about the effects of confinement but with ambiguous results. A popular publication used by criminologists, students, and puppeteers of penology is the *Canadian Journal of Criminology and Criminal Justice*. The January 2001 issue lists reports written about the effects of solitary. A problem not mentioned is that the journal, which is still published and used by many, is partly funded by the CSC. One should wonder if that is much different from a tobacco corporation keeping a doctor on the payroll to issue reports on the health effects of smoking.

The establishment of "control units" in the U.S. originated in 1963 and quickly spread after the closing of Alcatraz. Control units (or segregation) are now very common but not called "the hole" by most staff. The hole is really like a prison within a prison to further punish prisoners without any legal recourse. Prison staff may rightly claim some prisoners are segregated for their own protection or for the safety of the institution. A more appropriate term should be *isolated* since such prisoners are often housed in cells with solid steel doors to prevent communication with other prisoners. Many segregation units also operate by electronically controlled doors, further eliminating contact with any staff. There will be no communal dining, exercise, or religious services. The only noise may be another distant prisoner banging for hours on their door. A prisoner under administrative segregation in a federal system may be allowed books or a small TV. Provincial segregation has fewer privileges, if any, and will therefore be harsher.

In Canada, provincial and federal administrative segregation remains a grossly overused management tool. It was reported that between June 1997 and May 1998, out of an inmate population that averaged 13,504 federally sentenced prisoners, 6,848 placements in administrative segregation occurred.[xii] While half of all prisoners have experienced solitary at one time or another, and some stay there for weeks, months, or even years, many prison officials think the conditions should be harsher. Just as society prefers to lock up criminals, making them out-of-sight and out-of-mind, prison staff often use segregation to solve even minor problems.

If isolation is used in fear of losing a prisoner's life in population, that does not say much for the CSC's mission statement in "exercising reasonable, safe, secure, and humane control." Even calling it "twenty-three-hour lockup" is a misnomer since many days can pass without yard time, showers, or phone access being offered or accepted by a prisoner. That remaining hour, if it arrives, may really be only ten minutes to shower and maybe fifteen minutes in a very small concrete yard. Prison staff currently use the kinder term of *segregation* or *diss cells* (disassociation) instead of cruel terms such as *isolation*, *solitary confinement*, or *the hole*.

A charge may result from fighting, possessing contraband, refusing an order, or for something as simple as verbally irritating a guard who is in a bad mood. Anyone can end up in the hole for a couple of days without even being told why. You're supposed to be told what you are charged with and have a kangaroo court hearing within a few days. It's always your word against a guard or two, and the outcome is predictable. If you don't have any canteen and don't like to read, then you won't have any privileges to take away. And if you're sentenced federally, they can't take away any good time (early release during the final third of a sentence earned for good behaviour), as it no longer applies to federal time.

Some prisoners can't handle the solitude of the hole. Such a heightened sense of captivity and depravation, absolute or relative, provokes further frustration. A few prisoners, some even willingly, remain in segregation for much longer periods than the thirty-day limit under administrative segregation and still keep their privileges and some sanity. Even this can be difficult to accomplish with two to a cell 24/7. "Madness is the individual's response to the obliteration of his identity by others," concludes Peter J. Wilson, a professor of anthropology.[xiii] Triple-celled prisoners in provincial are common, with only one or two for solitary. Confinement to the hole or segregation can be quiet and peaceful, but never for long. You will eventually hear someone yelling, singing, or banging on a door, possibly for hours. It may only be someone making a low noise many cells away. Then, just as you are about to fall asleep, the prisoner in the cell next to you may bang and scream for the prisoner further down to shut up. Solitary time in a federal pen is usually more bearable (please see Chapter 8).

Lockdowns and Searches

Lockdowns for fights or any trivial reason are common and can last several days or weeks. Cell and strip searches, anywhere and anytime, are also very common. In some cases, reliable sources (a rat) or guard provide information, claiming a blade or drugs have entered the institution. This may allow the riot squad in Darth Vader outfits, nicknamed "turtles" or "goon squad," to exercise a full lockdown to search as well as get in some overtime and training practice. Guards will carry handheld metal detectors and tear apart the cells of any prisoners they wish. Some institutions use drug-sniffing dogs. Charges may be laid for the most trivial of acts, with privileges and visits suspended.

Some prisoners prefer lockdowns or doing time in the hole if they are not double- or triple-bunked. Sharing a cell with any befriended prisoners in solitary or on a locked-down range may not always work out. If you have ever moved in with a friend, that friendship could end once confined. In tight prison quarters of 8'x10', barely twice the width of a coffin, it's hard to remain friends even if you are compatible. Adding to this constant close confinement, every prisoner can be stressed out about upcoming court dates as well problems outside of jail. Occasionally, the guards will allow you to change cells.

Library or Schoolroom

Access to education or reading material in provincial DCs or superjails has become very limited now that most are maximum security. Many CCs are also maximum, but even the minimums may have little to offer. According to *Juristat*, across Canada, only 12 percent of provincial/territorial prisoners are housed in medium security, and 9 percent in minimum. Also, 34 percent of prisoners had a grade 9 education or less compared to 19 percent of adults in Canada. In the federal system, 46 percent had grade 9 or less.[xiv] According to the *Annual Report of the Inspector of Penitentiaries* (1905-1906), when there were only five penitentiaries, absolute illiteracy was 16 percent. Comparative rates still exist today.[xv]

A few places may have weekly volunteers push a book cart through the jail or assist with correspondence courses for an hour or so. Reading, writing, or drawing can be a short-term escape from the boredom of jail, away from the stress of all the other "troubled vegetables" around you. Trying to keep your mind busy or distracted may be the only way to stave off insanity. Doing time a hundred years ago without a TV meant more prisoners might have learned to read. Today, playing cards or watching TV is a passive escape. Reading, writing, drawing, and working out are active positive habits to take up when doing dead time.

However, reading fiction all day long to escape the ennui of confinement won't be of much benefit when your time is over. Many prisoners suffer from attention deficit disorder (ADD), hyperactivity, dyslexia, and depression. Some may have never made it out of grade school. Those who enjoy reading may find it difficult if they can't concentrate on a noisy range. Conversely, you cannot improve unless you continue to try. Pushing yourself into the daily habit of working out, reading, writing, or drawing is the best way to pass time in prison. Reading a book on any topic is better than learning nothing at all. Reading or playing Scrabble is better than spending the day playing cards or watching inane TV shows. Starting a school course, learning to draw, writing, and reading are good habits. When you're finished with court, you will have at least more to offer wherever you go. It's best to start new habits early. You won't regret it in the end.

In most provinces, you can begin a correspondence course as soon as you are incarcerated. The Independent Learning Centre (ILC) is an Ontario-wide correspondence school free to anyone. Several years ago, they began to require a $40 refundable deposit because some students started and never finished courses. Consequently, the deposit is lost if the student quits and doesn't return the course materials. Upon completion of a course, they used to return your deposit, so it was a fair motivator. They now keep the $40 as an administrative cost.

You can also take some identical courses for free through the prison school system. If you put in a request at the jail to see a schoolteacher or volunteer tutor, if they have one, these educators will list your options. They may have leftover courses of English or math on hand for you to start immediately. Smaller jails may have fewer educational materials or none at all, as budgets have been greatly reduced. You may also register for courses by mail or three-way phone on your own. No jails allow books or course materials to arrive to any prisoner unless the materials come directly from the distributor/publisher, although torn pages and photocopies can be sent in from anyone. Some institutions, especially DCs, where bored guards scrutinize mail, won't allow certain pictures or books such as this one—for security reasons. Some mixed material may slip past a cursory inspection.

With no bills to pay inside and so much free time on your hands, you may as well take advantage of the situation. Keeping your mind and body fit will make your chance of survival upon release better than if you only sit around doing nothing. In addition to keeping your body and mind in shape, it's important to keep your spirit alive. This task may turn out to be far more difficult than the first two. It's not easy to keep your spirit alive and well in such a cold and brutally cruel environment as a prison. With no supportive contact to the outside world, it's even more difficult. Idleness of the body, mind, and heart are prison's most evil consequences. Being cut off from the land of the living can become a terrible trap, and prisoners spend time sitting around dreaming of past days, hoping for better ones to follow.

With or without access to schooling, libraries, cards, or TV, prisoners are prolific storytellers for a captive audience. Fish stories get better and better with each telling. Prisoners reminisce and exaggerate about past events and scores and dream of future ones as they continue to grow older and infamously more impoverished. While art and writing provide meaning and confirmation of our existence, reliving the past gives a tangible sense of identity. It's a passive palliative way to kill time. Many prisoners tell themselves and others the great plans they have for their release. Unfortunately, most prisoners also do nothing to improve themselves while inside and will be sadly disappointed when all their big plans later fall apart. It's an easy escape to dream because there is no effort exerted. Doing this in excess only builds up false expectations that come crashing down the moment you are free. This can become a cycle too when one fails to take some advantage of doing dead time. If you don't push yourself to work on at least part of your life, i.e., body, mind, or heart, how can you expect the perdition of jail to make you a better person? Don't serve time—make time serve you!

Loneliness

Prison can be the loneliest place on earth. You may not know anyone upon arrival, or you may meet someone you once knew long ago or already know many others. Some prisoners know more people inside than they do on the outside. Many prisoners will give up calling or writing anyone on the outside. Friends may say they will visit or write, and when they don't, it makes being trapped inside feel that much more helpless. Few people on the outside realize how dispiriting it is for a prisoner to wait hours, days, weeks, or months for a visit or letter that never arrives. It's especially painful to lose a mate without even getting a "Dear John letter" explaining why. Many prisoners, myself included, know how painful it is to lose a loved one while inside. It's a memory that continues to haunt you because you are helplessly trapped. Even simple requests to those on the outside, such as asking them to visit, write, relay a message, or just send a picture, can be repeatedly ignored. And the more you continue to ask, the more helpless you will feel for asking. You may finally regret ever asking at all.

The only escape from prosecutorial pressures and the stresses of prison life, which can grow exponentially, may be to call or write a friend. If it's a female friend, you may grow mad with tenderness at the mere sound of her voice. Even calling buddies who are having a beer can make you regret not being there with them, but hearing them can remind you there is still life outside. Although it's easy for anyone to accept your collect call with the push of a button, visiting and writing take effort. Prisoners eventually discover who truly cares. For many, severing all ties with the outside world makes doing time easier. You won't miss friends on the outside or your freedom as much if you don't think about either of them. Struggling to save a relationship or calling friends to hear their happy or sad words can be difficult. Blocking out stressors may be your only controllable escape. But upon returning to the outside without friends waiting for you, your soul will take a beating you may never fully realize or recover from, provided other problems don't distract you first.

Keeping in touch with family and friends is sustenance for the soul. In dangerous and troubled times, we tend to draw closer to the ones we love—if we can. It can be difficult to keep ties alive when caged, especially if you feel someone out there let you down somehow, you can't understand why they don't visit, or you failed them. The longer prisoners remain incarcerated, the more people forget.

Your pride can take a beating from being caged and a beating upon release. If you forgot that one day you would be free again and wasted your dead time, don't expect to survive any better than before you came in. Being caged is a time of soul-searching. Having a friend on the outside helps you remember there is still a world out there to return to one day, a world no prisoner should return to all alone.

Some prisoners look much better upon leaving prison than they did upon arrival. Most don't! What's more difficult to understand is what has changed inside. Your experience in prison will depend on who you are: age, health, education, physical size, gender, sexual orientation, criminal history, crime, sentence, and security level of your facility. The way you come to jail and what you lose also plays a serious part in how you do time. This can have a great impact later on when you are released. If you have a wife or a long-term girlfriend, get ready for a shaky ride. If you met someone new or became close to someone just before ending up in jail, prepare to lose them. New relationships started just before being caged may only last a few weeks or months. Two sincere people can really fall for each other in this manner. The couple can see sensitive sides of one another, and a prisoner can really have a growing respect for a woman who was there for him to make time easier. The downside is that if she then abandons him just before trial, parole, or release, he will suffer the sad woes of a broken heart while also suffering such abandonment helplessly alone in a very cold cruel place! Losing a loved one is hell in the free world, but in prison, it's beyond hell.

Being in such a crestfallen state will not only make the reality of where you are harder to deal with, it can be fatal. The mind doesn't function well when feeling dejected and devastated. Prisoners may lose the will and strength to continue on with life. They may care less and less about an approaching trial or an approaching shank. Coming to jail may help prisoners realize how much this earthly world is a place of vanity and deception. Such insights may also influence them to attempt suicide—many do try. If you think about stringing yourself up every night you lie down, you may even be helpless in doing that.

If it's not depression that consumes you, it may be anger. Getting angry and snapping at another prisoner for emotional release is dangerous too. People with anger problems are often unassertive and may get dumped on repeatedly until they finally lash out. Letting out hostilities in "Casa Diablo" where anger grows in a pooling turmoil of anguished souls can have devastating results. For the violent barbaric prisoners, and there are many, intimidating and picking on others is a way of life. These prisoners get off on using and dominating others. Sometimes several prisoners join up to rule a range. Fights will be a common occurrence and you can't always avoid them, even if you don't start one. Fighting easily results in more charges against you. If guards are assaulted, additional time will be more difficult to serve.

People you thought were friends may totally ignore you once you're trapped in the belly of the beast. If a mate abandons you, they may steal your stuff or sell it to pay rent and bills. A mate may take your child and leave in your car, never to be heard from again. It's not like you can search for them. You won't even be able to drown your sorrows by having a few beers with anyone. How can you go on living when you're not even in the land of the living? You're trapped in a cold, dead, helpless place. You may become violent or suicidal—or worse, you could be suicidal and not know it. You may not even care. You'll feel dead inside, dead to the world, and have no desire to better yourself. But you can still play cards all day! This is the worst way to begin any prison sentence. The only choice you may feel you have left is to stop caring, to shut out the outside world and bury any pain. You emotionally shut down to survive the cold. It's like a slow unseen suicide that eats you from the inside while trapped in prison.

Few prisoners coming to jail are lucky not to have problems on the outside. They may not have any family or friends to let them down or screw them over. They may simply just not have anyone. It's not only the ones you know who can make your time harder, it's the prisoners, guards, police officers, news reporters, and courts as well. You must remember that many people have no concern for your personal welfare. After you go to jail, your difficulties are of no concern or value to them. Some police will only be too happy in hearing you aren't doing well. A weaker opponent for trial means an easier victory for the Crown.

After being arrested and sitting in jail awhile waiting for court, remand after remand, you may sadly discover people you once considered friends have little or no regard for your situation. Friends may refuse to take care of even the simplest matters for you on the outside. It can seem like there was a funeral—yours! People will take and fight over your property. Partners, friends, and family may not write or visit much, or at all. You may think they're ignoring your phone calls. Some will do nothing or do shocking things of which you may not even learn about until after your release, if ever.

Some people you know will want to accept your being guilty and believe that you deserve to be in jail. This not only excuses their conscience if they squealed on you, it also absolves them for not helping in any way, for abandoning you, or for profiting from your demise. One man's loss is another's gain. Business partners may welcome your departure. An ex-buddy may now be able to move in on your girlfriend. A friend who owes you money will now feel they don't have to repay you. The mother of your young children may decide to cover her tracks and flee with another man to make a new start. If anyone you once knew didn't make the slightest effort to help in any way to ease your situation, then they were never true friends in the first place. Unfortunately, this happens when you need them more than ever. Discovering this after coming to jail is very hard on one's mind. People you cared about may treat you as if you're dead and gone. Such painful memories can add up to haunt you daily. Despite being in such a helpless pillory pose, you will discover who truly cares.

When doing dead time, you are punished for alleged crimes before being tried. Your chances of being found guilty increase as well. You're in jail, so you must have done something wrong! This is a common assumption. You won't be free to work and be able to pay for a better lawyer. You also won't be able to easily find someone you know and question them about anything related to your charges. Once the police turn anyone you know against you, they may not accept your collect calls to hear your side, much less visit or help. When you're trapped in jail, cut off from society and awaiting trial, you're far more helpless to find or speak with anyone who can help in any way. The police certainly won't find any assistance for you. Friends may fade away and talk badly about you to others. Anyone who is jealous of you will be glad to see you fall. Those who are afraid of you or had anything against you may even go out of their way to make your situation worse. You're in jail! You're bad! You're probably guilty! You deserve it!

Getting jailed is a blow to the self-esteem. With your freedom gone you'll keep thinking about how it all happened. You won't just think about the crime alone; you'll think about all the other events and the roles played by you and others. "If only..." could be big or small thoughts upon which to dwell. Nevertheless, you will have nothing but time on your hands to think about it. Those on the outside will continue with their lives, but you will be helplessly trapped serving dead time. Although you have not left the world, you will have left their world.

When you were arrested, you may have had a desire to confess. If not, you may later feel anger instead of remorse in finding out which friends were untrue to you. Remorse and guilt are usually only felt at the beginning rather than the end of one's time in jail. If it were the other way around, maybe fewer would return to crime. You may feel crushed, lost, and broken after arriving in jail. Feelings take a beating in prison. By the time you are set free, bitterness and anger may be all you feel. Society has degraded you to a world where your human status is below common citizenship. Prisoners are viewed by many as base, sub-human, or as animals! Many will have no respect for you and won't want you to be a part of the gene pool. The only warmth you may get from the outside world may come from an occasional letter, phone call, or visit. Having buddies inside can make your time pass more easily. They may end up being your only friends, although hooking up with them after your release will likely contribute to your return to jail.

In the past, prisoners didn't mind receiving many remands while serving dead time, as it was the only way to get off the range for a day. Asking for remands, again and again, costs nothing to most prisoners on free legal aid. Sitting in the bullpen in court can be more boring than jail, as there is no TV or radio, but it's a place where prisoners can meet other cagelings. They may be able to score on anyone bringing in tobacco or drugs, speak with a lawyer face to face, or see someone they know in the courtroom and exchange a wave or smile. The ride to and from court may be a scenic one as well, if you're not in a windowless prison vehicle. The new superjails are now implementing court remands and legal aid interviews via video monitors. This is supposed to save costs, but it also eliminates being able to speak privately and face to face with your lawyer. It's a cost saving for management, politicians, and the courts but at the expense of prisoners' chances of regaining liberty. Will trials of the future and personal visits soon be by video monitors as well? Time will tell.

Visits

Visiting times at most jails are often limited to only two a week. Small-town jails often have better visiting access. They don't have pigeon machines (metal detectors) to walk through, like in the pen, or oversensitive ion scanners to refuse visitors. Many never even ask for ID, and visits can be extended. In the new superjails, each closed visit is timed to twenty minutes by shutting off the phones that visitors use. There is no longer any leniency in giving extra visits. Before, if the visiting room was not crowded, one could have much longer visits if the guard wanted to be lenient. Now most jails are strict. What's even worse is that family and friends may now have to drive quite a distance out of town to a superjail to see you behind the Plexiglas. Your visitors may have to drive an hour, wait up to an hour or more to see you for a fifteen- or twenty-minute visit, and then take another hour to drive home.

I will never understand how those in control of prison legislation can't see how this contributes to a rising crime rate. It saves money on paper in the short term by housing prisoners in a warehouse setting or on cheap land in faraway locations. Anything that lessens support to prisoners in cutting off family, friends, or lawyers from visiting easily weakens them and can cause bitterness and animosity towards the system. Prisoners will eventually be released again, and the less contact they have, the more likely they will be broken and return to crime.

Making visits more difficult is also unfair to those who care enough to visit someone. They may even have to wait outside the jail in the rain or a blizzard, as I once did after being dropped by taxi to visit a friend. Maybe management thinks discouraging visits means less staff will be needed, thereby saving a few more dollars. Their new hidden agenda may be that if prisoners are going to be released, it's best to have them as emotionally broken as possible so if they commit more crimes, they will get caught more easily rather than be "successful" criminals.

Correspondence

For years, prisoners were supplied with free writing materials to send out two letters per week. Canteen stationary or letters received are not limited or heavily censored like they were previously.

Anything mailed to you other than letters, cards, or pictures will be returned to sender, educational courses and religious and publishers' books excluded. If anything not allowed is mailed to you without a return address, it's supposed to be placed in your property in A&D storage for your release. For all you know, it could just be chucked in the garbage or scooped. How would you know? A guard who dislikes you or your charges may read a letter coming for you and just throw it away. Paranoia? Maybe, maybe not! Nude pictures from girlfriends, wives, and girlie mags are no longer allowed in provincial DCs or CCs. When they were, on two occasions, girls I knew sent me semi-nude pictures and I never got all of them. Tell friends to always number the pictures and say how many there are in the letter. I'm sure there are guards from every jail who still collect photos skimmed from their many victims.

Knowing emotions on paper are screened by guards, it takes away some of the intimacy. There were once many topics and subjects not allowed to be written about in letters. Years ago, heavy black markers were used by guards to edit out anything they felt should be crossed out. I'm sure some twisted guards had some evil fun then. Guards open all mail to check for contraband, and they may sit and read your letters and even pass them to other guards to read. Guards get bored! It really irks you when you actually see them do this, as I once did. Only correspondence with your lawyer, a member of parliament, or the ombudsman is supposed to come and go unopened by the guards. Guards still "accidentally" open such mail.

One thing that should exist in every visiting area of any jail is a number to call for complaining of a guard's treatment. There is the ombudsman for provincial complaints and the correctional investigator for federal complaints, but as most prisoners know, they are often useless. Anyone who has visited anyone regularly in prison will learn firsthand how nasty and uncaring some guards can be. This problem persists not just because there is no posted complaint number to call in *any* visiting room but also because visitors worry a complaint may fall back on the person they came to visit.

Canteen

If you have canteen money in your account, you can buy extra stamped envelopes if the two free weekly ones are not enough. Without money, you can't buy anything on the canteen list. In 1989, the free tobacco rations of two bails weekly were cut in half. A year or two later, they were omitted completely. Shortly after the tobacco freebies were gone, the weekly $6.50 allowance freebie also vanished. Smoking is banned in all DCs and CCs. Smoking was banned in all federal institutions in 2008. I'm glad about the non-smoking policy, since I don't smoke, but stress will be higher for those who are forced to do without upon arrival. The non-smokers will feel the stress from those forced to quit.

Jails have different canteen lists with chips, chocolate bars, shampoo, magazines, cards, and other items. To order from any weekly canteen, you must have money when arrested, have a visitor drop off cash, or have family or friends mail a money order to you directly. It's good that those forced to quit smoking can at least buy candies to help kick the habit, if they have money to spend. If you do buy any canteen items, there will be many disenfranchised prisoners who don't and who will ask you for some of yours. Like food, once you give away anything, expect prisoners to be back asking for more. "Sorry, I can't help you out." Be careful not to borrow or accept any loaned canteen items as well, since many prisoners run their own little private stores and charge two, or three, for one. The weekly spending limit is $60 to $90. Don't hit Grandma up so much that she has to resort to dining on cat food!

Spirituality and Death

You may find being in jail an extremely difficult time, and others you know outside may not know what you are going through. They may also be going through a difficult time, as well as worrying about you trapped inside away from them. Friends may truly not be able to find a ride or take a day off work to jump on a bus to visit you. Phone bills from collect calls add up quickly. Guys on the outside don't usually like writing letters very much, but some females do. You may become pen pals with those you never expected to care. Women often enjoy sending and receiving cards, letters, and poems. It's cheaper than phoning, and these can be read repeatedly. Getting a letter from the world outside reminds your heart there is someone out there who still cares. Sending a letter may ease their worries about you. Even if your "friends" no longer seem to care, at least drop Mom and Grandma a card to say hello, tell them you miss them, and thank them for everything they ever did for you. You may make their day just by sending a card and easing some of the worry you may have caused them.

Some prisoners feel uncomfortable keeping in touch with anyone on the outside. They may not feel very proud of being where they are. They may be angry with themselves or with others outside. Some prisoners' problems with family and friends may even relate to their incarceration, so they often would rather forget that the world outside exists for a while. Another sharp pain for some is when any stolen items, money, or benefits from a crime are taken and used by a spouse, partner, or friend while the prisoner is in jail paying for it. Those same people may have turned their backs on them or may have even turned them in. Dwelling on such memories really hardens the soul. Some will find praying to the Lord helps but not necessarily the one above.

There are chaplains at the jail to counsel you, along with Sunday services or Bible study courses, if you wish to converse with the big guy upstairs. Unfortunately, some institutional chaplains are overloaded with too many requests from helpless prisoners and help is minimal. Some prisoners who get crushed emotionally or have a traumatic epiphany turn to religion in jail. It's when prisoners are at the lowest point in their lives, disgraced, destroyed, and feeling alone, that the greatest changes, good or bad, can occur. They see the light in their darkest hours. Some turn to religion to escape their guilt. Some just fake it for a better shot at parole. Doing this was once quite common, and once free again, they would lose the faith. But some converts are genuinely seeking spiritual guidance and hope.

The death of a loved one can be more devastating to you when stuck in jail. You will not have had the chance to spend the last moments with someone before they died. Passes for funerals or serious family matters are now less common, and you can even be billed hundreds of dollars in escort costs.

Volunteers and Helping Agencies

In addition to the help from a chaplain, there is also help available from the Salvation Army, St. Leonard's Society, and the John Howard Society, who may assist in personal matters. Some of them offer rides for visitors or relay family messages on sensitive matters. They can speak with you on a one-on-one basis if needed. They can also help you get back on your feet after your release. The nicest part is that these organizations don't judge or condemn you in any way for your crime. Don't be afraid to put in a request at the jail to speak with any of their friendly volunteers. Best of all, when speaking to one of their representatives, your conversation will be kept confidential and won't become part of any prison files, unless it's a confession of a crime or intent to harm.

Taking the Dead Out of Dead Time

If you work out a few times a week and read an occasional book, you will be a better person for it—better prepared mentally and physically for a trial and your eventual release. If you keep in touch with a friend, they can help you hold onto any shattered sanity and hopefully help rebuild what's left of the past. After the dead time is finally finished, you will be set free or close to being free if you get a short sentence. Most prisoners are very relieved to start serving a sentence rather than doing dead time because of finally having a release date to focus on. If a prisoner receives a long sentence, the nightmare may begin anew.

In the past, many prisoners would stall court proceedings with as many remands as they could get, staying free outside or staying in the DC as long as possible, gathering dead time. This was a common practice by prisoners wishing to avoid a federal pen sentence and possibly also continue getting local visits and phone calls. By gathering as much dead time as possible, one could have a better chance to deal for a two-for-one time served or a sentence of less than two years and stay in the provincial system. Was it good that judges took dead time into consideration? If your lawyer asks whether this should be the case, the judge may simply give you a longer sentence. Instead of knocking six months off a one-year sentence for the six months of dead time you've already served, the judge just gives you eighteen months and says six off for time served. Recent legislation has reduced two-for-one time to one-for-one.

If nobody bailed you out or you were never granted bail, it may show the judge how unwanted and untrustworthy you are. At your trial and sentencing, with nobody you know in attendance to show they care, nobody will complain if the judge gives you a higher sentence. The judge can save lighter sentences for identical crimes when the accused has many family members and supportive friends in the courtroom. Then the judge will appear more compassionate.

The police and Crown know if they can keep you in jail serving dead time before your trial begins, their battle is already or partly won. Had you received bail, you could have worked at turning your life around. You could have completed some counselling, AA programs, volunteer programs, etc., and just stayed out of trouble for a while. A judge seeing this from an assessment report may then give you less time or none at all. If you serve dead time, you are far more helpless to show any changes. Dead time in the DCs and superjails is correctly named for those trapped in limbo waiting for court. For some prisoners, it's like waiting helplessly to die. Time is frozen. But the incarcerated continue to age and lose what they had on the outside. The terror is not knowing when, or if, you will ever return to the land of the living. If you waste all your dead time doing nothing, you will truly have done dead time.

Chapter 5

Detention Centres (DCs), Superjails, and Correctional Centres (CCs)

New Name, Same Game

Detention centre (DC) and correctional centre (CC) are the sanitized names for jails brought into use by the provincial correctional ministries in the eighties. Pretrial centre, sentence management unit, and remand centre are names sometimes used in Western Canada, with city lockup in Eastern Canada. By using these names, all jails in any town suddenly acquired a modern name even if the place was a crumbling rat-infested ruin.

The term *correctional* is used to imply it fixes something. An advantage for these new DCs and CCs is that now less of the public can easily see and believe the horrors of prison living. One fact many people outside such institutions fail to realize is that ever since the very first prison was built in North America (Philadelphia's Walnut Street Jail, 1773), they continue being built to keep prisoners in but also to keep the public out. Just because there are fewer dilapidated rodent-infested jails to be pointed at now, it doesn't mean that the new sparkling clean ones are blissful houses of repose. Horrors happen daily. Just no more "pets" allowed.

With all the superstores opening in Canada in the late nineties offering big financial savings to the public, the ministry decided that superjails could save money too. By 2000, many jails and CCs were supersized, and several new big-box ones were built. Superjail DCs detain you for court or to serve short sentences. A CC is where you get transferred to after you receive a provincial sentence of less than two years. After you've been found guilty and sentenced, you'll be taken, or returned, to a DC to wait there briefly before being classified then shipped to a provincial CC or federal penitentiary (pen). DCs, but not CCs, are also used as holding centres for immigration detainees, prisoners in transfer, short-timers, or parole violators on their way back to the system. Federal prisoners being returned to a prior place of incarceration are often referred to as being returned to their "mother" or "parent" institution.

Smaller Is Better

Most rural communities and small towns of up to thirty thousand inhabitants won't have a jail. A small police station might have a couple holding cells to house local prisoners for a day or two, but the nearest larger town with a jail would be used for detention. Small cities of fifty thousand to one hundred thousand people were likely to have a small jail capable of housing around one hundred prisoners. Jail populations fluctuate depending on the time of the year, peaking in late summer and early winter. For as long as I can remember, any jail where I was housed was often overcrowded. The reason? Money. Not only was there double-bunking in cells but triple and quadruple with two prisoners sleeping on the cell floor.

Any prison can be different from or more difficult than another to serve time in. In Ontario, a prisoner will likely be shipped hundreds of kilometres away from any family or friends. The upside is you are less likely to be double-bunked for your entire term as many prisoners are on the west coast. British Columbia recently closed many of their provincial institutions, increasing double-bunking dramatically. The BC advantage is that almost every prison, provincial and federal, is located within an hour or less of the Greater Vancouver Area. That means easier visits from a lawyer or family and friends and a cheaper phone bill to stay in touch. The big-box Edmonton Remand Centre, which opened in 2012, is the first in Canada to replace visits with video kiosks at another location.

Smaller jails, which are becoming extinct, were usually more humane and personal. Guards still gave you a strip search upon arrival, as the superjails do, but the smaller setting is better for doing time. Some of these jails would have a small library room or classroom where a tutor could visit. There would also be an exercise area with equipment. On a slow day, guards could allow visits to last over an hour. They were rarely as mean and violent as the ones in the superjails are now. Some small jails had more or less advantages and facilities than others, but the best benefit was being housed in your own community.

Ties to family and friends could be maintained through regular visits and local phone calls. Visits and calls to a lawyer were easier and cheaper. It was easy to keep in touch with the support you had in the community—a community you would be returning to one day. Being moved away causes more stress because of less or eliminated support. Prisoners housed in big, cold, warehouse-like settings are more stressed out. Along with higher stress levels among prisoners, guards will also be more hard-core in the larger jails than in the small community ones. Guards can be decent and humane, but there are always a few who are no less vile than the wards they keep. It's likely that harder meaner guards exist in the superjails because there are also harder malefactors in these larger facilities.

In the smaller community jails, guards and prisoners are more likely to know one another from the local community. Consequently, neither suffers as much from the stress of the big-city prison life. Guards in the smaller jails are less likely to be cruel to most prisoners for personal reasons. Staff could also know you easier from repeated returns. Being caged in a superjail, away from your family and community, means an extra loss of your identity and less freedom.

Long ago, communities would take better care of their own citizens. Families took care of their elders and the locals pulled together to solve problems. Any local person jailed was more likely better known as a member of that community. For breaking a law in these local areas, the accused would truly be tried by his peers, those who knew him personally, and be punished by and incarcerated in their own community. Nowadays, in an ever increasingly throwaway society of greed, communities care much less about the negative products (offenders) from their own area. Officials happily wash their hands of the unwanted by sending them off to a faraway superjail. Problem solved! Out of sight, out of mind! Money saved!

In the short term, supersized jails *appear* more cost efficient in saving taxpayers' money.

Count the Cost

According to Statistics Canada, on any given day in 2000-2001, there was an average of 151,000 adults under the supervision of the Canadian correctional system. The majority, 79 percent, was under community supervision, with 21 percent in custody. Of those caged, 40 percent (12,624) were federal and 60 percent (18,645) provincial. The system spent $2.5 billion the same year.[xvi]

In 2008-2009, the numbers doubled to almost 371,800 adults admitted to some form of Canadian correctional service program. With yearly operating costs totalling almost $3.9 billion, the tough-on-crime legislation will guarantee costs and keep prisons growing.[xvii]

Other costs are not so easily seen. It does make it easier for the "professionals" of the justice system to steal away the conflict, thereby robbing local communities of their ability to face trouble and restore peace. Sending the accused and the convicted far away results in long-term damage. What's more, the communities lose their confidence and their capacity and inclination to preserve, protect, and self-rule. They surrender their autonomy and are less likely to consider restorative justice measures. They become dependent consumers of police, court, and jail services.

Not long ago, if your crime wasn't serious or the sentence not too lengthy, you could possibly serve all of your time at the local jail. Those serving only a few months could be allowed to work on a city cleanup crew if they could be trusted. These lucky few could also keep their day jobs by serving only weekends, which would allow them to continue to support their families. You could also get a lesser sentence by adding volunteer community work as part of the sentencing. These programs kept prisoners feeling like a part of their community, one they should care about. This kind of sentence was not for everyone and was never seen as harsh. However, it allowed some offenders to prevent whatever life they had before incarceration from totally collapsing. They would still have something to return to one day. It also allowed the offender to take responsibility while the community had input and was a part of the solution.

In contrast to adversarial justice, community projects of restorative justice allowed healing, reconciliation, and giving back to the community. Those who couldn't be trusted, were violent, or had more serious offences would get longer sentences and were transferred away to serve them. In addition to possibly being transferred to distant facilities to serve sentences, anyone in smaller cities and towns may now be transferred to distant locations upon arrest.

Smaller city councils won't really miss the generous subsidies doled out to care for prisoners since they no longer have the expense of having a jail. Superjails in Canada are modelled after those in the American system, the ones rumoured to be the best and most efficient in the world. The fact that the U.S. also has the highest crime and recidivism rate is completely overlooked. Politicians and those in positions of power boast of financial savings through the building of superjails. It's a short-term saving at the cost of creating harder time for anyone trapped in jail, plus their friends and family.

Bigger—Better?

The new Ontario superjails, all maximum security, are located in Milton (Maplehurst, capacity 1,550), Penetanguishene (Central North, capacity 1,184), and Lindsay (Central East, capacity 1,184). Milton's was a CC and now has an adjoining DC built onto it. In the west, there is also the new Edmonton Remand Centre (capacity 1,952, with a future potential expansion to 2,816). London (Elgin-Middlesex) and Hamilton (Hamilton-Wentworth) still have large DCs, while Toronto has three DCs: the East, the West, and the Don, a medieval dungeon—all maximum security as well.

The larger jails and those built farther away in smaller areas on cheap land will save money on paper with their warehouse-style setting. In the long term, what can't be proven or easily shown are the mental effects on prisoners who are now cut off more from the world. How many will be released as colder meaner felons because of harsher incarceration? For more than a decade now, the provincial correctional ministries and the Correctional Service of Canada (CSC) have been growing rapidly with unchecked bureaucracies. The absence of priorities to rehabilitate or correct, as their mission statements imply, helps perpetuate the inherent problems. Many of the frustrated angry prisoners trapped inside and their advocates outside know there must be change. The current system is a disaster, and it is only getting worse.

Common Sense Cancelled

The CSC's mission statement states that it "contributes to public safety." It also says it does so by "actively encouraging and assisting offenders to become law-abiding citizens." Ha! The words *short term* and *rehabilitation* are never mentioned once. Just like judges, the CSC pretends not to be cruel and unusual while portraying compassion in its cause. But as the University of Toronto's Professor Alan Young says, "Compassion requires emotional engagement inconsistent with an adversarial ethic."[xviii]

Part of the retributivist's philosophy, or the hard-on-crime stance, is that if the system is harsher, it will deter offenders from returning by making them think twice about breaking the law. If this plan is successful in causing some criminals not to return to a life of crime, what effect does it have on all the others? The value of such deterrence is only limited to some individuals. I know the harshness and unfairness only made me bitter and more determined to vent myself upon society after my release. Feeling helpless, cold, and alone in prison does not help turn prisoners into more caring, productive, emotionally well beings for release. Deprivation and a cold environment affect prisoners negatively, and society will suffer eventually in the long term. It's basically cause and effect.

Violence 101

Larger jails look sanitized but are always more brutal than the smaller ones ever were. Jails can always play down the severity and sum of violence within its walls. It must do this in order to project an image of efficient control and protecting society. Critics who have studied penology and claim to be knowledgeable often compile their information from the management who run the jails, none of whom have likely ever served time in custody. These officials only see a fraction of the violence, pain, and suffering, and it's not in their best interests to report all they see or know. Statistics, of course, are relevant if they can support reasons for needing tighter security, higher operational costs, more danger pay for stress-related work, pay raises, or for needing more sick days. If it's so dangerous, why work there? Only the prisoners themselves truly see and feel all the violence. They suffer directly, but eventually so too will society.

I once did a short sentence of four months in Guelph Reformatory, or Guelph CC. I saw dozens of fights/assaults that were never witnessed by guards. Whenever a fight broke out, others would often "keep six" (i.e., keep a lookout) for any approaching guards. Unlike other prisoners, I could never stay and watch anyone fight. I would always turn away and leave whenever possible. I would never inform the guards, but sadly, prisoners rarely break up a fight. Why? For starters, people don't want to get involved in the problems of others. However, it's also a show of might when more than one individual gangs up on another weaker or disliked prisoner.

Many fights and assaults happen simply for entertainment at someone else's expense. Most people love to watch hockey because of the fights. Boxers get paid millions to smash fists to each other's heads. These sports may one day be viewed as slightly more humane than watching the Christians fighting the lions. In the penitentiary, whenever a fight broke out, I would walk away while everyone else gathered around to watch. If someone is fatally stabbed, everyone doesn't fade away from the scene like in the movies. They will want to see the action and carnage. However, if there is a chance of being blamed, prisoners will flee. Most will just stand back and watch. People have a morbid sense of curiosity, especially depraved prisoners living a cold uneventful life behind bars.

While I was at the Guelph Reformatory in 2000, a prisoner beside me was piped to death in the weight room as thirty others watched. I had just left the room a moment before it happened. I was the only one in the entire gym not to run over to the weight room windows to watch. The prisoners from the gym stayed at these windows for more then ten minutes looking at the bludgeoned prisoner lying on the floor with a pipe sticking out of his head. I heard what everyone saw but was glad I never looked. Why would anyone want such a sight etched in memory? It was the talk of the institution for weeks. The Guelph Reformatory has since been closed, but fights and deaths continue elsewhere.

There are now far fewer weapons—shanks, shivs, knives, etc.—in the DCs and superjails. The ranges are so sparse that there is almost nothing to break off or fashion into some kind of weapon. Pop cans in pillowcases were once popular, but neither can be found together in the DCs now. Bars of soap in a pillowcase or a wool sock were also corrected by giving out smaller bars of soap. The guards now diligently hold and count razors, but a thin razor is easy to hide if a guard slips up. I wished some prisoners had a razor to protect themselves or at least make bullies less of a bully. Even the biggest toughest bullies will use a weapon on smaller unarmed prisoners, and I've seen and experienced it personally as well. There are far more weapons in the penitentiary system. Not long ago, there were moveable wooden tables and chairs in the DCs. If a fight broke out, nearby guards could easily hear the noise of moving tables and chairs. With any banging or yelling, a guard could easily look up or around a corner and hit a panic button, and many guards would come a running. That is, of course, if they heard or saw it right away. In most fights, the greatest damage is done in the first few shots or minutes, so by the time guards arrive, people will already be hurting, maybe badly.

The Power of One

Large jails are mostly square in shape and modelled after U.S. prisons, using a hexagon design with a control pod in the centre. This spider-like layout allows one guard to watch several ranges all at once. Theoretically, one diligent guard could see everything. That is if they kept spinning their chair or had six compound eyes. The multiple circles can also be quite disorienting, especially when unable to see the position of the sun. This architectural innovation allowing no place for prisoners to hide from surveillance is modelled after Jeremy Bentham's Panopticon.

Bentham, a prodigy born in 1748, later founded the doctrine of utilitarianism. Followers stress utility over beauty and believe that the purpose of all action should be to bring about the greatest happiness to the greatest number. Unfortunately, those oppressed and suffering the most by the justice system are a helpless minority. Bentham believed that prisoners forced to undergo total surveillance would eventually give up their nefarious criminal ways and become the kind of citizen who has nothing to hide. It makes one wonder if this idea is what inspired George Orwell's *Nineteen Eighty-Four*. Placing surveillance cameras on more and more street corners is expanding such Dark Age reasoning.

To the Furies of the system, such a design appears to save money, be more efficient, and be safer. It is of little concern that the prisoners will feel uncomfortable being watched all the time or that a lack of privacy can be humiliating and shame-inducing. Shame leads to isolation, and in the cold storage of a prison setting, there is little hope of transcending shame. The danger is that a total lack of privacy can cause severe hardship for any prisoner. Such a stress-inducing effect on hapless prisoners may also cause them to compensate by victimizing those around them or upon society after their release.

There are many cameras in today's prisons. A guard who turns their back for a moment can miss a quick fight. If the guard is asked if they saw a fight happen, they are not going to admit being negligent during their vigil. They can simply say they just turned away for a minute. No guard will admit they were busy reading a car magazine, playing solitaire on the computer, or gabbing on the phone, even though prisoners see them do that all day. Another problem is sound. The guard in the control pod sits behind a Plexiglas wall, a hallway, and another Plexiglas wall. They couldn't hear a fight start anyway. There's a button to push to get the guard's attention and speak to them, but anyone who uses it during a fight to call for help will be instantly labelled a rat.

With only one guard needed to push buttons, monitor screens, and watch over many prisoners in several ranges at once, there will be fewer guards (i.e., money) needed to run each jail and fewer on the spot to break up any fights. Guards come running quickly from all over the jail if a code red is announced. This is not just because it's their job and they are bored but mostly to protect their kind. Caring about prisoners beating prisoners is not a priority. Guards come running to assist fellow guards. It's sickening to helplessly witness some guards running to the scene and assault a prisoner who never struck them. Guards quickly get prisoners into cells, away from other prisoner's eyes, before assaulting them. If the fear of six guards forcing you into a cell causes you to put up any resistance, it will be likely at least one of a dozen arms forcing you down will throw a punch, while others will quickly follow if you don't play dead. Next to being a street cop, being a guard is the easiest way to get away with assaulting another human being. Some guards really love their job for this reason. They will also all stick together if accusations arise. Who will be believed?

On the Level

Larger DCs have different security levels on different floors or wings. It's usually higher floors for higher security. The lowest level usually houses a hospital unit for faster and easier access to the outside hospital. The hard-core prisoners will usually inhabit the upper floors but will also be spread throughout the entire jail as well. One range may have more immigrants, blacks, or violent offenders than another range. Some quieter ranges will have more prisoners who have done prior pen time, while another range may have first-time offenders and small-time criminals. There is often a low-security range and perhaps dorms usually for weekenders or for those serving very short terms. Larger institutions may have a female range as well as a range for young offenders (YOs). Most ranges fluctuate in population, and adding or removing one or several prisoners can alter the entire mood of any range. Most guards don't want to work on a range that has more troublemakers, fights, and undesirable prisoners. Then again, a mean guard, pulling attitude on a more violent range, may also be looking for action. Non-violent prisoners won't want to be housed on a range with violent hardened prisoners, although prisoners wanting to achieve status may want to be located there. If a certain range becomes known as being very peaceful, most prisoners will want to be housed there and most guards will want to work there. Again, it only takes one or two prisoners to alter the stress level on an otherwise quiet range.

With many prisoners coming and going, ranges achieve a wide mix of personalities. On a range of younger prisoners, it often helps to add a couple of older hardened pen-timers to keep the younger ones quiet and in line. The guards know this but don't often know everything that is happening on the range, even when they hear whispers from rats. Guards don't live on the range. They only enter to lock and unlock cells, do searches, or escort prisoners elsewhere. Security officers in the newest jails are able to lock or unlock all doors from the pod. Wherever a prisoner is placed upon arrival will most likely be by designated chance of the available bed space. Prisoners could also be moved later for specific reasons never revealed to them. Rats!

Less fighting will be reported in these new jails. Researcher Jane Ireland underlines that "indirect and covert forms of aggression, not routinely identified as aggression, are successfully exploited in prison settings."[xix] Most bullies are aware that they can be spotted on camera and thus more easily caught, so they change their methods. A quick slap, punch, or full assault will happen off-camera in blind spots in the shower or cells. Even if a prisoner gets a black eye, broken nose, or broken jaw, most will know better than to admit what really happened.

Guards may try getting assaulted prisoners to squeal. Medical attention can be withheld until you confess. Prisoners who do are taken to protective custody (PC), which is considered the worst status in the prison. All other prisoners look down on those in PC. If you tell a guard that you fell and you need to see a nurse, you likely will. Guards won't write any lengthy reports about an assault if you don't admit that one had occurred. Why waste their time? A report will only make waves for prisoners and make it look as if the institution can't protect its wards. Fewer assaults on paper show that the jail is much more in control of the situation—super control for the superjail!

There is still much brutality in jails even though it goes unreported. Just because it's not seen, it doesn't mean it's not happening. Even greater is the unseen cruel stress of threats and intimidation that occurs. Many prisoners live in constant fear of being assaulted, and such fear over weeks, months, and even years can be more damaging psychologically than a fight alone. There are also prisoners who have too much fear and paranoia—a great destroyer. Some prisoners, and some guards as well, are very loud, aggressive, rude, crude, irritating, and down right evil.

There may not be a fight on one range for weeks or months, yet there may be daily fights on another range. This is because few know the meaning of "doing your own time," while fewer have respect for all human beings. It's bad enough being caged, worrying about problems outside or of an upcoming trial, without also being with some real dregs of society. There are always one or more prisoners ruling or trying to rule a range. These prisoners are often the ones who tried to control others on the outside, and after failing, they try to do the same inside. Such individuals feel even more helpless in jail and will want power and control inside. It's a power play for them to earn even small gains. Food, canteen, phone, and TV control all become tools for them to manipulate, obtain ownership, and achieve control. Many also want attention and will constantly try to achieve it. Guards do this too by manipulating prisoners into squealing on others, spreading innuendo, or inciting unrest amongst prisoners!

One small advantage to larger jails is they may have a small study room where a prisoner can ask to visit for an hour or so.

These rooms are for those involved in schoolwork. They may also be the only hope of escape from the madness of a range. A prisoner can also read or write a letter in peace if such a room is available. Some larger jails may have one teacher to attend once a week for a few minutes or more to answer questions about courses. There may also be a volunteer tutor to assist a prisoner for an hour or so with schoolwork once a week. After a prisoner leaves a DC and is transferred to a CC or penitentiary, options for schooling will be far better. Prisoners may find others doing the same educational course and help one another. Prisoners who take courses must keep pushing to finish whether they have help or not.

Shape Up or Else!

It's important to stay in shape both mentally and physically. Reading for an hour and pacing for an hour each day helps accomplish this. Some prisoners will quickly lose weight from the stress of jail time, while others will pack on the pounds from three fatty meals a day and sitting on their butts too long. The sedentary existence of prison life can be the worst environment to delay any diet or educational plans. Prisoners have more time on their hands than is imaginable. Prisoners who don't use time for self-improvement or at least self-maintenance will regret it. Whether you leave the DC to freedom or to another facility, you will have more time to continue on your regimen or notice how out of shape you've become. If you keep getting more brain dead, it's more difficult to notice; however, your body gradually getting more out of shape is obvious. It will be that much more difficult to survive inside as well as to get back up on your feet after your release. You may be happy the day you are set free, but when you look in a mirror, your self-esteem will take a hit.

If you start pushing yourself early to read, study, and workout, you will be more likely to continue later. Prison is an extremely oppressive environment, and the boredom alone can drive one mad. If you would rather not gain any education, then don't read anything, but keep yourself busy. To help pass the time, you could always work for "The Man" by doing some useless job such washing walls or sweeping floors. You can help your jailer and mop floors—for free?

There is usually only one person in a range to get the job of hall cleaner while the rest do nothing. There are very few jobs in the DCs. There are limited jobs for kitchen and laundry crews, but these prisoners usually have their own range, a lower security rating (minor charges), and are looking at short time. Even these jobs are ones you would never take on the outside, so why do them inside for free? Boredom! Time drags by at the slowest pace in the DCs.

With Friends Like These, Who Needs Enemies?

Can you meet new friends in jail? It's hard to imagine real friendships exist in such a cold barren environment nourished primarily by emotions of frustration and despair. I made many, but none lasted long after hitting the outside. Many prisoners I met inside changed upon their release. Most returned to being violent drunks, drug addicts, irresponsible, untrustworthy, or habitual liars and cons. There are many "bullshit slingers" behind bars, and many live better off in jail. Many have ingrained behaviours and bad habits built up over years. While inside, they don't worry about rent, bills, positive socializing, and other ways to get by successfully in the real world. Many have serious drinking, drug, and mental problems, and you can't always notice or see how bad their problems really are until they are set free. Some who abuse drugs and alcohol will claim they no longer have a problem simply because they haven't used any inside. Few will admit to themselves, much less anyone else, just how bad their ways really are or that they truly want and need to change.

Upon arrival to jail, some prisoners will quickly befriend you. Their friendship may be sincere, but they will most likely be looking for just another person to use. There is strength in numbers, and most prisoners want many friends for support. Many in the DCs don't have money upon arrest or in their accounts, so if you get conned into buying them a little something, don't expect to be paid back. Do expect their asking for more. Many will say they have money on the way, and some will know they are about to be transferred but won't tell you before borrowing anything. There are now more comrades than ever, and the poorest ones of all are the ones to say, "Everyone should share and help others."

The Lowest of the Low

People trapped behind bars have very few possessions to hold—a few pictures, letters, and some canteen items. When anyone steals from another in prison, it's called "box thieving." Anyone labelled a box or drum thief is often quickly pummelled by others. It's a bad thing to be caught taking another's property in jail. When people who have lost everything are tossed together and caged with few possessions, someone taking something as minor as a pencil can quickly develop into a situation of mortal danger.

In Joyceville Institution in 1996, in a range above mine, a fight broke out over a prisoner taking his cellmate's comb. That may not sound so serious, but the fight ended with one prisoner dead. Although there are more fights in the DCs than in the CCs or the pens, those in the pens can be fatal. One must always respect another's property and never take or use another's things without permission.

Sadly, some ruthless prisoners know how much everyone hates box thieves and will falsely accuse or label someone just to turn others against someone they don't like and want off the range. Many prisoners do the same by spreading gossip about a prisoner to start fights or justify beating someone up. There are all kinds of problems swirling about inside the heads of many prisoners. Taking something that's theirs or even being falsely accused of it, or anything else, may be the straw that breaks the camel's back, making one snap and lose it on another. Some prisoners also look for any excuse to justify jumping on someone they don't like or they know they can beat up to make themselves feared by others.

If you get into a fight and are spotted by the guards, you will both likely be carted off to segregation for a few days even if you never started it or raised a fist. This could last weeks or months with a loss of privileges (e.g., no canteen or books). For some, solitary is very difficult; however, for others, like me, it's a blissful vacation. The CSC sanitized the name to segregation because of the connotations associated with solitary confinement and disassociation.

Guilty Until Proven Innocent

Provincial DCs and CCs have now become so disliked by prisoners that more prisoners can't wait to be moved to a penitentiary. Prisoners are now more likely to try dealing with their cases as quickly as possible. Most prisoners used to try to avoid a federal sentence at all costs, but now many prefer the pen. With many smaller jails closing down and prisoners being sent away to larger jails farther away, in addition to CCs having less to offer, there is now less freedom and more stress. The federal government has succeeded in gaining more control over the most oppressed group of people in society, but the specialist of pain is no longer the executioner. That role is the province of the police, Crowns, judges, guards, and parole officers, all wielding a portion of the legal power to punish.

It is foolish to wholeheartedly believe that prisons, keeping the body of the condemned tucked away from sight, are a civilized replacement to flogging, the pillory, or the spectacle of the scaffold. Such ceremony of punishment is no longer used to deploy the pomp of justice. Anything easily viewed as barbaric or cruel can make a society and its justice system appear uncivilized. Now, more than ever, the brutality and damage prison causes is locked away from public view. Yet there are prisoners trapped inside who would gladly accept a whipping or the pillory in exchange for an early release from or to avoid time in prison. Could such physical acts cause less damage in the long run?

A flogging ordered by a judge can be less physically damaging than some of the beatings I've witnessed in prison. This includes one that put me in intensive care for several days with multiple lacerations to my body and head that required many stitches and more surgery years later. That pipe attack from four young prisoners also broke my jaw in several places. I can vividly recall waking up alone after surgery handcuffed to a bed in the city hospital recovery room with guards outside the door. The most painful feeling wasn't physical but emotional—and the memory remains. I awoke whispering, "Elsa," the name of my fiancée, who had left me unexpectedly months earlier without even a Dear John farewell. I lay there alone for days knowing that had I died, nobody I ever knew would have cared. Although that happened in a federal medium-security institution, much violence happens in the provincial DCs and CCs as well.

The public doesn't see the victims of violence in prison as victims. Prison walls easily hide the sights and sounds of "the guards' greatest hits" upon prisoners. The public can excuse responsibility simply by claiming that prisoners are the ones who put themselves there. Even before they have their day in court, the accused are weakened, punished, and some beaten by prisoners or guards, just for being accused. The longer they must stay trapped in custody waiting for a trial, the more they will suffer. The sad truth is that a person on remand who has *not* been convicted of any crime, and may even be innocent, can do harder time than a convicted murderer sentenced to life in a penitentiary. "Innocent until proven guilty" means nothing in the Canadian "justice" system, for the innocent are often treated worse than the guilty!

The superjails and DCs are the new unseen hearth in which violence bursts again into flames. For many trapped there, punishment, before guilt has been determined, rarely equals but often exceeds the savagery of the crime itself.

Chapter 6

Plea or Trial

Out on Bail

Upon being arrested, some people hire a lawyer, get bail, and never spend a day in jail. If they must wait a long time to find out what happens, the waiting may be the hardest part. You will be asked at an early court appearance if you wish to be tried later by judge alone or by judge and jury. Your lawyer will recommend which choice to make. Your lawyer should also inform you about the time you could get if found guilty. They may suggest you plead guilty because you're a first-timer and will be out on parole in no time. Unfortunately, lawyers know very little about parole and the differences between serving provincial or federal time.

If you remain free in society, you will have a slightly better chance of being found not guilty or you could cut a better plea bargain. If you go to trial and lose, you'll stand a slightly better chance of receiving a lesser sentence. With no dead time for your lawyer to barter with upon sentencing, your behaviour on bail may help, depending on the behaviour and the judge. A stressful year or more on bail with an 8:00 p.m. curfew, a radius limitation on movement, a ban on drinking, and other stringent stipulations will make a judge think they did you a favour. Forcing restrictions on you may help straighten you up. If you are single, your social life may have all but vanished just in time for a trip to prison. If you feel that being on the restricted freedom of bail was punishing, while the judge doesn't, too bad! You may soon think that ninety days in jail would have been easier than the year or two you suffered while out on bail.

When you're out on bail, many lawyers will postpone your trial date and set it as far in advance as possible. While the Askov ruling guarantees everyone to a trial without delay (usually about a year), those remaining in custody have more right to a speedier trial. Postponing is usually quite easy since many courts are so overburdened with cases. There are several reasons why lawyers and clients prefer to do this. There will be more time to gather evidence, and defence witnesses will be easier to find, locate, and speak with, especially if you are free on bail. Over time, Crown witnesses may move away, decide they don't want to testify, or their memories may fail or fade. Delays mean more time to prepare a case if your lawyer has taken on too much work. Dump-trucking solves this dilemma quickly. (For more on dump trucks, please see Chapter 3.)

If you can show that you've made some positive changes in your behaviour while you were out on bail, this may impress the judge upon sentencing you, but be prepared for it to have no impact. If you've attended Alcoholics Anonymous (AA) or Narcotics Anonymous (NA) for a year and claim you haven't touched a drop since the accident or incident, it may help you look like you've reformed. You can also appear more stable in the eyes of the court if you've attended family counselling regularly, married, become a new parent, found better employment, or received a promotion. If seeing a specialist, attending group therapy, or taking a new blue pill has made you a changed person, this will improve your chances in court, provided you haven't broken any bail conditions. None of these efforts will prove your innocence, but they can make a difference, both at trial and at the time of sentencing. However, all of these positive efforts can only occur if bail was granted in the first place.

If you fail to show any improvement or are found in breach of bail, you will be in worse shape than if you had never been granted bail in the first place. Getting charged a second time for the same crime before your court date sure won't make you look innocent. Any extra charges or bail breaches can result in additional time to serve and an angry judge adding more time to the original charge. However, if you've managed to turn your life around a little, a decent judge may sentence you to two years probation rather than six months behind bars. For more serious charges, you may be sentenced to two years instead of three. Some judges may care, whereas some don't seem to care at all.

The Importance of the Past

Some lawyers win big, or lose big, not only because of their skill and your crime, but also partly because of your past. Your past can play a minor or major role in a trial's outcome. If you decide to fight your charges and take the stand, you'll be questioned about your past. Behaving well adds to your image of innocence or lessens the length of your sentence. If you don't take the stand, the Crown can't question you or bring up your past, as it can bias the judge or jury against you. The Crown can only bring up a criminal past and immoral behaviour if you take the stand. This technique is to discredit you, although the media and the police may already do this to potential witnesses before the trial date. Professional witnesses used by Crowns can also destroy innocent lives.

In 1993, William Mullins-Johnson, a thirty-five-year-old Ojibway man, was accused of sexually assaulting and suffocating his four-year-old niece, Valin Johnson. On the morning of the tragedy, Mullins-Johnson, who often babysat his niece, was asleep downstairs on a couch. Within hours, doctors concluded that little Valin had been sodomized and beaten, and had been a victim of prior abuses. Without any semen, saliva, or hair evidence, coroner Charles Randal Smith's "expert" testimony was enough to find

Mullins-Johnson guilty of murder. The subsequent appeal failed.

Twelve years passed before new doctors viewed the evidence and concluded the original coroner was wrong. The enlarged rectal opening of the child was not proof of assault but due to the natural loss of muscle tension after death. The minute traces of anal blood? Natural seepage. The bruising? Post-mortem lividity (gradual pooling of blood after death). Mullins-Johnson was not only convicted of a horrific crime, he was convicted of a crime that never happened. Thanks to the enduring love of his mother helping him through many hard years in prison and the aid of the Association in Defence of the Wrongly Convicted (AIDWIC), he was eventually freed in 2005.

In the case of Guy Paul Morin, accused of sexually assaulting a young girl before taking her life, the police groomed the public before Morin even made it to court. Before Morin's arrest in 1985, the police released information from an FBI psychological profile describing the killer. Then, at another news conference called to announce his arrest, the police claimed he had been one of their five suspects and that "the profile matched him to a T." The defence lawyer argued this prejudiced his client's case for a fair trial because prospective jurors from the small community would suspect he must be guilty since he already matched the FBI profile. A police officer also voiced a statement at a news conference, saying, "You who should be chosen as jurors should remember this profile, as we cannot show it to you later when this matter comes to court." Announcing to the public after the capture, "I think there is a great sense of relief there now," implied the police had arrested the right suspect and that he was guilty.

Sadly, Morin lost twice at trial and did some very hard time. However, he was exonerated by DNA evidence three years later. Although the damage of Morin's tainted reputation will never be undone, such unfairness did produce the Commission on Proceedings Involving Guy Paul Morin (a.k.a. the Kaufman Report). Justice

Fred Kaufman concluded, "The police helped ensure that Morin would never get a fair trial."[xx] Although the police are permitted by law to use some forms of trickery and deception, they can go too far. It's unfortunate that only the highest profile cases with charges of murder—Donald Marshall, Jr., Romeo Phillion, and David Milgaard, for example—only draw such scrutiny now. How many thousands of less important cases go unnoticed where the police manipulate evidence and groom witnesses or the public?

Fact or Fiction?

If the police or any witness has it out for you, they will *always* make your crime look far worse than it may have been. By the time a witness for the Crown shows up for a trial, their memory may have mysteriously improved a great deal. As Dr. Tana Dineen writes in her book *Manufacturing Victims*, "Research shows retrospective memory is basically a reconstructive process. That remembrances are put together from partial memory traces and are remembered in such a way as to meet the needs or demands of the moment." Crowns want to make you look as guilty as possible any way they can. Regardless of the type of crime, any truths, lies, rumours, and erroneous statements may force you to go to trial whether you're guilty or not. You're less likely to plead guilty if facts are blown out of proportion from the very beginning. If you plead guilty and get twice the amount of time you deserve, you likely won't feel much guilt. In addition, if you are charged and convicted of other offences you didn't commit, it will likely vanquish any guilt you should feel for the charges of which you are guilty.

If your lawyer thinks you have a chance of winning (lawyers are usually optimistic at first), you may decide at the start of your nightmare to plead not guilty. You and your lawyer may also choose to have a pretrial to discover how strong the Crown's case is against you. This allows the police and witnesses to be put on the stand to evaluate their merit as well as review any evidence. After seeing the Crown's strengths and weaknesses, it may change your mind about going to trial. You can also opt to go straight to trial from the start without a pretrial.

For over twenty years, pretrial motions related to issues of the Canadian Charter of Rights and Freedoms have been used to delay a trial or toss charges out. No one wants to be on the wrong side of an incompetent counsel's allegation in the Court of Appeals for failing to have raised an issue of rights. Lawyers need not be so cautious now that most areas have been tested thoroughly. Gone as well are the days of winning on a technicality. Such outcomes are rare but still popular in TV land. Defence lawyers now have fewer opportunities to stall court with pretrial motions, alleging possible breaches to a suspect's rights. Prosecutors, however, under the new influence of victim's rights advocates, may sacrifice their time-honoured objectivity and, under pressure, overcharge or push the evidentiary envelope too far.

You can plead guilty at any time from the day of your arrest until the day your trial begins. I even had a judge thank me upon sentencing for saving the taxpayers' money by pleading guilty. I still received a nine-month sentence and will never know what would have happened had I followed through with the trial. My lawyer told me that the Crown had offered nine months, and I accepted. Had I gone through with a trial and lost, I would likely have received twice the time the Crown was asking. The unwritten rule is usually double or nothing. This type of joint submission by your lawyer and the Crown is common but never absolute. A judge does not have to agree to the deal after you've pled guilty. A judge may put more emphasis on certain facts of the case, facts the Crown or your lawyer had overlooked. The judge may decide to give a longer or shorter sentence. They usually agree to joint submissions and the punishment suggested, but they may occasionally alter it a little or a lot.

In the battle of lawyer versus lawyer, truth is always the first casualty. May the best man win does not necessarily apply to guilt or innocence. Exaggerated victim impact statements, erroneous police reports, faulty doctor's evaluations, and witness testimonies, whether accurate or not, all play a role manipulated by the system that will judge and condemn you. If you plead guilty or are found guilty, then guards, parole officers, prisoners, social workers, and doctors will also be added to the list of people who will use the statements against you. A guilty person can be found innocent simply by having a better lawyer, and an innocent person can be found guilty because of an incompetent lawyer.

When a case starts to fall apart for the Crown, they will *never* say you were wrongfully charged. The Crown will save face by stating that there is insufficient evidence to proceed to trial at this time. It's like saying you still did the crime but it just can't be proven—yet. For the Crown to come right out and say that you should not have been charged is like admitting they are guilty of wrongfully putting you through hell. Unfortunately, what few people realize is that once you are charged, even if those charges are later withdrawn or tossed out, the charges are still on record to possibly be used against you at a later date. Charging you, even for a crime that can't be proven, is a form of emasculation, an egregious lack of judgement by the police and Crown, which borders on the fringes of Crown misconduct.

Crown Misconduct

Some lawyers feel Crown misconduct should be made into a crime. It is difficult to catch or prove and is only occasionally pointed out by the appellate courts on appealed cases. The police and Crown will often try to show how horrible and damaging a crime was long before a trial begins. The media does the same to sell stories. Hopefully, disparaging comments about the accused will one day only be allowed after a conviction. The purpose of the trial is to prove one's guilt, not to sway a judge, a jury, witnesses, and the public with terrible facts of the case before a verdict is reached. It's as if the police and Crown strive to show that somebody must pay for the crime—the one accused—rather than let the individual who *possibly* committed it go free.

The depth of the damage has no point or value to an innocent person and only repulses a judge or jury and the public, inciting a hunger for blood. Showing how horrible a crime was doesn't necessarily have a bearing on proving who did it. The emphasis on the damage a crime caused, dramatizing the evil, should be reserved for sentencing purposes, not used as grandstanding by the police, Crown, or judge to manipulate the emotions of the jury, witnesses, or public.

Hear Ye! Hear Ye!

Many factors can influence a pretrial, plea offering, trial, or sentencing hearing. If a witness fails to appear or recants, or if an absent police constable is testifying at a more important trial, the Crown may not be able to ask for more than one remand to postpone the starting trial. Evidence may not be allowed by a judge or may be conveniently lost. Facts that were strong against you may have also changed over time. The plea offer can then suddenly change sharply. The Crown, knowing they may now lose the case, will want to at least get a plea for a conviction. This can also go the other way. If the police discover more incriminating evidence, or another witness talks even worse about you, your one-year offer may then jump to three.

If the Crown knows the judge better than your lawyer does, they may have an added advantage as well. The Crown may agree to a joint submission, knowing the judge will reject it and then, after you plead guilty, give you a higher sentence. The Crown who knows the judge better will be able to influence or manipulate them easier with a few selected facts about the case or you and your past.

Up goes the sentence!

An agreed deal that turns out bad is not the worst thing that can happen in court. Being found guilty for a crime you did not commit is not the worst outcome. Being found guilty and "crucified" for a crime that never happened is the worst nightmare. Guilty or innocent, if evidence against you is slightly wrong, it can set you free or make you get twice the time you deserve. If the police's, Crown's, or witness's words are inaccurate, it's unlikely your day in court will be just. Aristotle once said, "The least initial deviation from the truth is multiplied later a thousandfold." Sadly, justice can be denied, not only by errors of others but also by one's own lawyer.

"And in This Corner...."

Lawyers rarely give a guarantee. If they do, it won't be in writing. You may think a guarantee was implied, but remember that lawyers are practiced in the art of deception. In fact, their pitch to you may change from bad to good and back several times. Your lawyer may also be feeling you out for your reactions. Not all defence lawyers will ask you if you are guilty. They may try to search for the truth from you as well as guess what kind of witness you will make if put on the stand. Your responses help them judge what kind of offer you will accept to plead guilty.

In most cases, a defence lawyer will never put the accused on the stand. A lot of the time, a defence lawyer won't call a single witness. This puts the onus of proving guilt all on the Crown. Each time the Crown puts a witness on the stand, the defence lawyer gets the opportunity to question the witness after the Crown is finished. Your lawyer will only want you to testify if they are sure it will help and not jeopardize the case. If your lawyer intends to call any witnesses, this will begin after the Crown has finished calling all of theirs. The roles are then reversed, and the Crown questions your witnesses after your lawyer has.

Defence lawyers don't like putting anyone on the stand with a criminal past or anyone who doesn't speak honestly and convincingly. If you are innocent and your lawyer knows it, they may still not want you to testify. If your lawyer knows you are guilty, or thinks you won't hold up well under cross-examination from the Crown, they won't want you on the stand. If you insist on testifying, you will likely be the last one to take the stand. If your lawyer feels they are going to lose the case, they may not try too hard in keeping you from taking the stand because they can later blame you for losing. Your lawyer is also not supposed to ask you any question on the stand if they know your answer will be a lie. Lawyers have ethical guidelines to follow but don't always tell them to you. I suspect they bend such rules if it helps win a case.

Anyone who has never been on the punitive end of justice is not likely to believe it can be so unfair. First-timers who enter the system will hear stories from other prisoners that they think are impossible to be true. Upon learning more, it will shake the confidence of one who believed the system is fair. Some stories will be exaggerations, but once some turn out to be true, or happen to you, they will easily change your attitude. One may think such unfairness in the justice system would be a deterrent, but it can create corrosive consequences by making many prisoners serve their time in anger and bitterness at such an oppressively powerful system. It is also a two-tiered system of justice: one for the privileged and another for the less privileged.

Rightfully Convicted—Overpunished

Although the unheard cries of an individual against such a force and the unheard cries of the innocent in the prison wilderness are sad hidden realities, there is also the unfair justice on the guilty. A concept that can only be debated but can't be fully calculated or scrutinized is the cumulative effects of erroneous information used on anyone accused. *Wrongfully accused* should not only be a term to use on the innocent but the guilty as well. When the guilty are wrongfully accused, they are punished far more than they deserve. Being trapped in prison can be the closest thing to being lost in space where no one can hear you scream. Oppression rules once you are labelled a criminal and jailed! They don't do things like banish people to Australian penal colonies anymore, but even that sounds preferable. As for those justifiable words, "Don't do the crime if you can't do the time," how could any fresh fish know what they're in for?

Manipulations in shades of guilt can tip the scales of justice. Dictating guilt over innocence can also vary the punishment considerably. This may mean the difference between getting six months or six years. The harshness on the guilty is greatly overshadowed by the concern for the innocent, i.e., the victim. It's common to read or hear the public outcry about a criminal who receives too light a sentence or gets off with a kiss. Unheard is any protest or public concern when the sentence is too severe. As social theorist Michel Foucault wrote so eloquently, "the public execution is to be understood not only as a judicial, but also as a political ritual. It belongs, even in minor cases, to the ceremonies by which power is manifest." The ceremony of punishment, then, is an exercise of "terror" to make everyone aware, through the body of the offender, of the might and power of the law and justice system.

Lawyers will also admit that a court outcome can result from what was told as well as what was left out. Facts may have been solicited long before you even become a suspect. Positive or negative, and accurate or not, facts not only aid in determining guilt or innocence but also how much. If testimony or evidence is manipulated or exaggerated, it's harder to get bail after an arrest, and if you're found guilty, it can exaggerate your sentence. The police know this well and will begin their grooming process from the very start. In the end, any straying from the truth may never get straightened out, and you will receive a harsher sentence. This can make the experience of being arrested turn from a little bit of chaos into a big ugly monster.

Being pilloried by the justice system becomes even worse with a lack of adequate assistance. Many of the guilty can suffer far more than they deserve physically, mentally, and financially. Faulty witnesses, community assessment reports, doctor evaluations, police input, lawyers, guards, etc., can affect a trial's verdict and sentencing and will affect where, how, and how much time will be served. Few among the public understand this unfairness although many angry prisoners taste it regularly. This plants seeds of bitterness within prisoners until they turn against the system and the society to which they eventually return. Add to this any losses suffered after being busted, such as lost or damaged property, destroyed reputations, stressed friendships, terminated jobs, etc. These are not seen as collateral damage or taken into consideration by most judges upon sentencing.

In the sentencing practices of the courts, there is a term called the *sad life principle.* In certain cases, one may not be held to the same moral account as others when one's maturity has not fully flowered due to a difficult upbringing. Certain sentencing considerations will also be taken into account if you were a cop or upstanding pillar of the community with many righteous supporters. If you're tried for the exact crime as your twin brother and you're both just as guilty, except he has no life savings, legal aid will pay his bill. He may even luck out in getting off while you fall, but then maybe your paying for an expensive lawyer will increase your chances in court. However, a lawyer can't ask for a lesser sentence because you paid cash and lost a good job, girlfriend, or best friend because of your arrest, or that they have just testified against you. It's a painful personal loss, unseen by the courts, and off you go to prison. The pain is even greater if those friends had borne false witness against you.

Pleading Out

If you want to plead guilty to separate charges, you can often have them all brought together. You can also usually bring in existing charges from other jurisdictions. If you are charged separately on different matters, you can try them apart. However, if you are charged with several offences together, the Crown may not allow them to be separated. A Crown won't separate charges if it risks weakening any chance of winning. What some people prefer doing is pleading on small charges to get them out of the way. Then, if you and your lawyer think other charges can be beaten, you take those to trial. You then plead out the ones you think you can't win. This way you are clearing up some of your charges and doing the time as you wait for a trial on any other charges. If you win later at trial, you are then set free or are that much closer to freedom depending on the time you received on the earlier plea.

One note of caution: Pleading to certain types of charges may come back to haunt you. Prison classification and parole staff, or any future judge when attending court again, will focus on certain charges such as escapes, failing to appear, breaches, or even minor acts of violence. Charges you think can easily be cleared up with a slap on the wrist could add up to compounded payment later. Ten days for a breach and fifteen for an obstructing justice may be all that's needed to tip your chances for bail later or a parole decision that keeps you in for several more months or years.

Other important considerations when entering a plea or waiting for trial include when it will happen and whether it result in provincial or federal time. When you split charges up, usually of separate incidents, you may get lucky and get concurrent time. If the judge forgets or doesn't say it's consecutive, it's automatically concurrent to any sentence you are already serving. If you're serving a one-year term and two months into it you go to trial or plead and the judge gives you another four months without saying it's consecutive, you luck out. You are still only serving the original one-year term. Even if the judge gives you an additional year without saying it's consecutive, your total is not two years. It's only a year from the day you are sentenced again. A judge may even say it's concurrent time to any you are already serving.

The Crown may also agree to a concurrent term simply to gain a guilty plea from you, especially if the case is weak. Anything less than two years, or a sentence as high as a "deuce-less" (i.e., two years less a day), is a provincial sentence. If you get eighteen months and then a month later get another ten months to serve consecutively, you will have twenty-eight months to serve, which puts you into a federal prison. If the judge says it's concurrent time, you stay in provincial and the ten concurrent months mean nothing, unless you have almost done the eighteen when you get the ten. If you get eighteen and don't want to get a pen sentence from the next charges, you put off the trial as you serve some of the eighteen. If you serve almost a year of the eighteen and then get another ten or eighteen, you can still avoid the pen even if the judge gives it to you consecutively. You must have less than two years total to serve to remain provincial.

If any charge gets you two years or more, you immediately become a federal prisoner and remain one no matter what other time is added on. Not long ago, many would split up their charges to stretch them apart to avoid a federal sentence at all costs. It was once possible to be sentenced to a deuce-less back to back. That meant doing almost four years provincial. A judge could give you a deuce-less if they didn't want you to go to the pen. Then if another judge gave the same sentence, you would have served one after the other.

The Federal System

The federal system was more feared by many prisoners a decade or more ago. First-timers and younger prisoners would try hard to avoid a pen sentence, but this has changed. Provincial time is seen more now as minor crime time, and you are a tougher prisoner if you go "down below" to become federal. While a federal record is worse, many now prefer federal, as it is a different setting. It really depends on what pen you are sent to as well as your chances for parole.

On my first entry into the system, I heard many stories about the pen. I was only nineteen and worried about ending up there. Rather than pleading guilty to all my charges from the start and possibly get a federal sentence, I kept postponing some court matters, trying to stay in the city jail for as long as I could. I pled to some charges right away, remaining in jail for over a year serving time while dealing with other charges. By the time I was done with court, my total time was about thirty-three months. Since I had already served a year in the DC, my sentence remained provincial even though the total reached thirty-three months. I was then sent to a CC and released about a year later. Had I originally plead guilty to everything and received a two-year or even three-year federal sentence, I could have been released sooner. If granted parole, I would have done less than a year. Avoiding the pen by serving twice as much time provincially was a pyrrhic victory.

Over the last decade, the system has changed and so has the age mix of prisoners. Many prisoners who have done pen time prefer the pen now, as it has more benefits and freedoms than the provincial systems. Where you go depends on your past, type of crime, and security classification. A provincial deuce-less in a maximum security is far more difficult to serve than a two-year sentence in federal minimum, where you can have a TV in your cell, get a pay level, and, if at a camp, be one step away from freedom. (For more on camps, please see Chapter 8.) Places vary greatly, but the greatest drawback many federal prisoners now hate is being on federal parole after their release. If you receive a provincial sentence of a deuce-less, after serving two-thirds (i.e., sixteen months), you are completely free provided a probation order was not part of the sentence. If you serve a federal sentence of two years, you are placed on mandatory parole for the remaining eight months. Approximately 30 percent of all federal offenders released on mandatory parole (statutory release) end up getting revoked and returned to prison, the majority for a violation of conditions, not the commission of crimes.[xxi] If you are detained by the parole board, you will likely serve your entire term inside.

Federal versus provincial funding has surely had an influence on changing the system as well as influencing the public's attitude. Some proponents of the system think the entire correctional system should become federal. This suggestion can be quite scary to some people, myself included. The most hated by prisoners is the helplessness of being in maximum security and the restricted freedom of parole. More prisoners are now also being forced into halfway houses after having served most, if not all, of their sentences as well as being gated. (For more on gating, please see Chapter 11.)

Sentencing—A Roll of the Dice

For many, sentencing is a crapshoot. A judge may or may not take the gap principle into account for a repeat offender. This principle may be used for someone with a past criminal record who has stayed out of trouble for several years. My lawyer once said this principle should be used because I had not been in trouble for over seven years. To my surprise, the judge countered with, "Maybe he just hadn't been caught." There is also the step or jump principle used to increase the sentence length each time a person appears before the court for the same crime. But then, some judges just throw the book at first-timers anyway.

One person could get four years soon after an arrest by pleading quickly. Three months later they could be in a camp and three months after that be out on day parole to a halfway house. A decade ago, first-timers with no violence or breaches could get four years and plausibly be back out in under a year. Two criminals with the exact same past and charges can also have totally different outcomes. One may plead guilty right away, get four years, and hit the street ten months later. The other may be still sitting in the bucket, waiting for a trial before eventually being found guilty, or they may plead a year later and have to serve another year or two before ever getting out. In another scenario, one person gets four years, no parole, higher security, and is possibly gated, while the other gets time served at the trial.

Ontario provincial halfway houses were all closed in the fall of 1995, but minimum-security federal camps and federally funded halfway houses remain. For a few non-violent first-time offenders, a four-year sentence can be eight months, then camp or parole. For violent or repeat offenders, four years means four years, or longer if they violate parole stipulations after being released and their warrant expiry date (WED) is extended. One thing to note is that even though a person may be granted parole, *all* federal sentences are served until the last day. For some, the last day never comes. A minor charge that would normally receive a sentence of thirty days can be months and even years for a repeat offender, leading to life on the installment plan!

After you plead, you can't always depend on the information a lawyer gives you about where you will be transferred or about getting parole. Lawyers are only knowledgeable about pleadings and trials. If they show any concern or give you information about placement or parole, be leery of their advice. The best sources of information about the place you may be transferred to or the chances for parole are prisoners who have recently gone through the blender. Those who are just finishing a provincial or federal term or who are back for trials and parole violation will know best. The system, its rules, and the places one can end up are always changing. Asking those who know firsthand is important in helping you decide your plea or setting trial dates. As always, don't believe everything you hear unless you hear it several times from different people.

If you and your lawyer agree that it's best to go in and out of court for a year or more, it may mess up an early shot at parole. If you plead and then sit around waiting for another trial's outcome, you must postpone or lose any shot at parole. You can't even try for parole if you have outstanding charges and no bail on them. You also can't try for parole if your case is under appeal. You could end up serving your full sentence with no chance to ever try for parole by the time your appeal is heard. If you consider pleading guilty, your lawyer will mention the amount of time the Crown wants. Most times you will get what the Crown and your lawyer agree upon. If you have a lengthy trial for a serious crime and are then found guilty, the sentence handed down will likely be lengthy. In cases of murder, if you are found guilty, your time is calculated to begin from the day of your arrest.

A trial with a judge and jury is for serious (indictable) charges that carry sentences of five years or more. You can't ask for a trial by judge and jury for being accused of stealing the paperboy's lunch money. Jury trials also cost more time and money to taxpayers, you, and your lawyer. If you are paying cash instead of getting a legal aid freebie, good luck! You could save a buck and defend yourself, but it's been said that only fools represent themselves in court. Then again, I had two trials where I am positive I couldn't have done any worse than my dump-truck lawyer. Some lawyers really screw up and will never admit it afterwards. If you don't know how the "McJustice" system works, you have no choice but to hire a lawyer. With so many unknown laws in existence, it's wise to get a lawyer for anything that may get you jail time. It's lawyers who draw up all the intricate, confusing, and perplexing laws and loopholes. One may wonder if the common layman is intentionally bewildered to guarantee prolific survival for all the legal eagles who feed on us. It seems the days of defending yourself are becoming a thing of the past. Recently, severe cuts to legal aid have resulted in negligible support for anyone needing a lawyer in civil cases. Many civil litigants must proceed without counsel, withdraw, or defend themselves.

In a minor criminal or civil case, you can sometimes easily defend yourself without a lawyer. Just be careful if you think someone is being untruthful, because proving that in court can be very difficult. Witnesses who tell a story can never "tell the truth, the whole truth, and nothing but the truth"; they can only tell their version of it. What the accused knows means little if they can't prove it. If you go to trial and win, with or without a lawyer, you may be happy at first. Later, however, when you think of all the stress, lost time, and lost money, you may not feel like such a winner. The Crown and the police won't lose any sleep or money. They get paid, win or lose, just as your lawyer does. I find it very odd how the wrongfully accused or convicted who eventually win an appeal can say the system works. If the system really works, they should not have been charged or convicted in the first place.

There are two factors that must be proven beyond a reasonable doubt in a court of law. First, the Crown must prove a law was broken by a guilty act. Lawyers refer to this guilty act by the Latin term *actus reus*. This is the objective element of the crime defined in the Criminal Code of Canada. This must then be accompanied by a second part called the *mens rea,* which translates to "guilty mind." This is where culpability, intention, and blame come into play. No matter how good your lawyer is at defending you, a pro-Crown judge may lean towards the Crown and still find you guilty.

Down the Rabbit Hole: A Guilty Verdict

If you are found guilty, you may be surprised and feel numb to any words or sentence the judge throws at you. News reporters often say how the accused remains stoic or expressionless when a verdict is reached, as if the guilty are so cold they don't care. You could be sentenced moments after being found guilty or it may be postponed for several weeks or months. A postponement allows for a social worker, usually a parole officer, to compile information for a pre-sentence report. Information is gathered from an interview with you and possibly family members or others. The Crown and the judge then read this report to help determine an appropriate sentence. Victim impact statements, police reports, and doctor's reports may assist them as well.

Just before the judge passes a sentence, you will be asked if you have anything to say. Lawyers usually caution you not to say anything. Anything you say can be turned and used against you. Even trying to say you are sorry for any victims you hurt can be taken as a false apology in an attempt to gain mercy from the judge. If you try to protest or tell the judge they are wrong and made an error, you may as well just call them stupid. See if that makes them give a lesser sentence or change their verdict.

I have noticed that sometimes a judge will berate you just before they pass judgement on your being guilty or innocent. It may seem as though you are about to be found guilty and have the book thrown at you when suddenly the judge says you're not guilty. Sometimes it works completely opposite to this. Right up until the last moment, you think you are going to walk or get a light reprimand when *wham!* The next thing you know, five minutes have flashed by and you're back in the holding cells trying to remember what happened back in the courtroom. I even laughed once when a judge gave me a ridiculously high sentence. Was it odd that he didn't raise it even higher for my thinking his sentence humorous? Not really. He probably knew I was laughing out of nervousness and shock. Some people do laugh when suddenly shocked or when feeling afraid. If it were any higher, the appellate court would have likely tossed the sentence out.

When you are in custody, the judge and jury members are not supposed to see you in a pumpkin suit or wearing shackles and chains since this can make you look guilty, if not at least untrustworthy, before a trial begins. The judge or jury are supposed to enter after the accused so they won't know if you are in custody, as it can influence their opinion of you. Wearing orange prison clothes and shackles are insignias of shame, making you look like an outcast and pariah. Of course, the Crown can claim you are a security risk and protest that you should keep your chains on at all times as well as request having extra police present in the courtroom. This will make you look all that more dangerous and guilty before the public. It's a great photo op for hungry reporters too.

Besides your history of family, work, education, crime, etc., being put in front of a judge before sentencing, who shows up also matters. If only victims show up and are protesting outside the courthouse, it must affect a judge's decision. Any fanatic, or someone fuelled by wrongful facts from the start, can also start such protests. The police and victims can easily exaggerate facts to fulfill and exploit their role as protectors and victims. Those who are unemployed, retired, or with nothing important and interesting to do in their lives may be more likely to join and promote such protests, hopefully getting their fifteen minutes of fame.

If your family and friends can't take time off work to spend days in a courtroom, while Crown witnesses get paid to be there, how would a judge think that anyone cares about you? If someone at least shows up for your sentencing, it shows the judge somebody cares. Would a judge be likely to hand down the same sentence to an empty courtroom versus twenty victims versus twenty family and friends of the accused present? With nobody in the courtroom, the judge can have the impression nobody in the free world cares about you, so nobody will care or complain when they throw the book at you.

Victim Impact Statements

The police and victims rights groups will try to get victims to write a letter for the Crown to submit to the judge for sentencing purposes and/or parole hearings. If such letters are well written and if victims exaggerate their suffering, the judge will exaggerate your sentence. Victims can be very traumatized by a crime done to them and such input with a letter may help in their recovery. Sadly, a victim who was emotionally messed up before any crime can blame it all on the criminal. Even if the statement is from someone you know who exaggerates, there is nothing you can say or do to refute the statement. Victim impact statements are not open to cross-examination. You're the one on trial, being judged and then condemned. You are not a victim.

A Few Stats

In 2010, the Canadian crime rate reached its lowest level since the early seventies. The crime rate measures the *volume* of police-reported crime while the Crime Severity Index measures the *seriousness* of crime. Police services in total reported close to 2.1 million Criminal Code incidents (excluding traffic).[xxii] Reported crimes are evaluated then considered "actual" when police confirm they occurred and conform to the legal definition of a crime.

In 2008-2009, the Canadian adult criminal courts disposed of 392,907 cases involving 1,161,018 charges. Most cases were for impaired driving (11 percent), theft (10 percent), common assault (9 percent), failure to comply with a court order (9 percent), and breach of probation (8 percent). Together, these offences accounted for almost half of all cases.[xxiii] Three out of every ten cases were stayed, withdrawn, or dismissed.[xxiv]

In 2008-2009, the accused was found guilty in 66 percent of cases[xxv] compared to 58 percent in 2003-2004[xxvi] and 61 percent in 1997-1998.[xxvii] The highest Canadian conviction rate in 2008-2009 was traffic offences (80 percent), with Prince Edward Island having the highest and sending 90 percent of first-time impaired driving offenders to prison. Guilty rates for total crimes against the person were only 54 percent. In Ontario, 38 percent of all cases were stayed or withdrawn compared to Quebec (10 percent) and New Brunswick (16 percent).[xxviii]

Ontario police can lay charges without the Crown. In British Columbia, New Brunswick, and Quebec, approval of the Crown attorney is needed before a charge is laid, which may play a part in the above figures. (One in three Ontario criminal and civil verdicts are also later overturned.)[xxix]

The most common sentence imposed across Canada for 2008-2009 was for probation in 45 percent of the cases. Over half of all custodial sentences in 2008-2009 were one month or less, with 31 percent receiving up to six months. While only 4 percent received a federal term of two years or more, in 1997-1998 the rate was 3 percent.[xxx] Almost 371,800 adults were admitted to some form of correctional program.[xxxi] Total in-custody counts were 38,218.7 for 2010 (24,460.7 provincial/territorial prisoners and 13,758 federal).[xxxii] The 2003-2004 rates of incarceration by province were: Ontario, 41 percent; BC, 40 percent; Yukon, 39 percent; Alberta, 36 percent; Newfoundland and Labrador, 33 percent; Quebec, 27 percent; Nova Scotia, 26 percent; New Brunswick, 25 percent; and Saskatchewan, 24 percent.[xxxiii] Surprisingly, in Japan, only 5 percent of persons convicted serve time compared to 30 percent of those convicted in the U.S.[xxxiv]

In 2003-2004, most cases before the courts were crimes against the person (27 percent), crimes against property (23 percent), administration of justice (18 percent), and traffic (13 percent). A breakdown of 445,650 cases involving 1,028,681 charges disposed of in courts across Canada for the same year are as follows: impaired driving, 11 percent; common assault, 11 percent; theft, 9 percent; failure to comply, 8 percent; breach of probation, 6 percent; major assault, 6 percent; uttering threats, 5 percent; fraud, 4 percent; possession of stolen property, 4 percent; drug trafficking, 4 percent; break and entering, less than 4 percent; drug possession, 3.6 percent; failure to appear, 2.7 percent; mischief, 2.5 percent;

robbery, less than 2 percent; weapons, less than 2 percent; sexual assault and all sexual offences, less than 2 percent; and homicide and attempted murder, 0.2 percent.[xxxv]

Violent crime statistics can be blown out of proportion by the media, politicians, and others with an agenda. Serious violent acts make up a very small percentage of all crimes. Homicide, attempted murder, robbery, kidnapping, sexual abuse, and abductions each represent less than 1 percent of cases.[xxxvi] Up until 1983, the charge of rape meant rape. Now any assault deemed to have a sexual component or interpretation is labelled a sexual assault. Any unwanted pinch or slap on a person's ass becomes a sexual assault. The problem is most people now view anyone charged with a minor sexual assault as a rapist. Assault and sexual assault charges are defined in three levels. Level one is deemed to have little or no physical lasting harm. It can be as minor as pushing or verbal assault and, if sexual, touching, groping, or flashing.

Of the 2.2 million crimes reported to the police in 2009 (17 percent lower than a decade earlier), 181,570 were level one assault and only 3,619 were level three. For sexual assault, 20,460 level one crimes were reported but only 122 were level three.[xxxvii] Serious violent offences are not as common as many hard-on-crime electorates, spreading the gospel of fear, would like us to believe.

Dangerous Offender

Being declared a dangerous offender (a.k.a. being DOed), a slow version of the gallows' pull, is the worst sentence anyone can receive in Canada. It means an indefinite sentence, and few are ever released from prison. A prisoner with a sexual assault record can also be labelled a dangerous sexual offender (DSO). Unbelievably, it's worse than being sentenced to life, and you don't even have to kill anyone. Until the electoral win of Pierre Trudeau in 1968, a gay person could be imprisoned indefinitely using habitual offender laws. Rewritten and renamed, the DO designation is similar to the

American habitual offender law and the redundant three-strikes law passed by California's Governor Pete Wilson in 1994 that has spread to twenty-one more American states.

Two U.S. groups lobbied hard for the three-strikes law to pass back in 1993. One was the National Rifle Association (NRA) and the other the California Peace Officers Association (CPOA), a union that represents state prison guards, parole officers, and prison counsellors. Before the three-strikes law was passed, California guards made less than teachers (approximately $24,000 annually) and their union had only 4,000 members. Pouring money into contribution funds for a hard-on-crime politician paid off well. Shortly thereafter, guards' salaries rose to $55,000 and their union grew to 24,000 strong. The prison population of California was only 19,600 in 1977, but by 1998, it grew to 159,000. It is now estimated that one in four state prisoners is a three-strikes recidivist. This particular law was intended for violent offenders and yet a full 70 percent of all three-strikes prosecutions in California have been for non-violent and non-serious offences, with only 4 percent of those convicted for violent crimes.[xxxviii] Will Canada follow the American lead? It already is with the current push by many prosecutors trying to label more and more prisoners as "dangerous" or "long-term" offenders. Such moves keep the courts busy and guarantee the prison beds remain full and in demand by all those who feed from the justice trough.

In Canada, as of April 2011, there were 458 people designated as dangerous offenders, and the number is rising.[xxxix] This does not mean there are more dangerous criminals in our midst or that the courts are doing their job. Canadian statistics have repeatedly shown that crime has been level or even falling in some categories for the last three decades. What it means is the political climate uses fear to push for more retribution from the adversarial side of the system of justice. A hard-on-crime political platform (the new slogan is "smart on crime") always garners many votes for politicians playing the fear card. Today's society has been greatly fuelled with fear from the media and entertainment industry, industries that now profit the most from crime. Violence grabs people's attention and sells the most, whether it's on the front page of a newspaper, in a new blog post, or in a trailer for the next summer blockbuster. Second in line are the prison industry complex and the justice system. More laws, prisoners, and tax dollars mean more security and financial gain.

Even having more than one conviction of driving while impaired (DWI) can be used by the Crown to apply for a DO hearing. Any criminal charge that is deemed to have caused serious personal injury as well as *any* information that suggests a future risk/threat may be grounds to apply for a DO hearing. Hypothetically, anyone who drives after having a few can run someone over, but anyone with a criminal past is far more likely to be deemed dangerous. If you are convicted of robbery, assaults, or any sexual crime, the Crown can apply for a DO designation assessment before sentencing using section 752 (1) of the Criminal Code of Canada. If granted by the judge, this will allow the Crown to have the offender evaluated using doctors of their own choosing. The police will also then interview anyone from your past all the way back to kindergarten if they can to look for any negative feedback. They will focus on harvesting any useful information or allegations from your past and resurrect any unproven charges. A compilation of negative information will be gathered and recorded by the police to be used by the Crown. Unfortunately, unlike a normal trial where criminal allegation must be proven beyond a reasonable doubt, such accusations don't have to be proven in a DO hearing. Even worse is that any unproven statements of questionable morality will also be used.

After a guilty verdict is reached in court, it takes weeks or months to obtain and then proceed with a DO hearing. The Crown, after gaining doctors' reports, must apply to the Attorney General for the hearing since they are lengthy and costly, although the process is quickly becoming streamlined. Crowns will have "their" doctors assess a prisoner, if the defence and prisoner consent. They will then submit any negative findings along with the application. If the Crown's doctors' reports claim a prisoner is dangerous and incurable, the defence then has the option of having a second opinion from a doctor of their choosing. The disadvantage here is that if you are using legal aid, aside from the possibly of having an incompetent lawyer, you may only be allowed a small fee of $90 to $120 an hour for doctor's fees. Doctors will be needed for several days to evaluate you and then possibly spend several days in court as well. This can become quite expensive, especially for the best doctors, whom legal aid won't pay for. However, the Crown's virtually unlimited funds will allow them to use the best ones. Crown doctors may charge $250 an hour to evaluate you and then $2,500 per day to attend court and testify against you.

Using the *Diagnostic Statistics Manual of Mental Disorders* (*DSM*) for classification, doctors will ask if you were a bed-wetter, fascinated with fire, or ever cruel to animals and other children in your youth. Profilers classify these three traits as the McDonald triad or the triad of sociopathy. They will evaluate you and try to discover if you are impulsive, glib, irresponsible, and unable to stay in long-term relationships. They will ask if you had difficulty holding a job, maintaining a good a credit rating, or paying bills. All of these traits are considered antisocial and will be used to support a finding of psychopathy. The Crown will use their doctors' reports and testimony of witnesses to show the court that you have a repetitive persistent behaviour that is incurable and damaging and dangerous to the public. Psychologists and their kind will speak authoritatively, appearing to have answers using scientific references or even mystique to impress, convince, persuade, and sell their psychology. Then, once you are declared a psychopath by a judge, it's prison for life!

Until recently, everyone detained under a DO designation faced the parole board every three years. Facing the board never meant much since 90 percent of dangerous offenders are never set free while they can still walk. That period has now been increased to seven years. Once DOed, there is very little hope, if any, of ever being set free again. The time and research needed to apply for an appeal will take many years, far more than that of a murder trial. It will also be many years, if ever, before you will be placed into programs since you are declared untreatable and will likely never be fit for release. At least with a maximum life sentence one may still be paroled in twenty-five years. Dangerous offenders, however, many of whom haven't killed anyone, have *no* set release date.

The Kaplan-Meier survival analysis was used to calculate the average length of time first-degree murderers spend behind bars. The average time of incarceration is 22.4 years.[xl] Only Russia and our southern neighbours surpass Canada's incarceration rate. Information based on Department of Justice data also shows that democratic countries such as New Zealand, Scotland, Sweden, Belgium, and Australia only have an average of 11 to 15 years for most murderers.[xli]

Long-Term Offender (LTO)

The next worst designation now currently being handed out to many prisoners is the LTO, known officially as the long-term supervision order (LTSO). It has become popular since its inception in 2000 and has already been added to the sentences of 302 offenders.[xlii] It was made into law for use against repeat, violent, or sexual offenders, although it's also being used against first-timers. The maximum LTO one can be sentenced to is ten years, which is given to the majority of long-term offenders. Anyone who receives a federal sentence, even as low as two years with a ten-year LTO attached, gets ten years of parole after their warrant expire date (WED), i.e., after the entire prison term is served. The long-term designation means offenders will be supervised in the community by a PO for ten years. This may not sound too harsh except it can be to those having to abide by the conditions the police and PO impose. For many, getting a two-year sentence with a ten-year LTO added is worse than getting double the time or more without the LTO added.

Not only are frustrated prisoners denied parole, they must also serve their entire sentence since the LTO guarantees monitoring after any release. Many LTOs are now sent to halfway houses. Unlike other prisoners, more and more of them are not being released after two-thirds but sent to secure halfway houses. Some are even detained for their entire prison term and still sent to a secure halfway house upon "release." Many more released prisoners will be destined to return to prison even years later for non-criminal violations. So much for leaving one's past behind to start fresh.

If you are older and given a long sentence of, say, twelve years for burglary or robbery and have ten years of LTO added, it's almost the same as getting a life sentence and out on parole in twelve. You may as well have killed someone and received twelve years to life. You can get less time for killing someone and then be out of prison, totally free of the system. You could be sentenced for manslaughter, for example, and be out in only a couple years without the LTO attached.

The newest trick now being played by Crowns seeking attention is to scare an offender with being DOed, making them submit to the lesser designation of being LTOed.

Mandatory Sentencing

Mandatory means there are no variances allowed on the set sentence. Mandatory sentences are not well liked by judges, but politicians often use them as a tool for manipulating facts and latching onto any current crime headline in the news to stir fervour. Judges lose their discretionary powers as hard-on-crime politicians pass more and more mandatory sentencing bills. This means that a violent career criminal with a lengthy criminal record of multiple robberies will get a minimum sentence of five years simply for possession of a gun. That may seem fine, but it also means anyone who has never been in trouble with the law will also receive a five-year term. Applying such measures to other crimes can also be very unfair.

For example, let's say a new law sets a mandatory term of five years for anyone in possession of five grams of crack. This is now law in the U.S. There is also a mandatory life sentence for a third or even second such offence in some states. A criminal with a prior history of drug trafficking, robberies, and assaults will receive a mandatory five-year-term if arrested and convicted for having five grams of crack. The same applies to a nineteen-year-old female student caught holding five grams. Her plea of holding it for a friend, never doing drugs in her life, or that it belonged to her boyfriend, even if true, won't matter—five years. In fact, in the U.S., if the same naive female has 5.1 grams, the sentence rises to ten years.

Canada now has two dozen mandatory sentence laws, half of which apply to gun laws. Mandatory laws are proposed and suggested each time some victim group or politician complains about lax punishment. Such laws can be applied to any crime, not just gun or drug offences, but the more laws that exist means less freedom for all Canadians. The system keeps growing. For anyone on the receiving end, their innocence, their past guilt, and the particulars of the crime won't matter upon sentencing because the sentence is fixed with a mandatory term.

In the future, mandatory or "economical" sentencing may mean giving out brain-dead pills, castrating sex offenders, cryogenic freezing, or sending prisoners to age-accelerating clinics. Science will soon introduce gene markers for behaviour traits, evaluation, and predicted recidivism. Suspended animation is a real possibility for the future. Many prisoners might gladly be put to sleep for their entire sentence. They would come out older and the lost time on the mind could be just a blank. Maybe they would be less bitter too? The colder and deader prisoners are kept, the cheaper it is to house them. Privatized jails also have cold hidden horrors.

Appeals

Your lawyer may not want you to say anything before the judge passes a sentence, as it could affect your chances later with an appeal. If you express anything referring to sorrow, guilt, or blame, it can be viewed later as an admission of guilt. If you receive a pen sentence, your lawyer may also advise you not to participate in any programs, since taking any program requires admitting guilt or at very least an inference of guilt. Prison rule CD #730-17-D (1) states, "inmates who participate in a work assignment but refuse to participate in any other program assignment specified in their correctional plan…who are appealing their sentence and/or conviction and refuse a program assignment for reasons related to their appeal will receive D-level pay."

Upon arrival to a federal institution, it may be better not to admit right away that your lawyer has advised you not to partake in programs. It may take months or years to get into a program anyway, and if you refuse from the start, your pay will remain at the lowest level. It's unfair and unfortunate that refusing programs under advice from a lawyer will mean no pay level increases. It will also mean little chance for parole and possibly being detained and gated. In such a case, winning an appeal can be a pyrrhic victory at best.

After you are sentenced and taken to jail, you must put in a request for a prisoner's appeal package. Your lawyer will suggest what grounds for appealing to submit in writing on the application. In the package, you can appeal a conviction, the sentence, or both if you have grounds. It may be for an error the judge made, ignored evidence, Crown misconduct, or other reasons. You will also likely have to shop for another lawyer who specializes in appeals and not use the one who just failed in your defence, although your defence lawyer will most likely suggest an appeal lawyer for you to use. Some lawyers do trials and appeals, but many specialize in one area only.

Most lawyers who think you have the slightest reason to appeal will refer you to an appeal lawyer as soon as you are found guilty. Telling you that you have grounds for an appeal can alleviate your blaming them for losing in the first place. Your lawyer may say the judge "erred" or give you any other excuse. Lawyers will never confess to any of their own mistakes. Unfortunately, if you don't know what mistakes your lawyer made, you may never find out about them. If you hire an appeal lawyer your prior lawyer doesn't know, such a lawyer may be more likely to tell of any mistakes, but they may also wrongly blame the prior counsel. One fact to remember is that any information, evidence, or witnesses your lawyer fails to bring up at a trial, even if it was brought up at a pretrial, likely won't be allowed into an appeal hearing later on. Only newly discovered evidence or strong evidence that was missed can be resubmitted for an appeal hearing.

It may take several years to process an appeal and get a new trial. Successful appeals are difficult. The few that do succeed are then sent back for another trial, with even fewer tossed out completely. If your trial lasted only a day or two and you get a good appeal lawyer who can quickly obtain all the court transcripts, you may get a faster appeal. If your sentence is only a couple of years or less, you may end up serving it all by the time your appeal is done. If you're a trustworthy first-timer with lots of cash, you may be able to get released on what's called bail pending appeal. If your trial lasted weeks or months, it will take that much longer for the appeal lawyer to gather information, prepare the appeal factum (possibly up to thirty pages), and book time for the appellate courts. The appellate courts will have three judges hear your appeal. When it is finally heard, the judges may not render a decision right away. This is called a reserved judgement, and it may take several months for the judges to reach a decision. Appealing is a slow process, and you could wait several years for it to be prepared and then heard. You should also be sure to ask your lawyer for a copy of the factum.

In rare cases, when a crime is notorious and the media has fuelled the public, a lawyer can ask for a change of venue. This is so that the jurors, when selected, will not have heard anything about the case from the media and formed any preconceived notions about guilt or innocence. Judges claim exemption from media influence and will rarely grant a defence lawyer's request for a change of venue.

If you don't appeal the conviction, you may instead appeal only the sentence. Appealing just the sentence can be a quicker process because you're not asking for a new trial; however, don't get your hopes up too much. The system is always overloaded with many prisoners trying for a better deal and many lawyers filing appeals so they can bill clients or legal aid more. In a few cases, those who appeal with the hope of getting a shorter sentence only get it increased.

The Crown can also appeal for a retrial or a sentence increase against you as well. The Crown may also ask for a blood sample if you were convicted of a violent offence. Crowns will now ask every convicted offender of any violent or sexual offence to surrender a blood sample for entry into the new DNA databank which already holds over thirteen thousand profiles.

After Sentencing

You will be taken to a DC after sentencing to await a transfer to a CC or penitentiary. During this time, a PO will visit to gather information from you in an interview. Be careful what you say if you choose to talk with a PO, as they will later use any information you supply. Those who get pen time are transferred out much quicker than those who receive provincial time. You'll likely wait only a week or two to be transferred to the pen versus weeks or months to be transferred to a provincial CC, provided all your charges have been dealt with. After getting a federal sentence, you will likely be on the next load transferred out. If the jail is full and you have remaining court appearances that are more than several weeks or months away, you will likely be transferred. If you receive a pen sentence of two years or more, a jail official will immediately ask you to sign a fifteen-day waiver. The fifteen days are to allow you to see your lawyer and apply for your appeal if needed. You actually have up to thirty days to apply for an appeal. Not signing the waiver may not change anything.

The Goose is the slang term for the prison bus that transports shackled prisoners to and from different prisons. Long ago, there was only one vehicle. Now there are several in addition to trucks and passenger vans. They look like regular vehicles with tinted windows on the outside. Inside, they are cages with barred windows and wire mesh. One makes its way to eastern jails, one west, and another to other regions. Toronto's East DC was once the main transfer point for everyone. You could get lucky and ride the Goose for an hour to your destination or stop briefly in Toronto, or you could get stuck at the West DC in Toronto for several days on the way. With all the new passenger vans now added to the fleet and more bailiffs for superjail court transfers, prisoners may now avoid Toronto completely.

The worst type of transfer was called going on a "ghost chain" (a.k.a. "diesel therapy" in the U.S.). They were very popular only a few years ago, but they supposedly stopped. Whether or not anyone ever deserved such punishment never got to reach any great debate because this kind of treatment apparently never existed—that's why it was referred to as ghost chain. When CC or DC prisoners were difficult to manage, raised too many complaints, caused fights, were suspected of drug smuggling, or were a threat to guards, they were placed in this continuous transfer mode. If your court date was months away, you would be continuously transferred all over Ontario. You could be in Ottawa one week and Sarnia the following week. A couple of days later, you could be in some small jail up north. Forget about having visits from family, friends, or your lawyer. Your mail would also likely get lost before finally catching up to you. This was the prison's unofficial way of treating unsavoury prisoners who would cause trouble.

To explain putting you on a ghost chain, jail officials could use the excuse of suspicion, safety, security, or unavailable bed space. Many jails would just transfer their most troublesome prisoners to other jails, claiming they were overfilled. Although it's a management decision, the police on the street can influence prison officials to transfer prisoners to a faraway jail or onto the ghost chain. This not only weakens the prisoner from ties to their community, it also stops them from gathering any help to prepare for a trial. It also makes it difficult to fix any problems one has on the outside. If the police are investigating people you know, they won't want you having any contact with them or any help. Transferring you repeatedly weakens your chances for bail or a fair trial, and a lack of visits increases the odds of released prisoners to reoffend. With the current war-on-crime attitude of our society, jail officials, the police, and politicians will play down the sub rosa of divide and conquer or outright deny dirty tricks such as this and others to come.

Assessment

If you receive a federal sentence, you will quickly be whisked off to a federal institution that has a reception wing. Each province has one offender intake assessment (OIA) wing in one of its maximum-security prisons. Reception prisoners are kept separated from the high-security population there. The classification process can take anywhere from several weeks to many months. Most prisoners are classified within about ten weeks and then transferred. Fast-track first-timers and repeat offenders who have already been there may be processed a little quicker. Prisoners spend several days in a classroom setting for psychological testing.

One of the most important tests possibly given is the Psychopathy Checklist—Revised (PCL-R). If you score above thirty out of forty, you will be labelled a psychopath. Further assessment used to create a correctional plan is comprised of two core components: 1) criminal risk assessment (CRA) based on criminal history, severity of the offence, and sex offence history; and 2) case needs identification and analysis (CNIA). The CNIA evaluates factors related to employment, marital family, associates/social interaction, substance abuse, community functioning, personal/emotional orientation, and attitude. The data is collected and stored in the Offender Management System (OMS), an automated database. In addition to this, there are also the Reports of Automated Data Applied to Reintegration (RADAR).

If you admit you puffed on what you thought was a joint during a party at age fourteen, evaluators can interpret that as becoming a drug user at fourteen. What's worse is that you can be labelled an addict at fourteen even if you never smoked again until your twenties. Temporary case management officers (CMOs)/parole officers (POs) decipher the results, interview you, and assess your security/personality level before labelling you a schedule 1 (personal injury), schedule 2 (drug crimes), or non-schedule offender as defined by the Corrections and Conditional Release Act (CCRA). An overall risk and need rating of low, medium, or high is then indicated in the correctional plan. This correctional plan will, repeatedly, be referred to as *your* correctional plan even though they're the ones who write it. It will rate your security level, state where you will be transferred, and have reports and suggestions for what programs and conditions you need to complete to assist you in one day becoming a law-abiding citizen. It will also have opinions from facilitators as to what your chances are of rehabilitation and reoffending.

Along with the OIA process of collecting comprehensive data on mental health history, social situations, education, and other pertinent factors to determine criminal risks and needs, there is the Statistical Information on Recidivism (SIR) score and custody rating scale (CRS) to pigeonhole a prisoner. The SIR provides an estimate of probability that an individual will reoffend within three years after their release. *Probability* being the keyword here—it means guessing. A score of -30 means very poor risk while +27 means a very good risk.[xliii] The CRS consists of two independently scored subscales. The institutional adjustment subscale has five items and the security risk subscale has seven items. Potential scores can range between 0 to 186 on the former and 17 to 190 on the latter. Unfortunately, the scores can easily be inaccurate since police reports, reliable sources (rats), or even a guard's suspicion of a prisoner being involved with drugs or in an altercation with another prisoner will affect them. None of the data applied has to be proven or verified. The CSC believes these scales are very reliable, although a PO can chose to override them. The results will have a big impact on a prisoner's classification, program placement, chances for parole, and future.

POs and other authorities of the CSC's psychiatric profession present their reports and finding as if it comes from a hidden fund of superior knowledge. Nevertheless, it will have a profound effect on your future. The results can be similar to a pre-sentence report, but now a federal PO will focus on a prisoner's weakness, negative past, and tumultuous feelings and pay little attention to any positive strengths. Their knowledge is partial and imperfect but is touted as scientific fact. Much of their data is only speculation supported from an industry of prognosticators, an industry some believe is growing out of control. The psychology industry identifies pathology in everyone, as does the parole system (please see Chapter 11), to make subjects into victims in need of its services. Prison assessments of offenders are required to fill program seats and gather data, which guarantees extensive funding.

If you are looking at a short provincial sentence, you may be able to apply for the electronic bracelet program, but few places use it and very few prisoners can get it. You must be a good candidate: no escapes, few if any priors, and no violence. The program is rarely used in Canada. Introduced in the early nineties and used as an excuse for shutting down all Ontario provincial halfway houses, it was highly susceptible to signal interference as well as political climates, so it never took off. The provincial halfway houses were never reopened either. Just about anyone in a cage would prefer to be tagged with a bracelet and let go. The scary part with this new technology is that it may one day become a popular program to use. Some parolees will likely start being forced to wear such intrusive devices up until their warrant expiry date (WED). Young offenders could be shackled too, or anyone under suspicion, with a criminal past, or out on bail. Many law-abiding citizens claiming they have nothing to fear condone such programs. A cheaper consumer version could soon follow for your grandmother with Alzheimer's, your spouse, your kids, employees, and eventually everyone.

If a prisoner has a driver's license suspended for fines, some provinces allow the fines to be waived in and served concurrently with a prison sentence. Some people are also not aware that a suspension period may not begin until after a fine is paid. If you expect to be in prison for a year or longer on another charge, it may be wise to plead guilty to any traffic violation and have the time over with by the time you are released on other matters. Even if your license is fine upon arrest, the renewal fees should be paid to keep it active and extend your licensed history. This will assist in applying for a job or insurance again after release but also to avoid starting all over again as a graduated driver. Some provinces allow a driver's license to be frozen for up to five years. The cost is small, and a friend or family member can file it on your behalf at licensing offices. This allows you to retain your driving status without renewal or loss while you're incarcerated or out of the country.

In 2008-2009, 259,734 Canadians were sentenced (251,411 provincial/territorial and 8,323 federal). As far as having a criminal record, win or lose at a trial, there will always be a record. Even after obtaining a pardon, the courts and the police will keep the record on file. At any future date, if any government employee or anyone with connections wants to investigate you or someone close to you, up pops your file for them to use. This information can be used against you in court if you are investigated for anything else again or wish to testify for anyone else. The police and Crown will use it to discredit you as an upstanding trustworthy member of society. If you ever get any time for another charge, any prior charges will also be written about in your prison records, programs, parole reports, or community assessment reports.

Depending on the future political climate of Canada, anyone with a criminal record may have restricted travel, possibly even within the country. Offenders now on the National Sex Offender Registry (which is permanent) can be denied the freedom regular Canadians have in obtaining a passport or travelling without permission. The next step may be barring offenders from moving province to province or city to city. Soon to follow will be restrictions on anyone with a criminal record leaving Canada or travelling anywhere without permission from the police or a designated board.

If you do beat any charge with a "not guilty" record of the crime, you should be able to enter the U.S., although you will still have a record of being charged. You can also apply for a passport no matter how many charges you win or lose. Many people think you can't get a passport if you have a criminal record. The only people who can't apply for one are people currently on bail, probation, or on parole. However, Passport Canada may refuse applications from those who are deemed a national security risk, who are not permitted to leave Canada, or who have been convicted of a passport-related crime.

Even after getting a passport, the U.S. will deny you entry if they run your name and see you have a record. For minor records, you may fill out an American I-192 form, asking for permission to enter the country. It's best to travel there by car rather than by plane. A new passive/intrusive facial recognition system is currently being used in Florida airports for identification/security purposes. In the U.K., iris recognition technology is used at border crossings and high crime areas. Toronto now has a police vehicle that automatically scans hundreds of license plates per minute as it drives down any street. Such scanning devices are also currently being used at larger border checkpoints to the U.S.

Since 9/11, American border security programs with harmless names such as US-VISIT and CAPPS II have expanded. These programs have a sad result for trade and the freedom to travel. CAPPS II, attempting to skirt privacy issues, will gather as much personal information as possible from travellers, and those deemed high-risk are denied entry. The FAST program allows drivers with biometric security-clearance cards carrying pre-approved loads (i.e., truckers) to whisk through border crossings.

Since 2010, those crossing into the U.S. by car are required to show a passport, which will pose a problem even if you have a minor record. If you can stay out of trouble for ten years, or five years for a summary conviction, you can apply for a pardon by paying $631 (plus extra cost to provide documentation). You will also need to wait over a year for processing. This will clear most of your criminal file from the CPIC databank of the RCMP but not local courts or police agencies. A pardon also does not necessarily have to be recognized by other countries. Legally, you can say you don't have a criminal record, but if you ever get in trouble again, the past record will be fully resurrected.

Chapter 7

Copper versus Con

Coppers

The term *copper* may have originated in several ways. Long ago, an old guard told me that the name started from guards wearing copper buttons. In the *Oxford English Dictionary*, the term *copper* is said to have originated in the early eighteenth century, from the now obsolete verb *cap*, meaning "arrest." This word in turn originated from the Old French word *caper*, meaning "seize." Another origin may be that some guards seem to be wannabe cops. Those who can't make it onto a real police force to catch criminals can take to guarding them instead. Nevertheless, coppers and cons see each other as adversaries in the battle for justice.

The wages and benefits for police or guards were never great years ago, but they have improved considerably over the last decade. According to 2006-2007 statistics, to guard approximately 13,200 federal prisoners, the Correctional Service of Canada (CSC) required approximately 15,200 employees.[xliv] Federal guards are paid approximately $50,000 per year, just slightly less than provincial guards, and receive as much overtime as they can by exaggerating reasons to lock institutions down. They also have a powerful union.

Many prisoners refer to a guard as "copper" or "boss." Why not call them "master"? I have slipped on occasion and called a guard "copper," but not often. The indentured servitude of prison life makes some prisoners think they can con guards for small favours. Maybe toadyish prisoners feel that flattery will get them somewhere or something. Sometimes it just may. Personally, I'll stick to calling them guards. Today, many guards and other public employees parasitically feed financially off what many consider the dung of society: the cop's adversary often referred to as the con.

Cons

The term *con* is from the late sixteenth century word *contra*, meaning "against society." In the late nineteenth century, a con was a confidence man or swindler, and the courts used *con* to refer to someone *con*victed of an offence. In today's society, the term *con* denotes someone who is looked upon disparagingly. While any guard may like or prefer to be addressed as "copper" or "boss," most prisoners don't like to be called a "con," "offender," or even an "inmate," a name once applied to patients of mental asylums. A number of prisoners are under appeal and some are innocent, so calling them all offenders is incorrect. Whether someone is guilty or not, deserving or not, prison life is the ultimate form of oppression against struggles of recognition and self-determination. Since the terms *inmate*, *offender*, and *con* are oppressive, degrading, and derogatory, I usually refer to prisoners as prisoners.

Personalities

Guards' personalities can greatly vary. Some can be easygoing while others can be completely vile. Two decades ago, guards were all male, and when applying for the job, candidates had to appear physically and mentally fit. Now guards are both male and female of any size, shape, or age. I find it almost comical to see some very frail, obese, or old individuals working as guards. Some new guards have better personalities than the hard-core veteran guards do, although some can also be immediately cold and cruel. Some should never have been allowed to be guards at all. The attitude of some guards is very hard toward prisoners—if you do the crime, do the time, and the harder the time, the better! They don't seem to realize that tighter security along with the power attitude many guards express, along with frequent degrading cell and body searches, means more stressed prisoners, which increases stress on everyone. Treatment without at least some human respect will breed prisoners who will not make society a safer place once released.

Over the years, I have witnessed guards pulling some really sick pranks out of boredom or a sadistic sense of humour. One can only hope that a good guard will notice others abusing their power and have them reprimanded before they gain greater authority. Abusive guards should be suspended, if not fired on the spot, just as they would in any other profession requiring good interpersonal skills, except now they have a powerful union to protect them. Superior officers may have a hard time or not care too much about catching the cruel acts of the regular guards. When they do, they will most likely play it down. After all, many see prisoners as less than human—animals that should be punished. Prison is supposed to be a difficult place. But putting animals in cages is one thing, while degrading the animal and kicking the cage is another.

What sets a prisoner off is often unseen or not that important to a guard. Social learning theories analyzing patterns of prisoner misbehaviour such as no meds, missed yard time, or other matters such as the arrival of a particular guard can reveal much but are ignored. Confinement to a prison cell, especially solitary, like the sensory deprivation tanks of the sixties, tends to induce psychosis and bring out the animal within. Whether prisoner or guard, people can have a predisposition to brutalize in certain environments, and guards can lash out when questioned of their authority or may simply be sadistically bored. In the environment of bolt and bar, considering the nature of the beast within, it is almost impossible to rule by kindness. Using fear and brutality is much easier.

Attitudes

One time in solitary late at night I was awakened by voices. I had almost fallen back to sleep when I heard giggling. In the cell next door was a bug, an irritable prisoner that bothers others. Sadly, he was suffering from schizophrenia and could not be placed in population. He was waiting to be transferred to a treatment facility. What drove me mad was the sadistic guard who, each time he came to make his rounds, would whisper scary nonsensical sentences to make the guy freak out. I almost thought of it as funny myself except when I heard the soft weeping noises once the guard left.

The guard did this several times until I informed him he was waking me. He would have enjoyed being a guard during the era of whips and chains to increase the punishment of prisoners, when prisoners lived on bread and water. Few prisoners ever complained of any extreme abuse then, as there was a code of silence in effect. Those who informed or complained broke this code and were silenced by being placed in solitary confinement. Thankfully, today, with easier access to inform others outside, such tortures are gone. The tormenting of my schizophrenic neighbour stopped, and the guard never said a word to me about the incident. Years later, in another institution, I saw the same guard physically assault another prisoner.

Another occasion was on my way to the food delivery slot in the penitentiary mess. Entire ranges would each, in turn, pick up their meal trays and return with them to their cells. When it was our turn, I was in the front of the line on the way to the mess and the first to begin the return back to our cells. There was an entire line of prisoners behind me as I made my way back to the range. After the entire range had crossed an inspection area on the way to pick up their trays, a perverted guard decided to pull what he considered a prank. There, in the centre pathway everyone had to cross on their return to the range, the guard had placed an enormous carcass of a rat. The corpse had to be about eighteen inches long. No prisoners found any humour in this. Several guards stood to the side, snickering. I wanted so much to kick the carcass toward these idiots to wipe the smiles off their faces, but I held myself in check. I just stood for a moment looking at the pranksters and then walked on.

The guard's so-called prank is not the norm for all security staff. Violence, and the fear of it, was once often used by security to control prisoners in their care. Changing philosophy in the handling of incarcerated individuals has reduced such incidents, not necessarily for the sake of the prisoners but the CSC's image. If it were allowed, some guards would still resort to torture and act worse than many of the prisoners in their care.

Subtle Cruelty

Some guards can be far subtler with their cruelty. They might tell you repeatedly that they will let you out of your cell to use the phone or will give you some much-needed toilet paper. Conversely, they will also keep telling you they forgot. Some guards might not like you and have no intention of doing anything for you. Then, on their way home from work, they can chuckle to themselves, imagining you still waiting for the toilet paper. Years ago, I remember working in segregation and being warned about giving out matches to any locked-up prisoner who had lost all privileges (LOAP). Guards would occasionally dole out a cigarette to a seg prisoner with no intention of ever giving a light for it. One was better off with no cigarette than having one without ever getting a light.

In general, the group mentality of guards has little consideration for the prisoners they're assigned to watch. They not only consider prisoners the enemy but also entertainment and an outlet for their stress. Most guards perform their jobs by the book but may bend the rules when it suits their convenience. Sometimes, they may even bend a rule for a prisoner. It doesn't happen too often, but there are some guards who even act human. Sadly, a few treat prisoners like dirt with impunity. In the provincial system, guards seem to have meaner attitudes. It's very easy for prisoners to notice and suffer for this. Larger city jails and superjails are all maximum security. This greater security gives the illusion of a safer environment—for the guards. No weapons, fewer drugged prisoners, and more guards to respond when an alarm is pressed—all may make prisoners feel more helplessly controlled. As a result, do guards feel less threatened in a place more stressed-out for prisoners?

Shh....

It was the rule only thirty years ago in Kingston Pen that if one prisoner was caught talking to another prisoner or even caught looking at a guard he went to the hole. It may seem that things have changed for the better, but have they really? The more things change, the more they stay the same. There were serious riots then, and now they are rare. Is this change because prisoners are treated so much better? Certainly not! Is it because prisoners have finally been acknowledged as human beings? Hell, no! This change is because prisons, especially the new ones, are designed in a different style to avoid the chances of mutiny. The new style of higher security makes it almost impossible to riot. Prison staff and much of the public would rather not have prisoners riot as a protest against their treatment. It's best to just keep them helpless and silent about any questionable treatment. Riots cost money, and possibly lives, in order to get a point across. But once you take away the strongest means of collective protest, prisoners will suffer when protesting.

JFK eloquently said, "Those who make peaceful revolution impossible will make violent revolution inevitable." Prisoners who protest are targeted by the system and easily silenced. In the years to come, there will be no more riots, so prisoners must keep their anger inside them or at least until they are back on the street again. Experienced prisoner writer Jack Henry Abbott said it best in his book *In the Belly of the Beast*: "They go for your mind in prison today—where before, it was all physical suffering. The stakes are much, much greater today." All this under the banner of protecting society, at least until such broken-minded, angry, resentful prisoners are back in public feeling like aliens and expected to be productive members of society.

In the provincial system, guards can really treat prisoners like shit. If you are charged with any infraction (misconduct), you can lose your good time (early release during the final third of a sentence earned for good behaviour). This can result in extra weeks or months in jail for any mishap with a guard. You could lose all of your good time for an assault on one too. It makes me sick to remember having heard guards beating prisoners in their cells while the rest were locked up unable to help. It may not happen every day in the same bucket, but I know it happens every day in a different bucket or DC. A prisoner's only recourse is to complain to a white shirt, the regular guards' supervising officer. When one guard is reprimanded, other guards can then find some way to punish the prisoner for telling. Calling the ombudsman to officially file a complaint is often useless, and prisoners are too often considered liars. Filing a complaint may also make your time more difficult or may quickly get you transferred.

I myself have never been violent, but the police have assaulted me twice on the street. The police or guards can easily provoke someone to resist, especially someone they know with a criminal record or prior incident with them. The police and guards know it's a situation they can't lose. They can manhandle you, and if you resist at all, they can use excessive force. They know they can play it up if they get injured, not only to justify their actions and get time off work with pay but also to get a conviction later on. It's their word against yours....

Hair-Trigger Reflexes

I have witnessed countless situations where guards will overreact and push prisoners too far. When you arrive at any institution, other prisoners will often fill you in on whom to watch out for. A common new term I have heard prisoners call a despised guard is a *boot Nazi*. There's always a guard who pushes their role too far or simply responds to a situation in the wrong way. Guards, and prisoners as well, may even do just small things that add up over time. When the tension builds up, people, whether prisoner or guard, can also do stupid unexpected things. If a prisoner is arguing and a guard feels threatened, the guard could move first out of fear alone. The prisoner may not be violent at all, just extremely upset. Simply jerking your hand can be read incorrectly as an aggressive move. The next thing you know, a guard grabs you and then you yourself feel threatened in return.

Guards are not likely to touch you if they are all alone, but when several of them suddenly show up, they won't hesitate to overpower you. Their main goal is either to keep control or regain control of any situation as quickly as possible. When six guards pin you to the ground, you stay down. If it requires spraying you with Mace because you "may become aggressive," you get sprayed. I know this to be true from prior experiences. If you struggle when tackled and one guard thinks you hit him during the struggle, you could get several blows in return. Don't expect your version of events to be believed over a guard's. As a result, you could easily lose your good time and be targeted for intimidation again and again. Prisoners can also turn on you faster than any guard. Prison is not a place where the wicked cease from turmoil and the weary come to rest.

If the guards feel there is any danger of an uprising, a possibility of weapons, or maybe drugs around, they will institute a lockdown of the facility. The DCs are high security, barren, and easier to lock up. During this period, there is no yard time, phone usage, showers, visits, or any other privileges for prisoners. Guards may receive overtime during such times, as more guards are needed to secure the facility, search cells, strip-search prisoners, and deliver meals, which are usually brought in from the outside in DCs. They also assume other duties normally done by prisoners.

When a situation appears to be getting out of hand, the goon squad is brought in. Today's goon squad members are dressed in riot gear and can be fully or semi-armed. With their body armour and helmets, they're nicknamed "turtles" by prisoners. The goon squad is an extraction team and can be used to isolate and remove (potentially) rioting prisoners or possibly rescue any hostages. Security is a constant banner for the CSC to wave. Even though in 2005 the CSC recorded just two assaults on prison guards in the federal system, this did not stop it from clandestinely beginning a trial program allowing Tasers in two institutions.[xlv] Amnesty International indicates there have been at least 26 Taser-related deaths in Canada since 2001, while an additional 330 have died in the U.S.[xlvi]

Guards and staff continually push for danger pay, saying their jobs are equally as dangerous as an outside police force. It's in their best interests, financially, to exaggerate any incident about a prisoner to justify laying charges or needing extra time off with pay. Guards and their union prefer to inflate the chances of endangerment in their workplace. This tactic helps justify getting more power, support, tax money, and public sympathy.

"Correctional Annoyance Committee"

Every federal penitentiary is required by law to have a Citizen Advisory Committee (CAC). This committee is supposed to consist of appointees of the Deputy Commissioner. They are to serve as support to prisoners and employees of the CSC during lockdowns or concerns related to proper healthcare and other issues. They are supposed to represent the "community" and advise the Warden from that perspective. Their primary role is to act as a liaison between all concerned and give "impartial" advice as well as lean on administration to provide better service. Professor Peter Hennessy, who served on the CAC for Kingston Pen from 1992 to 1998, as well as helped gather data for this book, writes in his book *Canada's Big House: The Dark History of the Kingston Penitentiary*, "I believe there is a trend to selecting CAC members from security backgrounds, which results in a likely bias from the get-go. But I know we were different from other CACs in Kingston, some of which were in the Warden's pocket." The CAC's "Values" specifically state, "We believe that the protection of society must be the paramount consideration in the correction process." Does this statement sound like it supports prisoners?

The sad reality of the Citizen Advisory Committees is that to most of the CSC staff they are an annoyance if they take the side of any prisoner. They have no power and can only make recommendations, few of which are followed. If, on the other hand, the CSC needs support or advice, they will obtain it. However, is there a concern about bias considering the CAC's National Chairperson, Sean Taylor, is a retired officer of the Saskatoon Police Service?

Guard Life

When the night shift begins, you may hear guards talking, yelling, or laughing loudly down the corridors. They don't seem to care if you are sleeping or not. They will bang doors without regard that the noise will awaken sleeping prisoners. I recently heard a guard whistling while walking by my cell in the middle of the night, an action regarded as a prison taboo.

New guards and staff may begin working with an idealism that soon fades under the harsh light of prison reality and pressure from their peers. Some of the more educated guards who are not simply working just for a paycheque often work in institutions that are more treatment-oriented. The guards also must observe the line drawn between themselves and management. Management guards (white shirts) remain in their isolated offices, designing new procedures, while regular unionized guards remain in their bubbles and are required to implement these procedures.

There are also differences between provincial and federal system guards. In the provincial system, guards can be in your face all day long. Conversely, in the federal pens, you may not see them as often. In the provincial system, guards worry less about being cut or killed. There are virtually no weapons made or available in the new superjails, so guards have little fear of being stabbed. They can irritate or piss off any prisoner without that big worry. Ironically, the provincial guards are quite safe compared to those working in other workplaces. They could never act the way they do in a place of business, as prisoners are quite helpless.

In the pens, it's a little scarier. Not only are there lots of blades around, the pens are also full of more serious criminals, although if a prisoner is seen attacking anyone, a guard in a gun tower may shoot them. Compared to provincial guards, a guard in the pen, minus camps, is less likely to be disrespectful to anyone. Prisoners in maximum security can say just about any obscenity they want to a guard. A guard may not necessarily know that a prisoner is there for having stabbed someone. They may not even realize the prisoner they approached was the unknown assailant who stabbed the victim in the yard the previous week. A prisoner serving many years may have no qualms about assaulting a guard.

With the virtual elimination of riots, the employment of female guards has become more commonplace. Many of them can be meaner than their male counterparts. They are less likely to be violently aggressive but are more likely to be verbally abusive. Don't even try being too nice to one or she may think you are hitting on her. They may think every prisoner desires them because some lascivious prisoners will hit on them. While in the hole, I once stuck my hand out of my small door hatch to accept a meal and a large female guard threatened to break my arm if I put it out any further. When I asked her what her problem was, she snapped at me again, implying I might have been reaching for her. Attempted assault? If she had exaggerated or lied, who would anyone believe, guard or convict? One can easily lose good time over something that ridiculous!

Guards have nowhere near the education, training, experience, or respectability of the judge who gave you your sentence, yet many minions of the so-called correctional system can easily make your stay in jail harsher and longer. A guard's ego would likely get a kick out of exercising such power so easily over a prisoner, unlike a judge who takes years to make it to the bench. If you are a new or paranoid prisoner, you might also feel that the guards are out to get you, as some will be. It may only take one or two small forgetful acts by the guards for you to think they are intentionally ignoring requests or screwing you somehow. Guards will raise their voices or snap at you, which may fuel you to do the same to them or someone else. In the provincial system, any infraction of rules may result in your losing good time up to eight months or extra time added to your sentence if charges of assault, threatening, drugs, etc., are laid.

A few, and only a few, guards are easygoing and reasonably human. As in any large place of employment, there are always individuals who are liked, while others are disliked. Some guards don't even like other guards, while some guards don't seem to like anybody. Of course, there are the guards and prisoners nobody likes. Older ones may seem more peaceful and easygoing, but does this mean they were always so? I look at the older guards and wonder whether they were rotten at a younger age and have simply mellowed or burned out. I've also seen younger guards who didn't seem too bad. I've seen the same guards again two decades later and they look like hell—I've seen the same with prisoners too. It can seem odd how doing time in any harsh profession stresses individuals in different ways. Of course, one can't always know what other factors have played a role in this transformation. How an individual handles stress really makes a difference.

The Con Game

If guards around you are not your biggest problem, fellow prisoners will be. A guard may stress you out or start a rumour to get you assaulted or killed, but it can be one of your own cellmates with whom you have the biggest problems. An act as seemingly innocuous as accepting a cigarette from another person may set you on a slippery slope of ever-mounting obligation on your part, with ever-increasing demands from the uncharitable giver. Remember, very few will give you something without expecting something or some favour in return. Even guards may try to pacify you so they will have a peaceful shift. Be careful about owing anybody, and make sure you know the manner in which a debt has to be repaid.

The best advice for new prisoners is to do no favours and request none. Alliances with other prisoners are necessary at times, but you need to make alliances based on mutual self-interest. Even these seemingly solid alliances are built on ever-shifting sands, so beware. Volunteer as little information as possible about your personal life or your charges. Every fact that you reveal about yourself is a potential lever that someone else might be able to eventually use to manipulate you. Those who confide little run less risk of eventually being betrayed. The saying is, "Do your own time," so it's often best to keep your personal life and charges close to your chest upon arrival. Unfortunately, guards and other prisoners will talk about you, forcing you to respond.

Our prison system is a somewhat predictable destination for many individuals raised in institutions, poverty, or dysfunctional families. Many grow up in public housing, ghettos, cheap hotel rooms, and subsidized housing and come from single parent or broken families. Others were wards of the state, foster homes, or juvenile detention facilities. Some street people could have a vast array of experiences and contacts that may make their stay in prison much easier for them, as they've been toughened and prepared for their prison stay. Today's younger prisoners have the smarts and raw nerve required to persevere and weather hardship and adversity. They can survive in the concrete jungle, but at what cost? Many see older and disabled prisoners as easy marks for their cigarette and canteen needs.

Con-flict

Keeping to yourself is not always so easy in prison. It's bad enough being caged, having guards screw with you, but you're also trapped with others. It's not like camp or the army, or being forced to work all day for minimum wage with a crowd of people you don't like. It's much worse than that. Not only are you forced to live with society's assorted miscreants, they are your only companions 24/7. Just as you don't want to start off on the wrong foot with a guard upon your arrival, you don't want prisoners as enemies either. Even an innocent comment or benevolent look can be taken the wrong way in prison. It's best to keep to yourself as much as possible, but that can be difficult in such a small space full of wayward souls. The simplest thing can ignite a confrontation. Your intelligence, personality, size, age, and your fighting ability play a big role here. The majority of prisoners on your range won't be openly mean, hostile, or disrespectful to your face, although many will say things behind your back. You will hopefully get along with most of them. Of course, there will be heavies who think they run the range and are better than other prisoners. There will always be the range rats who carry tales to "the Man," but being a rat is risky business.

Con-fusion

There may also be racial tensions on the range, especially if there are minorities in larger numbers. In Western Canada, there are more Asian prisoners, while the Prairies have a larger First Nations population. Some larger centres, such as in Ontario, may have more immigrants and blacks. A large number of blacks may try to turn the status quo and make non-blacks number two in the pecking order. The mix on a range can include first-timers, repeat offenders, and one or more prisoner doing long sentences, such as lifers. Most prisoners gravitate to others for strength in numbers. Prisoners will also project the impression that they know others well and are "tight" with them. Conversely, they will avoid those they think are unworthy as well being in on questionable charges of morality. Calling someone "bro" is common when you don't know someone's name or want to pretend that you do. Some prisoners, or groups of prisoners, are offended by any nickname. Wherever you go, there will be a mixture of visible ethnic groups.

Con-fraternity

A low-security CC or federal camp houses mostly non-violent and first-time prisoners, while a max holds high-risk, dangerous, violent offenders. Those in between are housed in a medium institution. Repeat offenders will be found in all institutions. Many first-timers come across as normal people and are usually easy to get along with. Many won't have the hardened bitter attitude...yet. Some will have a home, family, and job still waiting for them. In such a case, they won't want to risk losing their good time or the chance of parole by hanging with hard-core prisoners. They will try to avoid running with shooters, or troublemakers, if they hope to get parole. They also learn to avoid the drug side of prison life. Such a prisoner must learn that whatever one has on the outside—a home, spouse, money, and business—should be kept private. Jealousy can be the root of evil in prison. Even a confident attitude is often mistaken as conceit and arrogance, although prisons are full of such prisoners. Prisoners can also be gregarious simply to gather exploitable targets.

Con-cede

Some first-timers won't have much waiting for them on the outside. They may feel they don't have much chance for a parole either. Some may take programs or school courses (upgrading) for their own self-improvement, a better chance at parole, or both. In some ways, it is easy to spot first-timers. They likely won't have a chip on their shoulder or be covered in tats, or tattoos, although that's not always the case. I have found hard-core criminals who are sometimes easier to get along with and nicer than some "newbies." First-timers may have ended up in jail because of a personality nobody likes. Even if most of them are placed in lower security CCs, or camps, it may not improve their personality. The lower security facilities, and those that have dormlike settings, have problems that higher security facilities don't have, such as more prisoners putting it on one another (squealing).

It may be much cheaper to house prisoners in such lower security facilities, with a more freedom-like surrounding, but that setting also makes many prisoners more free to squeal on you about any minor infraction you've committed. It also makes prisoners more free to use aggression or intimidation against others. Prisoners who are irritating to others around them can be twice as bothersome in a lower security setting. In higher security, they will be more reserved and careful not to offend anyone, but not so in a place where they can run to "the Man" and complain about anything. I have heard from many prisoners who don't like lower security institutions because of all the ratting that goes on. Some prisoners who have been transferred to lower security institutions have asked to be returned to medium security because of what they've experienced there. Even lifers can eventually make it to a low-security facility, usually near the end of their sentence, and regret it.

Any first-timer may quickly become a bad apple on the way to becoming a hard-core convict. They may vow to never return to prison only to be arrested and return repeatedly. This is known as "doing life on the installment plan." First-timers who enter and leave prison bitter, with a worse attitude than when they came in, are more likely to become repeat customers. The younger prisoners have more time to waste coming in and out of jail, but the older ones can return sporadically as well. Repeat offenders may last only a day outside before returning to the jail through the revolving door, but if they're lucky, they may remain out several years before returning. Early lawbreakers may have irritable, restless, or violent personalities that become worse or could mellow out with each return visit to prison. An older one may have become more irritable, restless, or violent as they lose more and more time as their bits add up. Prisoners can often be quick to anger, and when anger fuels aggression, it becomes a problem in the prison environment. Guards can be aggressive to prisoners, but most prisoners relegate their aggression toward other prisoners. Rage can erupt from a simple stare or off-hand remark.

Con-ceptus

Less than 30 percent of the federal population is under the age of thirty, and older prisoners tend to dislike younger prisoners who are loud and disrespectful. Some need to be "pulled up," or taught to be more respectful of others around them. Many of these youthful prisoners even continue their disrespectful attitudes when they reach the federal system. In the past, respect of other older prisoners was achieved mostly out of fear, as prisoners ran their own justice system. These days, however, prison life has changed somewhat with an increasing younger crowd and minority population. Some institutions also have a larger population of aging individuals, usually lifers.

Two decades ago, TVs with speakers were not allowed. Headphones had to be used. Stereos were rare, if allowed at all, and there certainly were no boom boxes. Now there are many of them. Before this, drugs were never much of a problem either. Today, the younger offenders seem to prefer momentary escape through drugs and loud music. Even some older prisoners resort to this lifestyle. Those doing longer provincial terms of two years will know more people and have learned to fit in by the end of their term. A long-term federal prisoner may be serving ten years to life and will likely learn to fit in well.

Con-gregation

Some long-term offenders don't associate much with the short-timers. Friendships as a rule don't last long, and former prisoners rarely stay in contact after release. Usually, those prisoners doing longer terms gravitate toward one another because they have known each other for a longer period. Seeing prisoners returning frustrates those with longer terms who have not had a chance to stay free. Often, when habitual criminals prepare for release, those who know them make wagers on when they will return.

For those who are lifers and those who have "got the bitch" (DOed), the system has them for life. A first-timer can commit murder and become a lifer, whereas a charge of manslaughter may get you life or only a couple of year's probation. Lifers who receive a life sentence may be given life-10, life-12, life-20, etc., with life-25 being the max. Life-25 means you can't get parole for twenty-five years, and if you do, it's parole for the rest of your life. Many prisoners would prefer a straight fifteen years for manslaughter than, say, life-10. For most, it's also better to do a few extra years inside rather than be on parole for life. Many pens also have a lifers group or 10-plus group for prisoners serving long terms. The pens may even have wings housing more lifers. These are the best blocks or ranges to be on. They will be the cleanest, quietest, and easiest places to serve time, provided you are not disrespectful of the lifers. You likely won't even make it there without a sponsor. Many long-term prisoners will be better to associate with, though they may not want to associate with you. They are in for the long haul, and they take their time more seriously. They will also have the most pull or influence inside. Remember, it's more their home than yours, as they'll be there longer. Many prisoners will also exaggerate or lie about their charges or length of their sentence, playing up their acts of violence to scare others and garner respect.

You don't want to have problems with a lifer upon arrival, or anyone for that matter. If you have a confrontation with a lifer who is just beginning twenty-five long years, while you are only doing three, giving them attitude may not be too bright. Even if the lifer looks feeble and half your size, they can cut your throat unexpectedly and not have any more time added to their sentence. Some are the most polite and easiest going prisoners, but you may later learn that they are the most violent.

Then there are disturbed prisoners only serving a few years who do kill other prisoners. These prisoners usually only get five or ten years added to their current sentence. Prisoners killing each other inside is considered less of a crime to the outside world.

Con-dition

Mental health professionals gather their diagnosis momentum of a prisoner's mental health from various disorders listed in an influential book called the *Diagnostic and Statistical Manual of Mental Disorders* (*DSM*), listing more than 350 mental disorders. Schizophrenia, bipolar disorder, and attention deficit hyperactivity disorder are but a few listed in the *DSM*. The disorders in the *DSM* are arbitrarily listed, delisted, or redefined by members of the American Psychiatric Association (APA). The decisions are based on the majority of members being in agreement.

The criteria for each disorder are encoded in the *DSM*. Doctors, insurers, courts, and schools all rely on these codes, just like a shopper's checklist. When anyone, especially those with criminal records, is evaluated and meets several of the criteria, such diagnoses are then used by the courts for sentencing, classification, parole, or possibly to keep someone behind bars forever. Many of these criteria can also be used to prove that the average citizen has deviant behaviour, so an argument can be made that the diagnostic criteria of the *DSM* are too broad. In reality, *DSM* divinations are inconclusive because psychiatry is inconclusive, and the manual seems to include more hypotheses than answers.[xlvii]

Society classifies anybody who breaks the rules or norms of society as being antisocial. The *DSM* classifies anyone who breaks the law as having antisocial behaviour. The prevalence of antisocial personality disorder in community samples is about 3 percent in males and 1 percent in females. Clinical estimates vary with the population being sampled and have varied from 3 percent to 30 percent.[xlviii] Even higher prevalence rates are associated with substance abuse, treatment settings, and prison (40 to 50 percent) or any forensic setting.[xlix] Someone with antisocial personality disorder (also referred to as a sociopath) can be further considered a psychopath. Since deceit, irresponsibility, and manipulation are central features of the disorder, these individuals usually have a history of behaviour symptomatic of conduct disorder. This is a persistent pattern of aggression toward people and animals, destruction of property, deceitfulness, or theft. It includes serious violations of rules and generally failing to conform to social norms regarding lawful behaviour. They repeatedly perform acts that are grounds for arrest, disregarding the wishes, rights, or feelings of others.

The list of characteristics that forms the pattern of antisocial behaviour runs the gamut of behaviour patterns of most citizens. It's when an individual breaks the law that the label of antisocial personality disorder is attached. Anyone who breaks the law is considered a sociopath. The worst label is a psychopath, which is reserved for those deemed the most uncaring, coldest, and notoriously untreatable. Whatever the term, after one has been arrested and assessed, it will be used as a tool to prosecute and condemn. Judges, Crowns, doctors, and parole officers then use such terms and related information in their files and complicated rituals of divinity.

DC prisoners are in a more closed environment, and being under the stress of just entering the system with looming court dates is enough to bring out the worst in one's personality. There is more freedom once you get shipped out to another facility, but there is also a bigger crowd of prisoners. These prisoners may be doing more time. Some are doing more time than they had expected. Many change in different ways: physically, mentally, and emotionally. Some prisoners befriend everyone simply to use them or feel secure thinking the more friends they have the better. Some just want to be popular, symptomatic of a narcissistic personality disorder. Some will be offended when you keep to yourself. Prisoners who start as friends may become your inescapable enemies. Conversely, those you didn't like at first may eventually become friends. It's difficult with everyone being forced to live together. Some prisoners will make their time pass easier, whereas others will make it a living hell. For those with social and emotional challenges, it can be devastating.

Chapter 8

Population, Protective Custody (PC), and Segregation (Seg)

Big-Box Pops

Prison is not just a warehouse of damaged souls to contain the broken, the beaten, and the damned. It's also a place of great suppression and suffering. Not only does each prisoner possess a different personality, so does each institution. Populations also differ depending on where and when you go. Regardless of which citadel of lawlessness, violence, pain, and despair any prisoner is sent to, the subterranean brotherhood of prisoners will still be governed by a herd mentality. A newcomer may find the reality of prison life hard to deal with. For some veteran prisoners, another day in the hermetic kingdom of the damned is all the life they have known.

A provincial detention centre (DC), remand centre (RC), or correctional centre (CC) can house as little as a dozen prisoners or, like the superjail in Milton, Ontario, nearly sixteen hundred. Warkworth Institution is the largest federal pen, holding around six hundred. Expansions are never-ending, and bigger warehouses are on the drawing boards. In the U.S., some state pens hold five thousand. Pens of that size would be much more difficult doing time in compared to Canadian ones. Larger populations mean more *short-term* savings for governments and more *long-term* pain, stress, and suffering for prisoners.

If you are the peaceful type of person who enjoys the calm living of a rural life as opposed to the crowds of a city, you won't like prison. Not that any prison camp should be compared to rural living—some have a farmlike setting with livestock and agriculture jobs. The cramped population of the CCs and pens (not as bad as DCs) are still a place where little or no privacy can be found. You will be double-bunked the first few months or years. Some cells will have bars, so those who don't get locked up roam around just outside. Some institutions have solid doors, which can make you feel more closed in, but at least you'll have more privacy. That's provided bored or needy prisoners you hardly know don't keep coming to your door, asking for a coffee, stamps, or munchies. Anything! Remember, once you give, expect them to be back for more. Jails are full of welfare hustlers.

General Population

General "pop" refers to the regular population of any institution, provided the entire place is not protective custody (PC). One of the hardest things to avoid in pop is population. Depending on where you go, the only time you may get any privacy is after full lockup at night. There is less privacy in any dormlike setting, although only federal camps and low-security CCs may have dorm settings. Camps have a far greater sense of freedom, and the populations there is not so hard-core. Some prisoners prefer a camp setting but can't handle its population. Many refer to the pop of lower security as a "kiddie camp" where prisoners are constantly bickering and squealing on each other like children. Guards in these places will also be more able to flex their attitudes. These guards know, as well as the prisoners, that it's very easy to transfer anyone back to a higher security facility.

Inmate Committees

Most places will have a range rep for each individual range. They may hold meetings to discuss what's going on in the range and within the entire institution or prisoner fraternity. Reps will also gather to voice matters with an elected committee. To elect range and committee reps, prisoners cast votes. Committees collect monies, arrange socials, plan events, and may stand up for your rights. The greatest problem, however, is that if the inmate committee stands up for someone they feel was wronged, whether by a guard or the institution, that prisoner may suddenly be transferred.

If any population elects a committee that becomes too strong, the institution's brass will easily dispose of it. Jail politics can be a frustrating nightmare. Some prisoners can truly make a difference in helping make the institution run a little smoother, but some prisoners will also abuse these positions. Still, whatever problem you may have, it's always better to discuss it with a range rep, or committee person, rather than inform a guard. You need to avoid talking to the guards or you may be suspected of being a rat.

Furbacks (Rats)

There is an old prison joke that goes, "When the Warden sees two prisoners whispering in the yard, he worries, but when he sees three, he no longer worries because he knows he has a man in there." Like street cops, guards will groom a prisoner for the specific purpose of obtaining information. There are even in-custody informer registries for such individuals. Prisoners must be careful speaking with staff or else they will become what they call a "reliable source."

Informants fuel distrust throughout any group. The guards know having informants makes their jobs easier as demonstrated in the book *Behind Bars: Surviving Prison* by Jeffrey Ian Ross and Stephen C. Richards:

> In a sense, the informer has shaken hands with the devil. Once you've told tales to [the cops or] guards, they've got

something on you: namely, the knowledge that you are a snitch. Threatening to reveal this to the other cons provides a club with which to beat you into informing again and again, until you're fatally compromised.

Big Wheels Keep on Turning

Some prisoners don't care much about their past or future and live only for the moment. Those moments inside can get hopelessly boring, so some prisoners will gamble, deal and/or do drugs, make moonshine, or just look for trouble. The higher security institutions will have more of these types of prisoners. They will float from job to job or not work at all. They may also feed off of or pick on other prisoners. In some ways, it's not different from the outside world, except in the free world, access to a weapon can even out a match. Not all prisons have shanks or weapons so easy to obtain. Many weapons may reduce instances of bigger prisoners attacking or muscling smaller ones. Having no weapons available to attack anyone also means having no weapons to protect yourself, and there are no guards to call for help unless you want to be instantly labelled a rat.

Ignorance is, of course, rampant in any population. Prisoners are not often people who have travelled the world or obtained wealth and prosperity. Most will never have owned a house, credit cards, or even a new car. Many have never even had a driver's license. Many will claim they had and did much and will often spread stories and gossip faster than wildfire. Prisoners trapped in cells seem to love nothing more than hearing and spreading gossip. It seems like there are more know-it-all talkers in prison than anywhere else on the planet. There too often will be prisoners who profess to know more about a crime than the ones accused of committing it.

In older days, when a new prisoner arrived, if someone said something against them later found to be a lie or rumour, the prisoner who spread it would be in deep trouble. Prisoners in each joint would even collect news articles, trying to verify facts about a prisoner's case. One could even go to the committee, "on the QT" of course, to express any knowledge of someone being a rat or rapist who should be ejected from population. The removal often meant either accosting the individual and asking them to leave or beating and stabbing them. Many mistakes were likely made, but at least rumours were investigated before any action was attempted.

Prisoners can become bitter and vindictive from friends, partners, or lawyers letting them down when they got popped. Most will blame others for a botched job or a leak of information that contributed to their fall. The majority won't accept the responsibility that they chose an untrustworthy partner or bad job to start with. It's far easier to attribute blame onto others for being stupid. Since angry prisoners feel helplessly trapped, they often focus their hatred on prisoners in PC or others whom they try to scare and force into PC. Just as many people in society look upon prisoners as scum, evil begets evil when prisoners do the same to others. Many prisoners think of themselves as better than the other prisoners around them. Even prisoners in PC will look down on others in PC and treat them degradingly.

Anyone in prison has obviously failed or lost in battling the law and going to court. Few people care to admit their faults honestly, much less completely, especially if the punishment and cost is harsh. How can anyone handle so much pain and guilt? Let he who is without sin cast the first stone. It's very difficult to deal with your emotions being trapped in a cage populated with so many other broken souls. If more people were kept segregated and alone, maybe more would reflect positively on the errors of their ways.

In population, you can become part of the worthless flow. Just as people in the outside world can quickly jump to conclusions or be easily swayed by rumours or the media, the same is true in prison. The difference is that this can often have deadly results in prison. It can happen much easier and have far more damaging effects over time. There are no police in jail. You can't go anywhere. Can't run or move. You can only fight or check in. "Checking in" means walking up to a guard and asking to immediately be moved into protective custody. Once you become a PC case, others will spread the news and you can't return to regular population.

Protective Custody (PC)

In the early nineties, the CSC brought forth a new plan called "Integration." What it basically did was forcibly mix higher security PC cases with lower security regular populations. They took groups of prisoners who had checked in over mostly non-life-threatening reasons and offered them transfers to other places of lower security. In other words, they offered them more freedom. This meant mixing up populations with all kinds of prisoner crimes and personalities. Maybe the PC populations were growing too big to afford two classes? Maybe wardens were not getting enough reliable sources to talk and squeal on each other? Maybe guards changed their tactics and more rats were easily discovered? Maybe the changing times just brought too many PC prisoners into the system.

Federal camps hold about 14 percent of all federal prisoners. They are the lowest type of security setting and are not considered pop or PC. Approximately two-thirds of the eight thousand federal prisoners are in medium-security institutions or areas of a medium that have what's called a dynamic security setting. Dynamic security is the combination of strong observational skills of guards, an understanding of each prisoner, open communication between prisoners and staff, and good practices of sharing information among staff. Such openness comes with a price in that prisoners can easily talk to staff but also talk crap about other prisoners.

Many stories get told about who checked in or who should. PC is supposed to be for rapists, child molesters, and informants. Many prisoners, however, especially new non-violent ones, check in simply out of fear. Gambling debts, drug debts, and borrowing are major factors causing many to temporarily check in. You may have done something unfavourable to a friend or someone another prisoner knows. By the time the story spreads and reaches others, it's like that fish story getting bigger and bigger. When you finally show up in jail or are transferred to another jail, trouble could already be waiting for you. Someone who testifies against you or rats you out can arrive somewhere before you do. They can easily spread their version of the story first, getting people on their side long before your arrival. If they are more popular, physically stronger, more conniving, or more dangerous than you, they will likely sway more prisoners to their side.

I have seen many occasions where guilty parties point a finger at others, deflecting attention away from themselves. I've heard many stories told to me in attempts to win my support only to learn it was the wrong story. When several prisoners go after a weaker, less known, inexperienced, or developmentally challenged prisoner, it's very unfair. Often there's little anyone else will do to help. Why stick up for someone you don't even know? Why take the minority side when you're trapped living with the majority? Survival! You are expected to stick up for those you live with and weed out any unwanted new arrivals. First come, first served!

It's sad to see how often prisoners assume another prisoner is a PC case simply from their appearance. Old or feeble-looking prisoners are the first choice to label as a diddler (child molester), rape hound, or rat. I have known educated prisoners who were unattractive, older, and/or overweight who others assumed looked like diddlers or informants when in fact they were in for fraud charges or property crimes. If you are simply quiet, geeky, nervous, or just keep to yourself, other prisoners may dislike you for that alone. The herd mentality is prevalent in prison. It's not just, "If you don't want to play ball, get off the field," it's go to another population. If you don't come across as hard-core or violent, yet are educated and polite, other prisoners can still feel intimidated by you. This is simply fear of intelligence. Is it best to pick a fight with you to show everyone who's number one? Intelligence only gets you so far in prison. Physical prowess takes you much further. Kindness is easily seen as an exploitable weakness in the prison environment. However, it's always good to be respectful if not polite to everyone. In the pen, it's easier to die because even a little guy can stab a bigger one. Not only are more shanks and razors to be found in most pens and CCs compared to the provincial DCs, there are more blind spots to attack a prisoner.

You may see a noticeable difference looking at a PC versus a regular range. There are simply a greater number of challenged, medicated, and non-violent prisoners found in PC. This does not mean they are all feeble, although being challenged or non-violent may mean it was easier for the police to trick them into squealing or pressure them into testifying. The worst types in PC are those who are violent. I expect they can rule easier in a PC environment. Prisoners who recently enter jail and break down emotionally are prime targets for colder prisoners to bully. Inexperienced first-timers may also escape by checking in hastily, only to later regret it. Fear and paranoia can easily contribute to the decision. Though the smaller population of PC may have some geeky-looking prisoners, it can also have the most irritable ones who couldn't survive on a regular range. Just as each regular population can have a varying group mentality from place to place, each PC pop can also vary greatly. There are sadistic psychopathic bullies in every population, both inside and outside. Prison has too many, and you just can't avoid them all.

Segregation (Seg)

Isolation, solitary confinement, the hole—they're all the same. Names vary from place to place provincially and federally. You may get a cell with a window. You won't get one with a radio. You will likely get a cellmate if it's a CC or DC. You won't get a cellmate in federal, but you can get a small TV. There are different reasons for being tossed into seg. If it's administrative seg, you are reviewed within thirty days. Administrative seg means you could be there for refusing to check in to PC and because administration fears putting you in regular pop. It could also be because your status is not yet known, or you may be en route to another destination, so they toss you in the hole for a few days. If you are an escape risk, file many grievances, have lots of enemies, pick fights with staff or prisoners, and act unmanageable, you will spend lots of time in seg.

Some prisoners complain to guards about everything. In some ways this can be good; in others it's not. Prisoners who often complain about treatment and rights are reminding others. If a guard fails to do seg showers or yard, prisoners will soon start yelling for a lieutenant because a guard isn't doing their job. The same goes for phone privileges. Using the phone while in seg is never as easy as in pop. Most places will let you out every day, or every other day, to use a phone for five to fifteen minutes. Some lucky places will hand you a phone in the cell. If one prisoner starts complaining, others may join in. Prisoners can also complain to other guards and management (white shirts). This is not considered ratting because guards are the ones with power to abuse.

The same goes for receiving meals three times a day, laundry every few days, canteen, etc. A frustrated prisoner may complain for guards to do their jobs, but they may overuse the complaint process. Some may bitch just for something to do and feel cheated over any minor loss. They may exaggerate any mistreatment or falsely claim of being threatened or even assaulted. Some will complain about there not being enough socks around and then take a dozen extra pairs, causing a shortage. They may whine about not getting phone time and then stay on it twice as long as anyone else. They may even file for an appeal, just for something to do or simply because they can. They will put in grievances against a guard or institution for any trivial reason. They will also overburden the system on purpose. This will cause more paperwork for guards, administration, or lawyers. Such acts drain needed attention away from more serious matters.

Provincial prisoners can easily lose good time (early release during the final third of a sentence earned for good behaviour) for offences such as assaults, drugs, possession of contraband, or talking back to a guard. Infractions result in being charged with an institutional misconduct charge. Prisoners awaiting results may also spend time in the hole. Federal prisoners don't lose good time. They just don't get parole, are sent to higher security pens, or get detained then gated. (For more on gating, please see Chapter 11.) Whatever the charge is, it will be your word against what the guards think or say happened. Two prisoners caught fighting anywhere will often go straight to the hole to be interviewed later. Acting suicidal or refusing orders can also get you tossed into the hole for a few days.

I remember in the early eighties that the guards would rush in when a fight broke out, and they would take whoever was involved to the hole and then lock up the range. They would then spend hours separately interviewing each person on the range, trying to find out about the fight. This rarely happens now unless it's a very serious assault. I guess the paperwork takes too much effort now, and guards don't care who pummels whom for whatever reason. Maybe interviewing everyone on a range caused too much suspicion, along with more violence to suspected snitches, or perhaps now there are just too many fights.

If you end up in the hole for misbehaving, you will likely get a label of LOAP or OP on your door. It means "loss of all privileges" or "off privileges"—no canteen, books, phone, and maybe no day mattress and blanket, although they should return your one-inch mattress at night. A "suicide watch" label means no blanket, sheets, towel, or razors, and guards are supposed to keep an eye on you. You will wear very uncomfortable cardboard-like clothing referred to as "baby dolls."

If you are seen violently banging your head against the wall, they will strap a helmet on you. Suicidal prisoners are dressed in baby dolls and left alone with nothing in their cell. Is this so they will feel better? No. The jail just doesn't want to be blamed for letting you die in their care.

The very worst is when the cell is cold or hot, you are naked, and the cell you are tossed into has walls smeared with human waste. Some hidden drastic measures are the five-point restraint—strapped to a bed all day, even sometimes while gagged.

Time in the hole can be boring and disturbing for many prisoners, especially if staff there are really nasty. Eventually, despite your best efforts to stay focused, the lack of human interaction will take its toll. Prisoners who are subjected to long periods in solitary confinement may suffer what psychologists call psychopathological consequences and sensory deprivation stress. Symptoms can include anxiety, hearing noises or voices, seeing ghosts, profound depression, perceptual distortions, hallucinations, and paranoia. The maximum punishment one is supposed to spend in the hole is thirty days, but prisoners can stay there for months or even years. Those who have spent years in segregation have been known to crack up and become violently psychotic, lose the ability to talk with others, and experience amnesia—they may not even recall their own names.

Administrative detention is common and is used to circumvent the legal requirements of providing a disciplinary hearing. It's also the easiest way to get rid of any complaining difficult-to-manage prisoners. The warden, or a white shirt, simply instructs the guards to remove you from general population and throw you into the hole. To circumvent the thirty-day review rule, institutions can keep transferring you to multiple locations as they did with nineteen-year-old Ashley Smith, who eventually took her life in 2007 as guards watched.

Medical seg is not necessarily the same as suicide watch. In larger places, medical segregation may be a separate range altogether. Prisoners could be there for medical watch or separated because they have TB in its contagious stage. Sharing a smoke can spread TB as well as herpes or hepatitis. Hep A is easily transmitted when people don't wash their hands after using the washroom, through contaminated food or water, and through unprotected sexual activity. Hep B and C and other new strains are caused by viruses that can be transmitted through bodily fluids by such means as blood-to-blood contact from sharing needles or unprotected sex. Sharing supplies used for snorting or smoking can also spread Hep C. I have seen many bloody fights, new tattoos, intravenous drug use, and some homosexuals who care little about diseases in jail. Almost half (45 percent) of prisoners have tattoos and 17 percent have body piercings. In 2004, it was estimated that one in four federal prisoners now have Hep C.[1]

Though the monotony of the hole causes many to go stir-crazy after a few days, it is truly the only place to find peace and quiet—to do your own time. That is, if you're lucky to get an empty cell and others prisoners next to you don't bug out. It's especially irritating when they bug out in the middle of the night. Some will just start screaming, singing, whistling, or kicking hard on their steel doors. In the DCs, people come and go from the hole constantly. Some restless, un-sentenced, or un-medicated prisoners don't care about being respectful to anyone. After leaving the hole, some prisoners may even get punched out upon returning to a range and not know why.

Working out can be plain and boring when trapped in the hole. It may become a problem to a cellmate as well. Preferably, you may both choose to work out in your tiny little space. Yard time is supposed to be given in the hole every day for twenty minutes (or an hour in federal). That's rarely the case. Guards may offer yard simply so they can toss your cell while you're gone. It might be at regular times or irregular times. Some guards may always ask if you want yard on a rainy, cold, miserable day. You're more likely to refuse and their job is then done.

The same goes with the phone. Most prisoners prefer to use

phones after supper, when people are more likely to be at home. In the DCs, lazy seg guards will go around asking if you need the phone right after breakfast. At that time, more prisoners will likely say no. The guards can then claim their day's routine partly done. Later, when everyone starts asking to use the phone, the guard can simply claim you were already given a chance but said no. However, not all guards are so horrible. Sometimes it's better to shift phone availability to after breakfast, after lunch, or before dinner, as lawyers on the outside are best reached at certain times. Most guards won't really care. Many are just there for the paycheque and consider pampered prisoners as less than human. Some guards feel prisoners should not be allowed access to phones at all. I'm sure there are many hard-nosed guards who would treat caged animals better than prisoners.

One popular conception of time in the hole is that it drags by ever so slowly but seems to have flashed by in the end. It's a weird thing to explain. It seems to drag because you sit and stare at a blank wall all day or pace for hours. It's what I did for twenty-eight straight months. It was the insanity of such boredom that led me to begin writing these words. When the end comes, it's as if it passed in a blink. I find it passes best if you're alone and reading or writing. I can read from morning till bedtime and shut out any noises. If you do this, the time flies by quickly. It's the best place to study or write out your thoughts.

If you never knew how to write poetry or draw, you may learn after time in the hole. If you get really bored, you can always write that letter to Grandma you've been putting off for too long. Just don't tell her you were bad and that you're in the hole. You can end up reading and writing more in the hole than you have ever done in your entire life. You can order newspapers and magazines, provided you have privileges and funds. Just remember, your paperboy won't be delivering your newspaper and the guards will pass it around taking their turns reading it first.

Chapter 9

Employment and Programs

Schooling

Schools will vary in size and curriculum between institutions. The same goes for workshops and programs. A maximum-security institution will have very limited access, while a lower security, in theory, will have more to offer. Places with similar security levels can vary in training, schooling, and treatment programs. Statistics Canada estimates that 36 percent of arriving prisoners (46 percent federal) had grade 9 or less compared to 19 percent of adults in Canada. Half were unemployed upon arrest and only a third was married.[li]

Most detention centres (DCs) have no schoolroom, and correctional centres (CCs) will have less than most pens. Any prisoner can begin correspondence courses from a DC and continue after being transferred. A larger DC may have one or more volunteer tutors visiting weekly. One teacher will likely visit different ranges in a larger jail to answer inquiries and offer applications for correspondence courses. They will also explain how some courses may be more difficult to enroll in or complete while in a DC. The teacher can obtain transcripts from your previous school and offer advice on courses needed to obtain a grade 12 diploma. Pens will have several teachers, classrooms, and prisoners who tutor.

Area county school boards may govern a provincial jail to issue diplomas. If you earn your final credits from them to get your grade

12 diploma, the diploma will bear their name on it. If the course is not done through an outside program, it will be done through the prison's own system. The name of the school for prisons in Ontario is Acheron, named in Greek mythology after one of the rivers leading to hell. If you are only one credit shy of obtaining a diploma and don't want the Acheron prison name to follow you for the rest of your life, you have one of two choices. First, simply take your last needed credit on the outside after your release. You may even be able to attend a night school class from your old high school. Unfortunately, after release, you may not follow through. The teachers and principal of Acheron know this and will encourage you to finish your last course with them. They benefit from using your success as another diploma delivered. Let's say you spent four years in high school but left with two credits shy of a diploma. If you obtain the final credits after arriving at the pen and earn your diploma from Acheron, they get to claim they gave you a grade 12 diploma.

If you don't want the prison name of Acheron on your diploma, the second way around this is to complete your final credit through a provincial correspondence program. In Ontario, the Independent Learning Centre (ILC) is open to anyone. You can take over twenty courses in the pen from Acheron, but ILC will issue the diploma as long as the final needed course is done through them. No prison school will inform you about this or recommend it to you because they won't be able to claim another successful graduate if ILC scoops the glory. Anyone, whether in jail or not, can take ILC courses. You can always hope that an employer, years later, won't know or ask about Acheron or notice the name on your diploma. However, it's best to get your diploma from ILC, just in case. ILC is also better recognized as a diploma.

Many prison school officials give preference to a prisoner wanting to obtain a grade 10 level of education. Since many have little education and grade 12 is a difficult goal, most institutions focus more on the teaching the basics up to grade 10. The term used is

10.9, although many who do achieve this certificate inside likely couldn't pass a grade 8 test taken on the outside.

Adult Basic Education (ABE)

Adult basic education (ABE) teaches four levels and is available in most cities and prisons. Prisoners entering the federal system without a high school diploma will have education goals as part of their correctional plan. They are paid to attend as long as they keep progressing. Education is considered by many to be the soil of survival in our current world. If you are already educated and wish to take college or university courses, you now have to pay if you are unable to obtain a bursary and do them on your own time.

To a more educated prisoner, or one trying harder than others, this may seem unfair. In a way, it's similar to applying for legal aid, where it's much better to be poor and have nothing. If you already have a grade 10 education and want to attend school, if there is a waiting list, you take second priority to anyone with less than grade 10. You may even be expected to assist in tutoring or only allowed more education through approved cell studies. Tutoring can be rewarding and is a paid prison job. Cell studies means you complete one lesson per week or a specified amount of work in your cell and possibly write a test in the school. With cell studies, you avoid classrooms and spend more time locked up in your cell.

Employment

The provincial system abolished all forms of incentive pay in 1993-1994. Therefore, if you come in penniless, that's how you will leave. If Grandma won't drop off any money, you won't be buying any goodies on canteen or registering in any school courses. As a result, the provincial system is now flooded with many mendicant prisoners. Pay levels for guards were cut by 5 percent in 1994-1995, but union strikes quickly raised their salaries. Prisoners in the federal system have never had a union or seen any pay increase in a quarter of a century despite the tremendous increases to the prices of canteen items. The pay is trivial to begin with, and with less incentive to work for peanuts, this contributes to contraband trade and the drug culture, which raises security concerns.

In the federal system, there are pay levels from A to F-zero. Prisoners can work a half a day at school and half at another job. Upon your arrival, you will receive pay level D, known as "welfare level." Handicapped prisoners can get paid if granted a warden's exemption. Prisoners who refuse work or programs stay at level D. After beginning school or work, you are placed on level C, which pays $5.80 per day. Performance is graded every several months, and if it remains excellent, you go up one level. The maximum level of pay is level A at $6.90 per day. Pay is deposited every two weeks for two 5-day work periods, 10 percent of which automatically goes into your savings, while another portion automatically goes to the Inmate Welfare Fund—the inmate committee's account. This pays mostly for cable TV and other activities within the institution. To earn slightly more pay is to receive overtime, which may be rare and only add about an extra $10 per pay. Larger payments are given to those employed in CORCAN, which has a limited number of positions and is only available in some federal institutions.

CORCAN is an industrial and agribusiness agency that claims to provide prisoners with work experience and training. Ha! They produce products that are then marketed to federal, provincial, and municipal governments as well as non-profit organizations. CORCAN applicants must have a 10.9 education. You can be fired if you refuse to take time off to attend psych programs. However, this also goes for almost any job or school program. Although CORCAN pays almost double compared to other jobs, employees must pay room and board, which can be up to $25 weekly.

Regular work jobs include cleaning, mopping, doing laundry, kitchen duties, maintenance work, etc. Work experience is not of much value. A job as a plumber will likely mean unplugging toilets.

As an electrician, it means changing light bulbs. The jobs in prison are often quite mundane, although they help keep maintenance costs down. If prisoners in the provincial system had banded together and refused to clean or help with kitchen and laundry work, they might still be getting paid. Even paltry pay is better than working for free. The pittance of a small weekly allowance to save before release also calculates to fewer humiliated prisoners reporting to welfare upon release.

Institutions have a small supervisory staff hired from the outside to monitor prisoners working under their direction. Provincial prisoners are more confined and will work for free simply out of boredom, exercise, and less confinement to a cell. With no provincial pay, fewer prisoners will be able to buy any canteen items. Goodies become a valued treat that prisoners will fight for, barter for, or con from one another, which causes problems. If provincial canteen disappears as the library books almost have, the only thing left of value may be a prisoner's good time. I expect provincial prisoners could one day follow the federal way of forced parole at two-thirds.

Guards may also suffer more as frustrated prisoners increase the prevalence of assaults. There is less incentive to behave if a prisoner has fewer luxuries, easily loses good time, and automatically faces parole restrictions upon any release. The only remaining deterrent to misbehaving is being sent to higher security. More prisoners ending up in higher security might subsequently become determined to not return, but others will come out much meaner from the experience. This does not protect society or save tax dollars in the long run. The lack of incentive pay makes prison more dangerous for guards and the public less safe from desperate penniless prisoners upon release. Not having the chance to earn and save any money means many of those released will apply for welfare and/or return to crime.

Programs

While schooling and employment are considered programs in prison, there are also behavioural modification programs. Provincial institutions have few programs, while those in federal institutions can vary considerably. Programs may be either weeklong or several months long. Their waiting lists may also be months or years. You can even be transferred to another institution to take a program and then be returned. If you only have a few months to serve, you won't likely get into most programs. If you are to be released and you missed getting into or were refused a program, you can easily be forced into a halfway house upon release to attend a program. This is now being done to many unsuspecting prisoners just before their release on mandatory parole. Many prisoners expecting to be released, if only for mandatory parole, are sadly surprised when told during a residency hearing weeks before their release that they are being recommended to a halfway house for programs or for security risks and a high chance of reoffending. If you have many years to serve before your release, you will likely be denied programs for years. Many prisoners are told by their POs to waive their parole hearings until they complete a program. Waiving parole because of a PO's claim about waiting lists for programs increases frustration levels and promotes an atmosphere of hopelessness. Prisoners often complain about being denied programs or getting them at the end of their term instead of earlier.

Political climates affect budgetary cutbacks to the number and variety of educational and apprenticeship courses offered in institutions. A decade ago, prisoners had access to trade training programs that would give them the required apprenticeship certificate needed to find employment on the outside. Numerous vocational and trade/training programs were discontinued due to budget cuts, some even in midterm. Motor mechanics, metalworking, welding, and other trade shops have almost completely vanished from institutions. Many prison barbershops have also disappeared. The infamous Alcatraz even maintained a barbershop. Go figure!

Many provincial and federal institutions have Alcoholic Anonymous (AA) and Narcotics Anonymous (NA) groups. Halfway houses funded by the CSC are also beginning to offer more programs. Additional funding is also now available for training, retraining, and salaries of staff needed to run programs. Such cost shifting may be higher in other ways when salaries are reshuffled for programs a minority of prisoners are honestly willing to take. Nevertheless, POs will evaluate a prisoner's openness to programs since openness to suggestion (synonymous with *hypnotism* and *fantasy proneness*) has been shown to be positively correlated with psychotherapy's outcome. Lester Luborsky, the celebrated researcher in psychotherapy, noted that "'successful' treatment was tied to the patient's mental health at the time of treatment: the studies 'indicate that the healthier a patient is to begin with, the better the outcome.'"[lii]

The CSC's mission statement contains five core values, the fourth reading as follows: "We believe programs and opportunities to assist offenders in developing social and living skills will enhance their potential to become law-abiding citizens." Some of the programs the CSC provides to change the behaviour (gather data) and thinking patterns of inmates while building new skills are:

General Crime Prevention

Alternatives, Associates, and Attitudes (AAA) Program
Basic Healing Program
Circles of Change Program (For Women)

Violence Prevention

Violence Prevention Program – High Intensity (VPP-HI)
Violence Prevention Program – Moderate Intensity (VPP-MI)
Violence Prevention Program – Maintenance
Women's Violence Prevention Program (WVPP)
New Spirit of a Warrior Program

In Search of Your Warrior Program (ISOYW)

Family Violence Prevention
Treatment Primer (Roadways to Change)
High Intensity Family Violence Prevention Program
Moderate Intensity Family Violence Prevention Program
National Family Violence Maintenance Program
High Intensity Aboriginal Family Violence Program

Substance Abuse
National Substance Abuse Program – High Intensity (NSAP-High)
National Substance Abuse Program – Moderate Intensity (NSAP-Moderate)
National Substance Abuse Program – Pre-Release Booster
National Substance Abuse Program – Maintenance
Women Offender Substance Abuse Program
Aboriginal Offender Substance Abuse Program

Sex Offender
National Sex Offender Program – High Intensity (NaSOP-HI)
National Sex Offender Program – Moderate Intensity (NaSOP-MI)
National Sex Offender Program – Low Intensity (NaSOP-LO)
Women's Sex Offender
Tupiq Program

Community-Based Correctional Programs
Community Maintenance Program
Community Relapse Prevention/Maintenance Program for Women
Aboriginal Women's Maintenance Program
Inuit Community Maintenance Program

Source: Correctional Service of Canada (CSC)

One caution to taking, or being coerced to take, any of the above dataveillance programs is the matter of confidentiality. Running a close second is spilling out your insides to a roomful of other prisoners you must live with 24/7. Third, the hardship of being trapped in a cage is difficult enough without letting others into your cerebral darkness. Being punished is one thing, having your captor force you to expel your insides while caged feels like double jeopardy. If you refuse to participate in any recommended programs, your pay level will be reduced or taken away. You can also be denied trailer visits or refused transfer for not taking or completing a program successfully. You won't gain early parole but will get more restrictions on mandatory release, be possibly forced into a community resource centre (CRC), or worse, be detained for your entire sentence and then gated. (For more on gating, please see Chapter 11.)

The rules and regulations that institutional staff and prisoners must follow are set out in what's called *The Commissioner's Directives*. CD #840-21 states, "...personal psychological information will be fully disclosed within CSC for the purposes of case management including release decision-making and the supervision or surveillance of the offender in the institution or the community." These CSC guidelines further state in section 22:

> ...pursuant to subsection 25(1) of the *Corrections and Conditional Release Act*, psychological information that is relevant to release decision-making or the supervision or surveillance of offenders must be given at the appropriate time to the National Parole Board, provincial governments, provincial parole boards, the police, and any body authorized by CSC to supervise offenders. Pursuant to subsection 25(3), psychological information must be shared with the police where CSC believes on reasonable grounds that an inmate who is about to be released on warrant expiry poses a threat to any person after release and where that information is relevant to the perceived threat.

The word *perceived* can be applied to justify the ransacking of confidential records, just as the word *security* can be used to deny almost anything. Under paragraph 23 of the above-mentioned CD, it says offenders are allowed access to psychological information, but subsection 23(2) "requires...inmates be given access to the same information...unless, except in the case of disciplinary matters, disclosure can be refused for reasons of safety, security, or to protect a lawful investigation." This means anything you tell a psychologist, or any member of the CSC, can be relayed to the police or parole board but easily denied viewing by you, often for *security* reasons.

Prisoners, especially first-timers, want to believe they will never return to prison. Some will genuinely want to change and be willing to take programs. Many won't consider that the information they surrender will be used against them later. I have known many who completed programs successfully only to be denied parole and angrily wish they had never attended programs. Those who unexpectedly return to prison have prior programs' reports, inaccurate or not, to evaluate and possibly condemn them in court.

In attending any psychology program, prisoners are expected to admit full responsibility for their crimes. While some prisoners have committed terrible injurious crimes, anyone can be unfairly and overly punished because of faulty reports. POs and program facilitators are guided by Crown data gleaned from ViCLAS (links to other cases), criminal profiling, forensic psychology, geographic profiling, polygraphs and other testing and studies, as well as input from the police, witnesses, and victim impact statements. Prisoners who contest any data errors will be seen as being in denial and failing to take responsibility.

Program facilitators may have lived sheltered middle class lives and have preconceived ideas of how other classes of people (the poor) should live. Not wanting to believe the words of any criminal, they may also not give much credit to existing studies showing that programs can increase the likelihood of reoffending.[liii] Prisoners have told me that in one such a program, instructors tell them that any woman who has even one drink cannot consent to sex. And if a fight starts with you being hit first, you are still to blame for returning such a gesture since you are the one in custody.

Anyone who was ever a player in the game of seduction will know how some tame people can let loose or turn "wild" after a few drinks. Some women the very next morning (or years later while being questioned and manipulated by the police) may act ashamed and blame the drinking/drugs, and then you for taking advantage of them. And if you show them little or no respect, they may be more inclined to claim they were taken advantage of. If they don't want to be known as promiscuous, they may even attempt to regain some of their lost virtue simply by claiming the sex was never consensual. The same applies to any physical assault. It doesn't matter that you discovered your mate in bed with someone else, she likes to fight, she slapped you first, or she is mentally warped. If you strike her for any reason, you are the one at fault and in need of reform. You must attend programs and profess a *desire* to change your ways. In the free world outside, people have the inalienable right to make choices that affect their own lives. You can seek or choose the help you want, but in prison, if you refuse programs, you will likely be punished by having to stay in prison longer with no chance for parole.

Free will is a necessary component to positive change. But under the iron curtain of the CSC, things are not always as they seem on paper. The Corrections and Conditional Release Act (CCRA), which replaced the Penitentiary and Parole Act in 1992, is legislation meant to improve the system. It claims first to protect the public, followed by helping victims of crime to be recognized, delaying eligibility for full parole, tightening the granting of passes, and making more prisoners serve their entire sentence regardless of their behaviour inside. Section 88(1)(a) states, "treatment shall not be given to an inmate, or continued once started, unless the inmate voluntarily gives an informed consent thereto." Further writings such as CD #760-12 states, "Offender participation in correctional programs shall be voluntary and based on informed consent." Their word *voluntary* really means "coerced." The propaganda fails to mention that any prisoner who refuses programs, even if instructed by their appeal lawyer, will have their pay level slashed and won't be supported for parole.

Participation in prison program groups can also have many negative results on prisoners that the staff never discovers. Group participants are instructed not to talk outside the group about what others have said, but gossip spreads and can help incite a fight months or years later.

One would think that the success rate would be greater if prisoners were given the incentive of earlier parole to a halfway house to attend programs in a setting closer to the real environment to which they will return one day. Unfortunately, the CSC values these programs, as they are a political tool and a tax money grab. However, the programs also help the CSC cover its ass (for the rare prisoner who is released and commits a violent act) while gathering information from the guinea pigs it monitors and plays with experimentally.

One would have hoped that all data pertinent to a prisoner would be held in strict confidentiality, since the CSC stresses that the operative words are *correctional service*, not *prison service*. The CSC states that their endeavours are assigned to assist offenders in correcting their behaviour and that society is best protected when offenders are able to re-establish themselves in the community.

A prisoner destined for the federal system is first sent to an assessment institution, where various psychiatric and psychological testing build up the prisoner's file with information for "treatment and assessment purposes." Ontario's assessment unit is Millhaven (MAU) in Bath. A prisoner is considered a risk to self and others; therefore, the privacy and sanctity of the therapist/patient relationship is overlooked. The CSC can then release information to "relevant" parties in accordance with the Privacy Act—and there is a wide audience that seems to be considered "relevant." Is there any wonder why many prisoners hesitate to open up to any counselling or are unwilling to take programs?

Treatment Facilities

Many correctional centres (CCs) and federal pens have some kind of program available or a treatment wing. The Ontario Northern Treatment Centre was once a popular location for provincial and federal prisoners, but it closed its doors to federal prisoners. Each of the CSC's five regions across Canada has a Regional Treatment Centre (RTC). Ontario's RTC is within the walls of Kingston Pen (KP) maximum security. It's a facility for violent prisoners or sex offenders, and it requires a stay of six months or longer. Bath, once a low-security federal camp, now has a new high fence and houses more sex offenders.

New arrivals will likely see a work/program board within the first week or two and be told what is available or what has a waiting list. You will be seen by your caseworker, sooner or later, to fill you in on what type of programs you will be expected to take, as well as possibly where and when you will take them. Prisoners were once told shortly after arrival the exact dates when their training/program would start and be completed. If not, they were at least assigned a number on a list. That gave prisoners focus but put too much stress on POs to live up to, so dates are now only vaguely suggested. Again, priority cases will bump those waiting.

In the provincial system, you may not see a work board at all, and there will be no PO/caseworker who can help. Management accountability lacks in the prison system. POs inside often do very little work to help most prisoners on their caseload. Some institutions have POs who juggle a caseload as high as twenty-five. The more prisoners they have who are non-priority or doing longer sentences the less work they will have to do and the more time they will have to focus on the easiest ones to support for parole. Unless you are prone to psychological disorders and/or are a first-time non-violent, prisoner, you won't get much help from a PO. First-timers see their caseworkers quickly give them priority on programs and more attention in helping them move on to a camp or apply for early parole.

Unlike professional medicine, where practitioners can be judged for harming or neglecting patients and face charges of incompetence, program facilitators, POs, and the CSC are immune. Many studies about programs are even funded by CSC-contracted workers. That's like a tobacco company writing a report about the health effects of smoking. Research shows that appropriate correctional interventions are more effective in reducing reoffending rates when they are delivered in the community compared to those that take place in a prison. Unfortunately, the federal system is gaining more power and tax dollars for programs even though community-based alternatives are also less costly than imprisonment in human, social, and financial terms.

Meanwhile, repeat customers are being denied chances to better themselves. While they are in the same settings as first-timers, with the availability of treatment or education, the chances at parole or a transfer to camp and eventually freedom will seem very unfair to many. This only increases the possibility of returning to prison after another failed attempt in society. Not only do many prisoners fail to be released early on parole, they lose again by returning to crime. The protection of society fails as well, but the CSC wins another repeat customer.

Chapter 10

Idle Hours

Boredom

The word *boredom* hardly describes what it's like being trapped in a cage with nothing to do. In the buckets, there is less to do, and prisoners have much stress dealing with court and recent losses. Anything to take your mind off your troubles is a welcome distraction. The detention centres (DCs) are the worst, especially in the hole and off privileges. Even reading all day, playing cards, or watching TV can become maddeningly monotonous. Add to this other restless prisoners, seeing a fight may be the highlight of the week to escape the monotony. If you are the type of person who has difficulty standing still and strives for autonomy, you really won't like prison. Unfortunately, many prisoners who get restless and bored seek entertainment at another's expense.

Pulling pranks is one thing in the free world, but in prison, they can be quite cruel. Prisoners suffering from their period of attenuation sometimes attempt to deprive others of their strength and dignity. Stressed and helpless people may intentionally stress others as a form of control. Wardens know a restless and bored crowd of prisoners is harder to manage than content, working, busy ones. Jokes and storytelling are quite common. However, prisoners looking to vent can target an innocent quip or comment. A prisoner may want to beat up on someone simply because they look like someone they don't like. A once popular joke pulled by younger prisoners was with matches and lit cigarettes. Bored prisoners would put a lit cigarette in the pocket of a prisoner sleeping on the range floor just to watch the reaction. Thankfully, the ban on smoking eradicated that entertaining prank. A more devious prisoner will trick or pressure another to fight another, spread rumours, or start something, all just to escape the boredom.

Once finished with court and set free, or at least transferred out, you won't feel so trapped, provided you don't receive a long sentence. Though some places are more boring than others, boredom really depends on the type of individual. My dad always said, "Boredom is an insult to oneself." If you can't think of something to dispel boredom, then you are a boring person. My dad's words stayed with me and sunk in deeper after I came to prison.

Over 95 percent of any population on a DC range, except the work range, won't have jobs. If there is a gym, study room, or library, there will often not be enough guards working to escort prisoners there. Even when there are, they use this excuse to deny daily usage.

Prisoners desperate enough to escape the helplessness and boredom of prison will desire drugs. Those who have never done harder drugs may try anything in prison for escape. The easy availability of drugs, if not brought in by staff, comes from the high turnover rate of prisoners. In the DCs, prisoners arrive daily from the street, after arrest or trials. They can swallow a package before court or when being chased by police. *Hooping* means hiding the drug package where nobody can see the light of day. Such methods are easily employed just before arriving to face the judge. If you are well known or have friends inside, you will be expected to bring something in to be well received. Often, packages such as these are also delivered for a small cut, usually a quarter of what's brought in.

The smell of pot is easily noticed by other prisoners and passing guards, but consumption often mellows out aggressive or violent prisoners. Since THC lasts up to thirty days in the system, some prisoners/parolees prefer harder drugs that leave the body sooner to avoid failing a piss test. Unfortunately, homemade brew, shine, pills, and heroin can cause major problems. If guards notice that prisoners appear wasted, the entire place may be locked down for several days and searched. A few indiscreet users make the entire population pay. Lockdowns mean more loss of freedom and unwanted searches, with cells torn apart and items seized.

Urinalysis

Urinalyses, or "piss tests," don't happen in the DCs but are common in the pens, halfway houses, or for prisoners on parole. Random urinalyses are scheduled for all prisoners/parolees to check whether they've been using drugs and for estimating the prevalence of drugs throughout the system. Suspected individuals can be tested more often, while others may have only one or no testing. Charges are laid for failing a test or for refusing to surrender a sample. These charges are made in an inside court, and the penalties range from a reprimand or fine to a stay in the hole. Failing a test will be a strike against you when trying for parole, and a parole officer will increase the frequency of testing after your release. Failing a piss test on the outside can be grounds to yank anyone's parole.

Visits at the DCs are in an enclosed area with glass windows, so hooping or bribing a guard are the only ways to smuggle anything into most DCs or correctional centre (CC) max facilities. Throwing drug packages over a DC's yard wall was once quite popular in the nineties until nets popped up to cover them. Trusties, prisoners who would work on outside maintenance crews, were also once an easy way to obtain drugs, since a friend could always stash a package outside to be retrieved. Now, most DCs, CCs, and pens no longer have maintenance crews, trusties, or any prisoners outside the walls—but mysteriously, the drugs are still getting inside.

Hobbies and Social Groups

After transferring out of a stressful DC, your next stop will likely have hobbies and crafts for you to toy with. Most will have the standard activities—leatherworking, woodworking, music, or art—and a craft room, or possibly two. Your placement and security level play a role here whether in a provincial CC or federal institution. In the provincial system, the only programs or groups will be Alcoholics Anonymous (AA), Narcotics Anonymous (NA), church, the John Howard Society, and the Native Brotherhood. In the federal system, there are many more, such as the inmate committee, Black Inmates and Friends Assembly (BIFA), French, Muslim, Italian, lifers, etc.

Groups hold monthly or yearly fund-raising drives selling food, T-shirts, sunglasses, pizza, or other approved items. Prisoner committees help organize and raise funds for purchasing needed equipment such as microwaves, toasters, and other items for individual ranges or family trailers. Signing bulk lists to purchase items or donate money to any group or charity drive was common, but many institutions are eliminating the easy use of bulks.

There are hobby craft and fund-raising projects carried out for outside charities and local causes. There may be a toy drive where woodworking prisoners make toys, a canned food drive for donating to a local shelter, or Christmas support for the less fortunate. Groups may offer some kind of help for senior's causes, raise donations for a transition house or memorial, or put on a yearly event such as Field of Dreams and other events for developmentally challenged children. Recycling cans is the only environmental project to have caught on.

Native prisoners may have their own activity room to do some exceptional craftwork. Making dream-catchers, carvings, drawings, and leatherwork are popular. The Native Brotherhood has sweat lodges and special gatherings in reserved garden spaces. Some

Canadians feel First Nations individuals deserve special status, even in prison, since Canada was once their entire domain. Some prisoners think they are treated too well. Muslims also have extra status by being allowed special conditions related to their religion, such as prayer mats and specially prepared pork-free meals.

Some places, more often pens than CCs, will have a common room, pool room, and a music room to play instruments. A craft room, library, or canteen may be accessible daily or weekly. In the federal pens, such rooms are more functional, as CCs hold smaller populations serving shorter terms. Since prisoners in the pens can work for small wages, buying outside supplies is an increasing desire. This includes ordering small stereos, TVs, gym clothing, fans, and craft supplies. With the exception of some craft supplies, none of these luxuries are available in the CCs. Although federal prisoners can buy typewriters, purchasing computers is no longer allowed. Fewer than six hundred federal prisoners have old computers in their cells, but they have no Internet access. Scanners were never allowed, and old printers were only allowed black ink. Computers can be taken away for suspicion or the most trivial of security reasons.

Recreation

The yard, gym, and weight pit in any federal pen will likely be much bigger and better equipped than any DC's or CC's. Many prisoners who put off working out claim they will wait until they are transferred out of a DC. They may know the pen will offer a far better area in which to exercise. Unfortunately, many quit shortly after their transfer. The same happens in the land of the free. We get all worked up and inspired over the idea of starting something new and positive. Some people spend more time thinking about starting than actually doing it.

I have always worked out or jogged. In solitary, it helps pass time and stay fit, although showering may mean birdbathing in a little sink. My reason for frequently jogging outside was not simply for health or because I gave up smoking. Fewer could accost me while I was moving at a faster pace than hundreds of others roaming the yard. If they did, I often increased my pace or claimed I needed to do so, and then I politely lost them. This was not simply because I thought most prisoners were undesirable as friends, although many are, but because it's easier to run and be alone. Also many others smoked.

Many prisoners would try going a lap or two at my pace but would tire because of their smoking habits. At times, I would even run for hours alone in the yard on the coldest of winter days. Many prisoners at one time or another avoid others by jogging, going to an area at times when they are the least busy, staying in their cell, or taking trips to solitary. As alone as prison is, it can be very difficult to find time alone, especially if double-bunked for a long period.

Most prisoners go outside to socialize as soon as "rec-up" is called. I prefer going outside when there are just a few prisoners. Jogging sucked when you had to dodge around clouds of smokers. Smoking is gone, but baseballs still run wild. If you go outside to sit or stroll, there are always others who may join in, or they may join in on conversations you are having. It's as if nobody will leave you alone. That is unless they can't jog for long. Some prisoners exaggerate their I-hate-everybody attitude, just to keep as many people away as they can, although they'll suddenly be nice to someone when they need something.

The Weight Pit

Weight pits are usually indoors during winter months and moved outdoors for summer. There will likely be a limited number of benches available in the spring with an unlimited number of mosquitoes. During prime-time rec-up just after supper, most benches will be in use. As a result, you may have to wait for a bench, know someone you can join in with, or ask to share equipment. Weekday afternoon hours in the gym may only be for rec workers, guards, or a protective custody (PC) range.

It's best to leave an area just as you found it or better. It's a common courtesy in any gym to put weights back where they belong. Some prisoners still think their mothers should be picking up after them. It may be a good idea to discover who else uses the bench you wish to use and let them know. Benches and equipment areas are used like shift work, and just because someone isn't using the area at a certain time, it doesn't mean that the area is technically vacant. Someone may have just taken a few days off.

Much of what happens in prison weight pits would have most prisoners permanently banned from a gym on the outside. Spitting, yelling, throwing weights, or dropping them (sometimes on other's heads) happens more often in prison pits. Any trainer from the outside would be aghast to see the mistakes made by know-it-all prisoners in the pit area. The main source of exercise knowledge comes from others or from reading workout magazines while skipping unfamiliar words. It's one of those things where a little bit of knowledge is dangerous. New and veteran prisoners may have all the determination needed to begin and stay with a program, but muscles become torn and ligaments damaged through improper training. Prisoners have more time than ever, so this means more time for overstraining and overtraining.

There are no longer any certified trainers to assist prisoners, although just about everyone will come across as an expert. Even if they're built like the Incredible Hulk, they don't always know what they're talking about. There are many genetically gifted well-proportioned meatheads. They can lift more than most people and claim their methods are wise. Genetics plays a major role in body shape; active knowledge plays a major role in avoiding injury. Injuries may not only end your workouts, the damage can last for years. Don't go overboard or exercise too strenuously for the first few months. Wait until you know what you're doing. Some prisoners will have lots of experience and good advice about working out. They may have been training diligently for years, having learned through trial and error. These are the ones you need to learn from. Workout partners, or those who offer proper advice, will push each other safely to work harder and continue to learn.

Any exercise or activity helps you keep a healthy body. It also relieves stress and boredom along with preparing you for release. Any self-improvement you undertake in prison lifts you from hitting rock bottom. You won't feel as bitter and lost after your release if you stay engaged mentally and physically. Discovering something new and positive will also decrease any desire of stringing up for Christmas.

Working out, getting an education, discovering a new hobby all helps pass many idle hours while trapped in prison. Time inside can be especially difficult for those who have no family or friends to stay in touch with. Mental and physical decay seems to accelerate for some prisoners. Sadly, most prisoners don't push themselves to become better at anything that will improve their situation or strengthen them for release. Many are weakened survivors, damaged from abuse of all kinds and living day-to-day with only the hope of getting high. It's no wonder that many downtrodden prisoners long for such easy escape to avoid the reality of lost autonomy. Loss of freedom and all the collateral damage of one's arrest make many a prisoner feel helplessly lost and forgotten. It's quicker and easier to enjoy the pleasure of endorphin release from drugs rather than from working out.

Religion

Finding God is another popular event for many down-and-out prisoners. Every institution has a visiting chaplain or possibly two. There may also be part-time volunteer or visiting clergy of other religions such as Buddhism, Islam, Judaism, Quakerism, etc. Some will be hired full time by the CSC, as they know supporting religion makes for a more manageable prison population.

Prison fellowships with any religious sect can help just about anyone make their time pass in a more positive light. They are often the only outside people many prisoners can speak with openly and not worry about information being recorded for CSC use. They can be a good source to seek counsel and comfort from without fear of appraisal. They are also becoming a stronger outlet and supporter for sharing circles and outside support networks that can help prisoners after their release.

Homosexuality

New friendships are easily formed in prison. I have never seen any acts of homosexuality, although they do exist. It's not like the prison scene in the movies where others rape the new fish in the shower upon arrival—at least not yet in Canada. Such acts are common in the much larger overpopulated U.S. prisons. Violence itself is very real between prisoners with beatings, stabbings, and pipings, but rapes are uncommon. There may be the occasional homosexual or two in the entire place. At the Don Jail in Toronto, there is an entire range for them. In the federal pens, it's not as if there are dozens of them roaming around, but there are noticeable homosexual and bisexual prisoners, as well as much innuendo. Most keep their actions out of sight, although some seem to advertise, wanting everyone to know they are out of the closet and available.

Some straight prisoners think it's unfair to be cut off from sex in prison while gays are not. Some prisoners who can't hold back their hunger for sexual gratification will openly or clandestinely associate with a gay prisoner. They may tell themselves or others that they are not gay or that they're just temporarily "institutionally gay"—a popular justification. One blatant fact is that some prisoners, particularly older and/or long-term ones, will groom a younger one with advice, goodies, protection, or threats to obtain sex. Some younger prisoners will profess they are only using the older prisoner but not engaging in any sex. Some will be telling the truth but some won't.

Visits and Phone Calls

Anyone (excluding lawyers) wishing to visit a federal prisoner is required to fill out a visiting application form in advance. This multi-page form now available online has simple standard questions but requires two passport-sized photos of the visitor. Anyone with a serious criminal past or any outstanding charges may not be approved to visit. In the provincial system, anyone can usually visit just by showing up and possibly being asked to show ID. The federal system once allowed this method for your first visit until your forms were processed and approved weeks later. Recently, this first easy visit is no longer allowed, and prisoners must wait weeks before getting a visitor approved and having visitors added to their approved visitor's list. CD #770 (2008) states that visits are normally scheduled at least twenty-four hours in advance, but many institutions now require all visits to be booked forty-eight hours in advance.

Making collect phone calls in the provincial system is easier than the federal screening process. Names and numbers of those you wish to call must be submitted weeks earlier for approval to the Inmate Telephone System (ITS) (formerly called the Millennium telephone system). You may regularly call people added to your "call allow list" by using an assigned PIN. You are allowed up to forty numbers. Toll numbers are only allowed on a pre-approved list of thirty-five agencies that any prisoner can call. The claim of this security measure is to stop a prisoner from contacting victims. It seems rather strange a prisoner would call the owner of the car they stole, the owner of the house they broke into, or the clerk they robbed. Though perhaps there are a few violent and/or disturbed offenders who may cause problems. Most victims of crime, however, are unknown to prisoners. It's the people who were once *friends* that helpless prisoners are likely to try contacting. Ex-girlfriends complaining to police were likely one reason to control and restrict phone use in prison. Harassment charges should have sufficed even if a prisoner used a three-way call to contact others not on a call list. Also, prison staff and the police prefer to record phone calls in case they need to review them later. With fewer people than ever writing letters, and with texting not being allowed in prison, phone restriction cuts many prisoners off entirely from reaching the outside.

In 2007, federal prisons began allowing prisoners to use Bell/CSC phone cards charging $0.11 a minute to a prisoner's account. While this is one-third the cost of making collect calls at the regular rate of $0.28 a minute, it's still very expensive for prisoners and a monopoly for Bell and the CSC. Few know that Bell charges the CSC almost nothing for staff using phones to make long-distance calls.

Specific times and days are set aside for phone access or the visits of family and friends, but they can vary slightly from one institution to another. A lockdown the night before can also disappoint anyone who drives for hours only to be turned down at the gates. It's always best for visitors to call before departing to make sure there are visits allowed. Visits take place in the V&C (visiting and correspondence) section of the institution. It's a contained area furnished with tables and chairs, and it may even have comfortable sofas. Visitors can usually walk with you outside in good weather, and attending children usually have a play area as well, both inside and outside the building. A bank of vending machines with food and beverages, hot and cold, is also available. Each visitor is allowed to bring in $30 to put into these machines. They can also usually bring in photos as well. A prison photographer may take pictures if requested.

Visits and phone calls remind prisoners that their actions and crimes have brought pain to those who stay in touch. It can be very traumatic to the children of prisoners. Children's behaviour may deteriorate with the changes brought to a family with the incarceration of a parent. Young children may start wetting the bed, become aggressive, withdraw into themselves, get low grades at school, and push or break the rules. They may think that being bad will allow them to be with their lost parent. Children of imprisoned parents are also five to six times more likely than their peers to later become incarcerated themselves.[liv] A parent must also realize the dangers of not telling the child where their other parent has gone. For example, boys who don't have a father tend to be more aggressive and are at higher risk of ultimately becoming incarcerated.[lv] Agencies such as the Canadian Families and Corrections Network, the Salvation Army, the John Howard Society, and others offer advice and possibly rides to different institutions.

Socials

Another advantage of the federal system over the provincial system is socials. There are semi-annual socials for the entire institution and annual closed socials for groups, i.e., BIFA, French, seniors, the John Howard Society, etc. Each group usually has volunteers from outside that attend. They are invited to socials or "food night" and "events" as they are sometimes called. Visitors already cleared for regular visits may be allowed to attend socials provided their names are submitted in advance. You're allowed to invite three, or possibly up to five, people to come and spend the afternoon in the larger prison yard or some other designated area where there will be a barbecue and possibly entertainment of some kind. There can be a greater atmosphere of freedom than that of just the regular visiting room. There are also more prisoners moving around as well. Even the paperboy can come to a social if he gets official paper approval first.

Trailers/Private Family Visits (PFVs)

The extent of tactile exploration with a significant other from the outside is limited to secretive petting during visits. However, this must be done discreetly, as there are usually children around as well as other visitors who may be offended by overt demonstrations of consensual fondling. Provincial DCs across Canada mostly offer closed and short visits, but CCs and pens can have open visits that last for hours. Many pens also have private family visits (PFVs), often referred to as "trailers," in a small two- or three-bedroom cottage-like building. Prisoners can apply for one as soon as they arrive. It can take months to be approved and finally get one, and then you can book one for every ten or twelve weeks thereafter. There can be a waiting period depending on where you are. Approval for family trailers can be delayed if a PO requests a prisoner first complete a program for such things as anger management or family violence.

You can marry your significant other or make that common-law relationship official and then spend your honeymoon in a trailer. I think this is fine if two people are truly in love and can't wait or if a prisoner is doing a lengthy sentence. It can help secure the relationship of two people. The idea of a marriage and honeymoon in prison seems rather bizarre, but, hey, if two people wish to wed, why not? Waiting years for your release may not be enough to secure a mate into waiting—marriage may. For those who are out of the closet, provincial laws now allow same-sex marriage.

However, you don't have to get married to obtain a trailer visit. Anyone who comes to visit regularly and claims to be your common-law spouse since before your arrest can apply for trailer visits. A requirement is that you have to prove you once lived together or have a lawyer send a letter. Since most lawyers would type up such a letter of confirmation for their clients, getting trailers is not too difficult. To counter such easy ways of obtaining trailer visits, institutions now push for more program enrollment and psychiatric evaluations first. Sadly, stalling trailer visits until a prisoner completes a program may contribute to ending a relationship. If you are serving a sentence greater than five years, you can also request quiet time alone in a trailer for three days, provided you don't have any recent suicide attempts or seem unstable. If so, you must then be evaluated briefly by a doctor.

Immediate family members can also apply and spend time in the trailer. Parenting from prison can be difficult and frustrating, but having a three-day visit with your children can be the most cherished moments inside. When you are with your children, talk to them about their lives. Reassure them that you love and miss them. Don't lean on them for comfort or support or dig for information about your spouse. Such adult things can confuse children and make them anxious. Describe your environment and how you spend your days without telling them of any bad experiences or worries. Be consistent in your contact with them by phone and letter if visits are not common or possible. If you are a new parent, it may even be a good idea to take a parenting class either at the institution or through correspondence.

The trailers are fenced in and located at an area not readily visible to the rest of the prison population. The only requirement other than possibly having to speak to a doctor or do a program first is paying for the groceries needed to stock the trailer. You can also order videos. There should also be a few toys for any kids to play with.

Some prisoners prefer not to ask those they know to come for a trailer or even come to visit. Too often "friends" say they will visit or come to a social event, and they don't show up. It's very painful to wait and wait for a visitor who stands you up. It may be difficult to decide to send out a visiting form if you think someone may never show. With nobody on your list, you know for sure you can't have any visitors. If you send out a form, you may keep waiting and waiting for a visit that never happens. Then you will regret ever sending out the form. If a friend didn't abandon you in the provincial system, they may after you reach the federal one. This can make a prisoner feel quite depressed getting their hopes up only to crash lower than before. Maintaining contacts with the outside will help make the eventual release less painful. Having no outside support means you're more likely to be turned down for parole as well as possibly being gated. (For more on gating, please see Chapter 11.)

How prisoners spend their time with or without outside contact is up to them. Many refuse to try keeping in touch, thereby avoiding the roller coaster of emotions. Cutting off the outside world is a form of pain control for many. Prisoners can forget the outside world and vegetate by spending all their time watching TV, eating, and sleeping. The proliferation of obese prisoners shows this is the chosen life of many, although I don't know how they can consume so many of the crappy meals. Conversely, prisoners can get off their butts and get learning jobs or go to school for upgrading. They can join groups and develop hobbies. They may end up selling the products of their labour and even continue doing so after their release.

Maintaining contact with the outside can keep one's spirit alive, but many prisoners eventually lose contact with those they know. Many are leery of attending institutional programs and offering intimate details of their crime, past, and psyche in fear that they will be used against them later. Attending programs to listen and learn without being judged and recorded would be more attractive as it once was when early release was common. CSC programs can appear to help prisoners with rehabilitation as part of correctional plans, but for most prisoners, having contact with the outside world can make the greatest difference to their sanity. The challenging use of spare time to prevent boredom, to educate and improve oneself, and to maintain ties outside is what helps prepare prisoners in facing their return to the community.

Chapter 11

Catch and Releash

Parole

I often wonder if the existence of parole does more harm than good. Although this may sound a little odd, difficulties arise in measuring unseen damage its existence causes. I'm not speaking about the infinitesimal number of prisoners released early only to commit mayhem in society. In viewing those granted parole, it is easy to statistically compile successes and failures by number, but there are flaws in such a system with a political agenda.

First, the parole board is always under pressure from society not to release anyone deemed a risk to society. Any act of violence done by one parolee now means that even *potentially* violent prisoners are a risk. The board is not always accurate in evaluating each prisoner when determining the chances of their reoffending if granted parole. The problem is that they only focus on and choose the "safest" prisoners for release. No longer will they take any chance in releasing anyone who they believe is a "risk." This covers the parole board's ass. Now, the only prisoners with any chance for parole are first-timers, non-violent prisoners, or servile prisoners who completed parole on a prior sentence. These docile manageable prisoners may never have come back anyway even if parole didn't exist. Parole granted to these lowest risk prisoners makes the board seem as though it's contributing to prisoner rehabilitation, public safety, and even saving tax dollars. The operative word is *seem*. The truth is that little can be gained in life unless a risk is taken, and the bigger the risk, the greater the gains. Short-term savings or claims of protecting the public can easily cost tenfold in the future.

A second flaw in the existence of parole, and one you will never hear about, is the damage done in denying a prisoner parole. In the psychosomatics of penology, the parole board hides their disorder of being short on statistics while pretending to be long on theory. It's simple to view the right and wrong decisions when a parole is granted by viewing the successful completion or the revocation of paroles. But what of the damage done to those denied? It can be assumed they were bad risks to be turned down or released with heavy restrictions. There is no way to know for sure if they would have successfully completed parole, or failed, because no risk is taken. Although this second reason concerning risks sounds similar to the first, the difference is in the damage to the prisoner. Any chance of successful reintegration into society is not only denied at a hearing, but those with the lowest self-esteem take a heavy blow. This may help the parole board in their mandate for the protection of society, but what is the effect on the future danger to the public? Longer prison terms drain public coffers and increase recidivism rates. A rejected prisoner eventually cut loose at two-thirds on mandatory parole or no supervision at all on their warrant expiry date (WED) is likely to feel more alienated and angry and may return to crime.

The hope that a prisoner fosters in being granted parole is a motivating factor to behave, take programs, and plan for release. People without hope lack optimism and incentive, prerequisites for survival as a human being. When a judge sentences you, they often direct degrading comments at you. Then your hopes may climb after you serve a portion of your sentence and face parole. But you are belittled and admonished again when the board says you're not good enough for society. As stated in previous chapters, all that you lost as a result of coming to prison is of little significance to your PO or the parole board. Losing everything—family, friends, job, home—translates into no outside support, which means you are a higher risk if granted parole.

Good time (early release during the final third of a sentence earned for good behaviour) no longer exists for federal prisoners because at two-thirds, parole is mandatory. Prisoners who refuse to bare their innermost thoughts and feeling to their captors will not be supported for early parole and will be given tighter restrictions on mandatory parole. Excess conditions meant to make you extra cautious overstress some paranoid parolees causing them to flee. You can refuse parole and even serve your entire sentence but then risk the chance of being gated. Gating results in being on court-imposed restrictions for a one-year term after you are released, and that year is renewable.

Decisions made by both case management officers (CMOs)/parole officers (POs) and the Parole Board Canada (PBC) are based primarily on a prisoner's "estimated risk" of reoffending or "low integration potential." In addition, criteria for release under Section 132 of the Corrections and Conditional Release Act (CCRA) states that offenders may be detained until their WED if they committed a violent offence or may commit a violent offence. Fear drives many prisoners into taking programs that may not help them gain parole. This can generate a report that detains you until your WED or that may be used the next time you face a judge. Risk is also judged (and punishment executed) from viewing any prior criminal allegations.

The CSC *Case Management Bulletin* of July 2004 entitled *Info to Be Considered in Completing Risk Assessment* angers many prisoners. It states, "...the withdrawal of a number of charges as part of a plea bargain leaves open the probability that the offender actually committed the underlying conduct alleged in the charges."[lvi]

Therefore, if any of your charges were bogus, you will be treated later as guilty if they were withdrawn as a part of a plea bargain.

The two fundamental approaches to prediction are statistical and clinical. Professor Jeffrey S. Rosenthal says the following in his recent book *Struck by Lightning*:

> Of course, probabilities can never prove that inappropriate activity was committed. When we arrive at a conclusion of criminality based on probabilities, the question we must ask ourselves is, what is the probability that we are mistaken? The justice system is sometimes too quick to minimize the possibility of mistakes because it uses faulty reasoning to estimate probabilities.

Canadian scholars such as Simon Fraser University's forensic psychologist Stephen Hart recently released a study published in the *British Journal of Psychiatry* confirming that risk assessment models long favoured by social agencies to predict the likelihood that a convicted criminal will reoffend are "fraught with problems and give a false sense of security."[lvii] A higher risk assessment translates into punishment resulting in placement to a higher security, being compelled to do programs, being delayed from programs, having fewer chances for early parole, and having a more restricted release or, worse, further detainment.

Prisoners may take programs suggested by their CMO/PO because they know they likely won't get parole if they don't. They also don't want to risk being detained past their mandatory release, forced into a community resource centre (CRC), or gated. Many will be asked to delay their parole hearing, sometimes more than once, because they have not yet entered and completed a program or because the paperwork and reports are not yet ready. This will be out of a prisoner's control, yet they will be asked to pay for this by waiving their hearing. The parole board prefers to have all paperwork and reports months in advance.

Before any hearing, prisoners are allowed full viewing of all documentation the board has, but full viewing rarely happens unless you can afford to hire a lawyer. According to Don M. Gottfredson, Leslie T. Wilkins, and Peter B. Hoffman in *Guidelines for Parole and Sentencing*, "The information possessed by the criminal justice system, whether contained in police, judicial, or correctional files, is frequently incomplete, inaccurate, and ambiguous." Unfortunately, any institutional, court, Crown, or police reports with erroneous information won't be up for debate. Their words will be seen as accurate, and your objections to anything contained within them, without proof in hand, will only make you look manipulative and like you're avoiding full responsibility for your incarceration. They are the patriarchs of righteousness, and you will be expected to admit full responsibility for your crimes and past negative lifestyle or behaviour. After belittling yourself, the board will likely tell you more reasons why you're not good enough to return to society and turn you down for parole. Then, as many others will agree, this will make you angry and you will regret even trying for parole.

Unlike the courts, which must follow guidelines set out by the Charter of Rights and Freedoms, the Parole Board of Canada (PBC)[lviii] has its own refined set of rules. One tenet of the Charter as used in Canadian courts is that one must be presumed innocent until proven guilty beyond a reasonable doubt. This right no longer applies after you are sentenced. The Supreme Court of Canada (in Mooring v. Canada (1996) 1 S.C.R. 75) has ruled that the "traditional" rules of proof and evidence that govern criminal trials do not apply to PBC functions (and, by extension, to administrative decision-making within the CSC). The CSC and the PBC consider all "relevant" information about the conduct of an offender. Unfortunately, their interpretation of the words *relevant* and *conduct* means anything negative ever written or said about you, even if unproven.

If you have several charges and are later found guilty of only one that puts you behind bars, a PO, the CSC, or any parole board will evaluate current and all prior accusations and suspicions. You will be judged as if you were guilty of any and all prior allegations. It won't matter if prior charges were stayed, dismissed, or withdrawn. You will be expected to own up to any prior charges regardless of any court results. You will be expected to take full responsibility for any accusations or charges ever laid, as well as concede to any and all written information from the police, witnesses, a doctor's report, or even statements from jailhouse informants.

The board will consist of two members (three for lifers) plus your PO. Member may be ex-cops, ex-Crowns, or retired judges. Does this mean you should feel more at ease? Most prisoners think the board makes up their minds even before you enter a hearing. This may be true. A member of the parole board will have preplanned questions to put you on the spot as well as elicit a reaction from you. You can't argue with them about facts you know are faulty. As soon as you start to deny, get frustrated, become angry, pass blame for wrong information, or minimize your criminal actions, you will be shooting yourself in the foot. Your PO and the board will expect you to admit guilt, show remorse, and tell them how you have changed for the better. In the U.S., if you don't admit guilt, parole is automatically denied. In Canada, if you are under appeal, you can't even try for parole. In fact, if your lawyer suggests not talking about your charges to anyone in the CSC until your appeal is heard, you can't do any programs, which may also be viewed as an admission of guilt. The board will ask you outright about your charges and why you think you should be granted parole.

I cannot speak for every prisoner in saying that a parole hearing lights a small spark of hope within you. You try to do it with a positive attitude and can genuinely feel and express a desire to live a better and crime-free life. Your conscience and reasoning tell you that you will try to succeed if the board gives you parole. However, with the pressure of being so helpless in prison, and knowing the board has the power to set you free, can you really be so honest? Like interviewing for a job, you must sell yourself to the parole board. Unlike trying to land a job, however, if you can't sell yourself to your PO and then the board, you stay in prison.

If you are in a treatment-type provincial correctional centre (CC), you may get a caseworker to help plan and prepare you for a hearing. In a non-treatment CC, you likely won't have a caseworker to help but will receive a visit from a PO four to six weeks before your hearing. They will ask where you plan to live, work, etc. The PO will interview anyone you may plan to live with by phone or in person. A community assessment (CA) is then compiled within thirty days. For federal prisoners, a CA is prepared six months in advance. If a CA was previously completed for sentencing purposes, it will be reviewed and likely rewritten word for word.

You may feel pressured into doing programs because your PO implies they won't support you if you don't. Without their support, it's almost impossible to obtain parole. So if they screw up and don't get you into a program on time...too bad. If they don't have reports completed on time or claim to have a heavy workload and say you must postpone your hearing…too bad. If you are bumped on a program waiting list so that non-violent or first-time prisoners can take the available seats ahead of you…too bad. Just as a lawyer may give you positive encouragement about your future, a PO will mislead you into cooperating if only to make their job easier.

By law, you are entitled to a hearing when one-third of your sentence is completed, unless you are serving life or are deemed a dangerous offender (DOed). A judge can now order half of any sentence to be served before trying for parole. But without a competent or helpful PO, it's pointless to even have a hearing. Program completion can help you emotionally and help your chances for parole, but you may later regret submitting to programs if parole is denied.

It's one thing to feel upset the day the judge sentences you, but you can feel it again when you are turned down for parole. Judges spend years working hard in their professional career to become judges to judge and sentence you. Then a glorified guard or PO has the power to make you serve a third of your time or more with the stroke of a pen. Their judgements, efforts, or whims are major factors in dictating your chances at parole. They are a second judgement to punishment and can make you serve more time than the judge expected.

Day and Full Parole

Not every province has a provincial parole board. Statistics Canada states that in 2010 there were 10,916 provincially sentenced prisoners across Canada with only 658 on parole, compared to 3,753 in Ontario alone in 1993.[lix]

In the federal system, fast-tracking (also called accelerated parole) was used sparingly for some first-time prisoners. It was abolished in 2011, although POs still prioritize efforts towards a few first-time non-violent prisoners. This priority, or special treatment, means a better shot for parole or transfer to lower security. If your PO thinks you don't have much chance, they won't expend effort to help. Informing a prisoner about getting support for early parole is good news for the few, but many others get less, if any, attention and must wait longer for transfers or release.

The federal system has day parole allowing prisoners to be paroled to a halfway house as early as one-sixth of a sentence. It's not total freedom because you must reside in a halfway residence, but it's the closest and fastest way to freedom. Day parole is rare for most federal prisoners, although the public thinks otherwise. I have never known anyone who tried for day parole. Such prisoners are usually sent straight to low-security camps before applying for day parole.

The Parole Board of Canada (PBC) posts grant rates on their website that may mislead the public. For 2009-2010, it lists the number of conditional releases at 8,709. Below this it states that the parole grant rate for day parole is 66 percent and full parole is 41 percent, making it seem as if more prisoners get day parole than full.[lx] In 2007-2008, the rate was 73 percent, giving the appearance to the public that thousands get out early.[lxi] What it doesn't show is that very few prisoners even apply for day parole. In 2007-2008, there were 13,582 federal prisoners with only 1,240 on day parole—this is five fewer than the previous year.[lxii] Even this number can mislead, as it contains parolees from previous years as well. Prisoners are also often granted day parole long after eligibility dates. Of the approximately four thousand on full parole, many postpone early hearings and get paroled to a halfway house only months before statutory release. The number of prisoners getting parole on their actual eligibility dates is far less, but such transparent data is not made public on the PBC website.

Longer prison terms do not reduce crime or make society safer. A meta-analytic review of research literature found more prison time was associated with an increase in reoffending.[lxiii] Further research has shown that appropriate programs delivered in the community, especially for high-risk prisoners, reduce reoffending.[lxiv] Analyzing fifty studies about the effects of prison on reoffending, researchers found that harsher and longer prison time produced slight increases in reoffending. Community-based programming also tends to produce greater results than programming delivered in custody, yet parole granting has been plummeting for two decades.[lxv]

I first headed to the pen with a four-year sentence. One of the prisoners with me had just received seven and a half years. When I went up for early parole, I was turned down. A month later, he was sent to a camp. Months later, he was in a halfway house. He had almost double my sentence yet made it to freedom long before I did. We were both non-schedule offenders, but I had a previous provincial record. Just weeks before my release, he came back on a violation. I was not surprised.

My first pen sentence was given with remarks from the judge saying I was unlike other criminals in that I was intelligent and therefore more dangerous. I later wondered about his words and reasoning for giving me such a high sentence. If he felt I was smarter, would I have a better chance in obtaining early parole? If he thought I should spend at least two years in prison, then he had to double the sentence to make sure I was not out too soon. I was denied parole.

The only small happy thought after being turned down for parole is that you won't have to kiss up to your PO any longer while inside. You will then be able to focus on the set date of mandatory/statutory release, provided you are not detained until your warrant expiry date (WED). The freedom that federal prisoners once obtained on mandatory release is no longer a happy one for many. Since the nineties, parole has clamped down on many people being released. Freedom on a provincial release at two-thirds won't have stipulations, provided there's no court order of probation to follow. Although more prisoners now prefer doing a federal sentence of two years versus a provincial one of two years less one day, most are learning that they would prefer a provincial release with no parole.

Passes/Temporary Absences (TAs)

Passes, or temporary absences (TAs), for work or a family emergency have almost disappeared in the provincial and federal systems. It's possible to obtain one if classed as low security, but you will likely still be escorted by guards, have to wear handcuffs or leg irons, and, if provincial, possibly a pumpkin suit. Who wants their family and friends to see them like this? You may also be required to pay for the guard(s) salaries if you are not eligible to be taken by an outside prison volunteer.

In 1998-1999, there were 4,429 TAs activated in Ontario, compared to 20,583 in 1994-1995. The decrease in TAs for academic and employment purposes—from 3,119 in 1994-1995 to 335 in 1998-1999—was particularly disturbing since these activities are important factors that contribute to reducing recidivism.[lxvi] Ironically, the Provincial Auditor observed that those serving a provincial sentence of six months or more were increasingly waiving their right to a parole hearing. Many prisoners stated they felt they had little chance of having a fair and unbiased parole hearing.[lxvii] Many likely didn't want such limited freedom upon release. This attitude has grown among federal prisoners as well.

The Solicitor General of Canada 1998 statistics show that 30 percent of prisoners (49 percent First Nations) waive their full parole hearings.[lxviii] There are three reasons for this, but you won't see them on any reports. First, prisoners may feel they have no chance at parole. Second, they may not want it. Third, no matter how much they ask their POs to be put into a program, they are deferred, delayed, and denied. Denying a pass to a halfway house, stalling entrance to a program, or simply not finishing a report on time is less paperwork for any PO, but this forces prisoners to waive parole hearings. The more times a prisoner waives away parole while waiting to finish a program, the less encouraged they feel. Like the rolling hope of Sisyphus, it's an emotional path one tires of travelling.

CSC statistics claim that the number of successful temporary escorted passes for 2003-2004 was 7,865 men and 677 women.[lxix] These figures seem to indicate that many prisoners were granted passes. What the numbers don't indicate is that most escorted absences were granted not for work or compassionate reasons but medical reasons. This disparity can be seen in viewing the number of unescorted temporary absences: 750 men and 78 women for the same period. Passes were once managed as a *strength-based* approach to rehabilitation. Unescorted passes for a day visit to a funeral or federal halfway house before parole are now *risk-based* and rarely used. It's only a few first-time non-violent prisoners who apply for such passes. Low-security prisoners might be granted a hospital trip to visit a family member, but your PO/caseworker must fully support it.

Transfers

Transfers can happen involuntarily after a fight or any security claim. They can happen in a matter of hours after an official decision, although transfers from a provincial CC/DC to another province don't occur unless there's an outstanding charge to warrant the transfer. In the pens, well-behaved prisoners may be transferred to lower security after serving a portion of their sentence or to higher security for misbehaving. Transfers mean double-bunking again and placement on a waiting list for programs or jobs. It may also mean having to waive or postpone a parole hearing.

Prison computer databanks compile lists of non-compatible prisoners. Prisoners who have had fights or altercations or who testified against others are listed as incompatible. Federal transfers can take hours or months or unwillingly with a PO's input. An interprovincial transfer takes at least six months, and you need a good reason to be approved. Being from another province or having family in another province is usually a good reason. Your life being in danger is another one. Some transfers occur just before a prisoner's release when there is an outstanding warrant that extends to other provinces. A checklist called the Security Reclassification Scale (SRS) is a 30-point scale used to rate prisoners for transfer, placement, and release. Below 27 eventually can get you to medium security, but an SRS of 15.5 is needed to make it to a camp. Most never make it below 20, and the rate easily rises with institutional infractions.

Halfway Houses

The 1995 closure of all Ontario provincial halfway houses for the implementation of the electronic bracelet program that never arrived has kept many prison beds filled. The bracelet program was discovered to cost far more than estimated and had less rehabilitation value than suggested. Without a place to live, there is no point in applying for parole. The John Howard Society or the Salvation Army may be the only places able to help you if you have no family or friends to help. In facing the parole board, it's helpful to have a letter from an employer offering a job. This goes for both provincial and federal systems. Any job offer is better than none. Once you get parole, you can be laid off the first day out. This is not grounds for revoking parole as it is in some U.S. states. You simply tell your new PO that you will look for another job right away.

If you are in a halfway house, keeping a job is important. You won't want to get off on the wrong foot with the staff or PO. Many will file a report to quickly send you back to prison. You will have a curfew, have many restrictions, and need a day pass to venture outside. You may break one house rule and be revoked, or you may get away with several screwups before they throw you back in. If you abide by the house rules or parole conditions, these conditions will be lessened in a few months or years. It all depends on what they think of you, the amount of time you are doing, and where you are. Some regions are more restrictive with rules and supervision.

Community Correction Centres (CCCs)/Community Residential Facilities (CRFs)

High-risk and/or repeat offenders with little chance of early parole may later be involuntarily paroled into a community correctional centre (CCC) before, on, or after their mandatory release date. The newest screw applied to some prisoners expecting to be released on mandatory parole is being told they are having a residency hearing. It's more a notification that they must live at a halfway house or CCC upon mandatory release. CCCs, also called community residential facilities (CRFs), are high-security halfway houses found in larger cities. They are often welfare-like settings with barred windows and locked doors to keep parolees locked up at night.

They will have many rules to follow. Breaking or even suspicion of breaking conditions or any laws will quickly send you back to prison. Although the Parole Board of Canada policy manual states, "Imposing a residency condition is regarded as an exceptional provision," more and more prisoners, especially those with a long-term supervision order (LTSO), are being forced to reside at a CCC upon release. Prisoners waiting years to finally be free from the system's oppressive grasp can become quite angry when told unexpectedly, weeks or even days before release, that they must reside in a CCC. A forty-five-day notice is supposed to be given to prisoners so they can contact a lawyer, but this notice is often ignored. The policy also states under the heading Duration of a Condition to Reside that "there can be negative implications for reintegration if the offended believes that a condition will necessarily remain in effect until warrant expiry."

Detainment and Gating

Between 2002 and 2004, 279 prisoners were detained by the Parole Board of Canada (PBC) and forced to stay in prison until their warrant expiry date (WED) because they were deemed a high risk to reoffend. Surely, such an action didn't make them any less bitter toward the system or feel a part of the community upon release. They were held under a federal law that allows the parole board to deny a prisoner release if it suspects they may commit a violent crime or serious drug offence. According to *Juristat*'s data on risk and needs profiles, nearly half of provincial prisoners (49 percent) are deemed as high risk to reoffend. In the Yukon and PEI, that classification rises to 78 percent and 68 percent, respectively.[lxx] The risk rates rise for federal prisoners, but risk is also something used when picking lottery numbers. Simply shoving someone can result in a conviction of a level-one assault offence, which is still a violent offence. Imagine a future when judges send people to prison for suspecting they may commit a crime. That guessing and playing the probability game already can and do double a person's sentence from a judge as well as keep people in prison much longer by denying them parole.

I first heard the word *gated* back in the late eighties before it became something different today. Back then, the police and Crowns had a nasty way of extending a prisoner's sentence on their release date. For example, the police want to charge you with four burglaries but only charge and convict you of three, so off you go to serve your entire sentence. The fourth charge would purposely be held back until your release, and the police would be at the "gate" to arrest you. The first sentence could result from a plea bargain or a trial outcome and be served concurrently. Two years for each burglary to be served concurrently means you only serve two years, or the judge may give you two years for three or four burglary charges.

Holding back any charges to gate you with later meant whatever time you receive from them can't be served concurrently since you were technically released into the custody of the police the moment you walked out the gate. You will then get a completely new sentence to begin all over, maybe even another two years. Many saw this as cruel and abusive, especially prisoners who thought they were getting a new start on life. Such practices are now well hidden by the police, who easily claim that they never got around to fully completing their investigation, they didn't know the suspect was in custody, or paperwork delayed filing the charges earlier.

The word *gating* currently has a mixed definition from prisoners and others who confuse it with *detaining* or an 810 order of the Criminal Code of Canada. Detaining happens when the parole board thinks you will reoffend. They keep you jailed until your WED. An 810 is a one-year peace bond (renewable each year) forcing court conditions upon anyone released at their WED.

Prime Minister Brian Mulroney recalled Parliament during the summer of 1986 and brought gating, also referred to as detention or 810, into the limelight. The move followed a series of murders and violent crimes committed by offenders who were automatically released on mandatory parole. Although the parole board played no part in the release of the prisoners who committed the horrendous crimes in the eighties, it was frequently and wrongly criticized for what had happened. Now many prisoners pay for what only a few did. Just the fear of possibly being gated can pile unnecessary stress on a prisoner, just as the press and Parliament did to scare the public into the need for the new law. Gating laws, a cosmetic form of legislation, were passed to show the public something was being done, but holding prisoners for as long as possible is a short-term solution and not necessarily the wisest choice.

Release

When granted parole to a halfway house or community resource centre (CRC), you may be released that day or wait weeks for an empty bed. If you have a home to go to upon release, you will be released the same day. The first order of release will be to report directly to the parole office, where a PO will tell you all your restrictions. You will then have to go to the police station to sign in. Neither of these two priorities will leave you feeling free. Your so-called freedom will be even more limited if the PO considers you an intensive supervision practice (ISP) case.

Larger cities have a program called team or tandem supervision (TS). It's a very strict type of parole requiring two weekly face-to-face visits with two parole officers. It can be forced on anyone with mandatory parole. It's alleged to be used for unmanageable or potentially violent prisoners and those deemed a higher risk of reoffending. If you are put on TS for suspicion of being a risk or for whatever reason, you may despise it. If you feel bitter or angry about parole, you will feel it even more on TS. With so many restrictions to follow, it's easy to breach parole and return to prison. Statistics claim that the majority of parolees get revoked within the first three months of release. The parole board can cite such failures to support their risk assessments.

Whether you are put on TS or have many stipulations after release, you may live in constant fear of being revoked. This fear can haunt you even while staying out of trouble. A parolee may even flee simply out of fear of being revoked, making their situations much worse and increasing the danger to society. With 72 percent of prison staff being punishment-oriented, getting fair treatment from POs outside will be unlikely if they are oriented towards punishment rather than rehabilitation.[lxxi] High-intensity supervision may force most parolees to behave better, but it can also push some to the edge, causing them to snap and commit terrible crimes.

Anyone can be revoked, especially for suspicion of drugs use, having a beer, failing a urinalysis, being ten minutes late, or by anyone claiming you were at a crime scene or even a bar. Then, in serving the remainder of your time, you may wish you really had committed a crime. Later, upon your release, there may not be much, if any, parole time left to monitor you. There will be no parole for the public to blame either if you strike back at society in anger. This is now being resolved by detaining then gating more and more prisoners on their WED.

One call from a nosy neighbour, paranoid relative, or jealous friend, or being questioned by the police for anything, and you may be back in custody. Even the fear that you may commit a crime is enough to send you back. Neighbours, the police, or anyone can be paranoid or suspicious, and anything they say will be believed over the words of a parolee. The PO or the police are the ones who will exercise exclusive ownership of the truth. A PO won't risk staining their record by taking a risk, and neither will the police. A PO may give out a few easy breaks before revoking you, but the police may be quick to arrest you for anything. A PO may try to get you back out within thirty days, but don't hold your breath. If you committed any serious breach of conditions or get any criminal charges, you'll likely be transferred back to the pen to appear before the parole board again. If you sit in jail for a year and are found not guilty or have the charges tossed, you will be released again on parole. Of course, you don't get a year of your life back. You only get a little angrier at the system.

Very few prisoners are now granted early release, which does not seem to make economic sense since most revoked paroles result from a violation of a parole condition rather than the commission of a new offence. Very few (2 percent of provincial paroles and 7 percent of federal paroles) were revoked for a new offence.[lxxii] The statistics for federal parole are more complex, since there are more types, although fewer prisoners than ever are being granted an early release. Prisoners today consider mandatory parole a limited release they look less forward to after prison.

When prisoners are released, there are different agencies that provide support. Many offer counselling, emotional and spiritual support, clothing, food, work references, or even temporary housing. The best part is they don't all judge you, write bad reports, or pull your parole like your PO can. However, you should be careful of any agency linked to government funding. For example, halfway houses may have CSC beds, and outside programs may write reports about you and answer to the CSC. More organizations and services are becoming linked to the justice and punishment machine.

A few agencies and groups across Canada are the John Howard Society; the Elizabeth Fry Societies for women; the Salvation Army; St. Leonard's Society of Canada; Quakers Fostering Justice; Mentorship, Aftercare, Presence (MAP); and Circles of Support and Accountability (CoSA) for sex offenders. There are also Canadian Families and Corrections Network (CFCN), Bridge House, Project Reconciliation, Just Us (a support group in the Toronto area), the Society of St. Vincent de Paul, Alcoholics Anonymous (AA), Narcotics Anonymous (NA), the chaplaincy or any religious affiliated organization, sports organizations, and volunteer groups. The list is long, but the range of assistance offered and the number of staff and volunteers involved vary from one organization to another.

Larger cities list services in the *Yellow Pages* under Social and Human Services Organizations or Volunteer Services. Although larger cities may appear scarier and more intimidating to some newly released prisoners, these areas will have more help available as well as more employment opportunities. In any case, the private, religious, and charity-funded organizations offer more for your rehabilitation than government agencies offer—and this is executed with less red tape and fewer reasons to be paranoid.

Chapter 12

Back to Life

After serving two-thirds of your sentence with a third off for good behaviour, you expect to be set *free*. In the provincial system, if you haven't lost any good time and have no probation to follow after serving two-thirds of your sentence, you will truly be set free. In the federal system, when you are let out on day, full, or mandatory parole after two-thirds, it will be a restricted/conditional release. After being caged in a hate factory and dreaming of the day you will be released, when that day arrives, you may not be so happy. You will be ordered to report to a parole office immediately upon your release. *Release* is not an accurate term and *conditional release* is oxymoronic. You will leave your caged, controlled, and oppressive environment only to be told a list of things you are not allowed to do and places where you cannot go. You may feel you're not a normal member of society. Parole stipulations will remind you of this every day. Just as when you were sentenced by the judge, then fail to obtain an early release, you can now feel a third blow to your self-esteem leaving the parole office with your list of new stipulations and restrictions. It can feel like your foot is still trapped in the prison gates.

Rules for mandatory parole will be easier to follow for those who are responsible and have a good support network, but that's not the situation for most. Many were broken up mentally and emotionally prior to their arrest and will be much worse after serving time. Many don't want or seek the proffered help inside. If prisoners refused help inside, how will curbing their freedom and forcing them into programs on the outside help? Many prisoners take the CSC behavioural programs inside simply to play for early parole. They may get something positive or negative for their efforts. Once on mandatory parole, they could be ordered to attend the counselling they were denied or had refused while inside. Forcing a prisoner to get help by threatening a loss of freedom strikes at the deepest core of bitterness.

During my first incarceration long ago, a counsellor told several of us that it was difficult to understand why some prisoners screw up near the end of their sentence rather than at the start. Losing good time for fighting, drugs, or escape didn't make much sense to him. It did to me. I remembered being almost rude to him for his ignorance when I answered. Here he was, twice my age, educated, and with a career in corrections. I, the novice on the other side of the fence, could easily decipher his dilemma. Sure, it's good to feel you will soon be released, but then the reality of all you lost hits you hard. You will be released with much less than what you had before your arrest, which includes missed opportunities and time that can never be replaced. The only things you may gain are parole conditions that make you feel more shame and even less worthy. Deep-rooted shame can make anyone feel forever lost to wander the halls in the palace of forgiveness.

No one can tell you how you will feel the day you are released. Each one of us are individuals, but for someone in corrections to write or express what it feels like to get out can be absurd, like a young male doctor telling a pregnant mother of five what it feels like to give birth. Can he really speak from experience? The 2005 edition of *Basic Facts About the Correctional Service of Canada*, published by the CSC, under the section Conditional Release, states, "Offenders who are incarcerated until their sentence has expired (known as warrant expiry) and then released into the community without any controls or supervision have an increased chance of committing another crime." Of course, that is true and expected, but who wouldn't be pissed off at the system and society for being forced to serve one's entire sentence? They fail to address that. When the judge sentences someone to, say, three years, the prisoner expects to be released after two-thirds. Not anymore. Even if you behave in prison, as well as partake in programs (or fail to enter them because your PO was slow with the paperwork), you can still end up serving an entire sentence. More and more prisoners are being forced to waive parole, go to a high-security halfway house at two-thirds, or even serve their entire sentence. That would make me angry at society after my release.

Prisoners can sit inside for months or years planning what to do upon release. Even those who plan to never return often do, and they don't even have to break any laws to do so. All they have to do is not let a PO rummage through their brain, and then break a few parole stipulations. The PO only has to *fear* that you will break the law. A common reason why many prisoners are returned is ironically termed *suspicion of being suspicious* or *deteriorating behaviour*. Rather than take risks, it's safer for POs to revoke parole than get blemishes on their work record.

The experience of decarceration after being released may make people want nothing from any PO or authoritarian figure. They may feel glad at first to finally be out of a prison cell, but as days turn into years, the stress of returning to society builds. Trying to find a job, a decent place to live, and a partner, or just walking down the street like a citizen again, can be restricted by a PO telling you what to do and the fear of being revoked at anytime.

The police can charge you with just about anything, even while knowing the judge won't find you guilty. They know laying charges is often enough to terminate parole. The term for justice workers bending rules or even breaking laws for the greater good (to convict or punish) is known as *noble cause corruption*. Justice workers committing wrongdoings easily dismiss any self-guilt by telling themselves the criminal deserves it anyway. You then stay in jail until your trial, and if you beat the charges or if the charges are tossed, you just spent time in jail for nothing. An inexperienced person in such a situation quickly learns why so many others have little or no respect for the law. Once memories like these build up, so will your animosity and distrust of the system.

After release, your body may still be fit and your mind may actively hold hope, but your soul can feel broken and damaged as reality sets in. Returning to a better life may seem forever out of reach with thoughts of a life that might have been endlessly haunting you. Even if you are physically fit, your mental health is more precious than flesh and bone. You may have recovered from a beating or stabbing, but you may never recover that peace of mind robbed by the terror of time behind bars. You may feel as if you are forced to pay again through the turmoil you will suffer. Lacking job skills or education and having a criminal record will mean few job prospects. Even after having served your court-ordered penalty, it may feel as if your debt to society will never be paid.

Extra Stress

If you are a first-timer or cooperative parolee, you may be given only standard release conditions: no drugs or drinking, a curfew, and a radius to limit movement. You may have to ask permission for simple things such as a travel permit. You may also be ordered to attend counselling, see *their* psychiatrist, and sign in at the cop shop weekly. If you don't have any family or friends to return to, these conditions will constantly remind you of where you just came from and that you're still not free. It may feel like a cloud of shame is following you. While feelings of guilt focus on behaviour (a bad act), feelings of shame focus on character (a bad person). Guilt is less painful. It allows one to feel empathy and make reparations.

But shame is painful and destructive, as it focuses on the self and makes one feel worthless and exposed. It can make a parolee want to hide, deny, and blame others for their failings. For many who dream about their day of release, being placed on parole will resemble a pseudo-freedom, purchased for the price of chains and slavery to the system.

Tragedies in life can bring people together or tear them apart. With caring, compassion, and sharing, there can be a light at the end of the tunnel. This is not always the case for the person released from prison all alone. Most of the people on the outside believe a prisoner released would be thrilled to finally be free, but many are not, and POs and the police continually remind them of why. Then there is the painful reality of learning how much you have lost while struggling to get back on your feet again. It will be difficult to deal with stress and emotionally related issues, as well as financial ones. When stressed, parolees longing to regain control are more likely to reoffend, and the last person they may want to turn to for help is a PO who has the power to send them back.

Being released from a provincial correctional centre (CC) without a probation order can be better for some prisoners but not for others who need and want help. A federal release at two-thirds can be easy for some but very restricting for others. I can vividly remember being released alone on mandatory parole my first time at age thirty-two. A month after my release, my PO said I was still not allowed out past my ten o'clock curfew. I said I still went to clubs and left early. I asked whether I could at least have the time limit extended an hour or two to stay out later on weekends or for taking a girl on a dinner date and a movie. She told me I had to notify her in advance and that I should also notify my date that I was on parole. I laughed at her preposterous suggestion. "Hi, my name is.... I'm on federal parole.... Wanna go on a date?" Little did she know that the only women to whom I could offer such quick honesty without garnering an instant rejection were the bad girls.

Feeling ashamed after your arrest and knowing you have caused pain to the ones you love may have made you sever contact long before your release. Dragging a girlfriend or loved one along while inside may make your time more difficult. You may have missed your freedom even more by staying in touch. However, if they are there for you in the end, it can really make a difference on how you will feel and will improve your chances for success. Even Grandma or the paperboy being there to meet you is better than no one there at all.

With no friends, job, or money, and little else, you will feel empty and restricted in searching for companionship, which is something you will have missed more than anything. Parole may allow the freedom of having a couple beers like everyone else, but smoking a joint could cost you years behind bars. A cop may spot you having a beer with your buddy, or you may get nabbed for breaking curfew while driving back from a movie with a date. Unauthorized medication or THC lingering in your body may cause you to fail a urinalysis.

Deciphering the heavy blow to your self-esteem while incarcerated is deleterious at best. It's only when your release date approaches and/or after your release that the trouble begins. The day you get out can be far worse than the day you went in. The damage upon your soul before your arrest compounded with all you've lost now comes crashing down for real when you return to the land of the living. The aftereffects of prison can have devastating results when trying to regain your dignity. Being on parole may constantly remind you that your existence is below that of the poorest commoner.

You may last a day, a week, or a couple of months. For some, the easiest escape will be to get wasted to numb of all the pain, only to get tossed back in prison later after failing a urinalysis. Being on parole can turn out to be worse than being on bail. If you get into any trouble, even minor, you may wish to flee and start over again somewhere else, but federal parole warrants extend across Canada. You'll feel powerless but want to feel in control. Many oppressed parolees have no family, friends, money, car, home, or possessions and will seek any method to bring quick financial and emotional results. The less one has, the more intimidating and helpless it may feel on parole. For the troubled ones, committing a crime is the easiest and fastest way to again feel control and exorcise some spite.

Publicity

To most people, publicity about a criminal in their midst takes precedent over the right to privacy. Communities have a "not in my backyard" (NIMBY) mentality when it comes to learning about a proposed halfway house or parolee destined for their community. Sex and violence sells. The police and the media know sex with deviance and fear sells even more. The police can now release information that a "potentially" violent offender or sex offender is living in a neighbourhood. Even though people without a criminal record commit approximately two-thirds of sex crimes, the police seem to want to destroy any parolee's chance at a fresh start or just drive them away. Informing and inflaming the public can do more harm than good. It's often done to sell news and protect the police from possible lawsuits. Notification tightens the leash on a newly released person, decreases their acceptance to a community, and adds extra stress that can contribute to reoffending or going underground.

If you are prone to violence or if there are cops who know and dislike you, they will be watching and riding you every chance they can. Targeting or harassing a known criminal for selective incapacitation is easier than catching an unknown one without a record. Police may drive by your residence daily, pull you over every time they spot you, or lean on others for information about your activities. If you are forced to be on a sex registry, even for a minor offence, you will be a suspect for the police and your neighbours to focus on. Whatever your record, it will be viewed for any similar crimes recently committed. If your neighbours know you have any criminal record, they may quickly suspect you as well.

It's possible to be charged with a minor sexual offence that does not even warrant any time in prison and still be placed on the registry. A number of non-sexual offences (breaking and entering, abduction, kidnapping, trespassing at night, manslaughter, criminal harassment, living off the avails of prostitution, and soon likely any act of violence) are also included if the Crown claims there was an intent to also commit a sexual crime. For those convicted and wishing to appeal their name being on the registry, an application to legal aid under the "grossly disproportionate" test will likely be refused. The police and Crown know that minor offenders will be denied legal aid assistance or removal from the registry for life and will therefore place as many people as they can in the database for future use. Even if you become an accepted member of your community, if a crime is committed near your residence or workplace, a cop or someone can destroy your reputation by unfairly labelling you a rapist or pedophile. Newspapers will jump to spread news that you are on a sex registry without admitting it's for a minor offence from years earlier.

It's easy for people to be prejudiced against a prisoner, parolee, or person with a criminal record. It's also easy to abuse power by using fear or statistics to manipulate the public view of criminals. In 1971, Stanford University psychologist Philip Zimbardo famously concluded that the capacity for evil is not only found in bad people. It's possible for anyone to do bad and hurtful thing to others depending on the situation. Yale psychologist Stanley Milgram, a childhood friend of Zimbardo's, commanded test subjects to administer shocks to unseen victims. Two-thirds willingly delivered what they thought were painful shocks when ordered to do so. Many people excuse abuses of the prison/justice system by simply saying, "If you break the law, you get what you deserve."

Another sad statistic from the 2005 *Basic Facts* is that it claims First Nations people represent about 16 percent of the federal prison population, yet only 3 percent of the population of Canada. According to the 1904 *Annual Report of the Commissioner of Penitentiaries*, the First Nations population of prisoners then was only 1.5 percent and the black population was only 3.5 percent. It's easy to deceive the public with fear of others when using race. Although there are not yet statistics to show rates of justice system abuses or violence by race, there are ones that show violence. According to *Juristat*'s 1996 data, only 22 percent of federal inmates (63 percent provincial) were currently incarcerated for non-violent offences.[lxxiii] Statistically, if a person receives a thirty-day sentence for even a minor crime against a person as well as a two-year term for a property offence, that prisoner is technically still serving federal time for a violent offence. If you have any violence on your record and are a minority, your chances of parole diminish. The news and music media often portray blacks as more violent than whites. This may seem believable, but what can easily be left out of the equation is that blacks are targeted more often than whites overall and have fewer education, work, and survival opportunities than whites, and such racist attitudes divert more of them toward a criminal lifestyle. Systemic racism throughout the U.S. in particular is the major reason why so many blacks are incarcerated.

Returning

If being in prison has made you bitter or more violent, your reintegration back to society will be that much more difficult. If you feel angry that the police, your lawyer, your ex-friends, or the system in any way screwed you, that pain will be with you upon release. It might not be a good idea to express this to your PO. If you are openly honest with them and say you are frustrated and feel like you are going to lose it, they may revoke you just to be safe. Safe to them means protecting their ass from blame. A PO's job means more to them than any prisoner's freedom. There can be no gains without taking risks, but fewer and fewer POs take such a gamble. They and the Parole Board of Canada (PBC) don't want the public in an uproar blaming them when someone they released screws up. Claiming they do it for the protection of society is a common answer to keeping more prisoners and ex-prisoners locked up. This protects society for the moment but only increases the chances of greater dangers to occur at a later date. This is a fact everyone ignores and no one wants to accept. It's a short-term saving on public security that can cost society much more in the long run.

If you move to a large city, you may be able to live in anonymity. With a larger population and many more police and criminals to monitor, the police may not pay close attention to your arrival. They will be notified, and the local ones who cruise your area will be informed. If you are returning to a large city where there are cops who don't like you, they may hassle you every chance they get. A larger city may have more employment opportunities and family support, but there will be more anxiety in larger cities, especially for anyone who has served a longer sentence. On the other hand, moving to a small town after serving a long sentence can be peacefully relaxing. The downside is fewer employment opportunities and the few local police will all know and watch you. If it's a really small community, your arrival may be the talk of the town.

Being on parole can feel as if you are paying twice for your crime and will either help you stay out or help you reoffend. You won't feel as if you were set free, just moved from one prison into another. Getting a low-paying job will feel similar to a work-release form of indentured slavery, just like the one in prison. Many prison systems have officially repudiated the idea that they're responsible for rehabilitation. Given the explosion in prison populations since the drug wars began in the eighties, the idea of rehab is no longer seriously considered feasible. Inside programs are a band-aid solution for emotional injuries, with the majority of tax dollars used for paying and training staff to gather data.

Society will have little, if any, sympathy for a prisoner recently released from prison. Many people will expect you to have learned your lesson and that you will work hard and be a reformed person. Whatever you may suffer upon release will be seen as your own doing. No matter how out of sync your life feels, no matter how hard the aftermath hits you, no matter how difficult the crush of unseen darkness assaults you, you'll want to forget it ever happened and catch up to all you have lost. But the sticky ghost of a prison past may never abandon you. Having been arrested, condemned, and hauled away in chains can create a trauma-associated dead spot. Suffering such anguish is compassionately understood when it comes to soldiers with combat fatigue or people with post-traumatic stress disorder (PTSD). Unfortunately, with attitudes regarding the war on crime, prisoners are denied such empathy, no matter how much loss, injustice, murder, and mayhem surround them.

The psychological effects of imprisonment are very disabling. Many prisoners, especially first-timers, don't know how psychologically deteriorating being in custody is, much less what they are in for upon release. Estrangement prevails in a caged atmosphere of cellar beasts where the light of grace cannot shine. For example, prisoners will lose their capacity for intimacy. They suffer bouts of moodiness, have an inability to settle, and feel a loss of sense of purpose and direction. Shortly after release from prison, many ex-prisoners will suffer withdrawal and be unable to relate properly to much of the world and people around them. Some will have panic attacks and symptoms of paranoia and will feel socially isolated. They may have chronic difficulties in sleeping and be very irritable to live with. Sadly, they may also feel a permanent loss of joy. Some will experience a profound loss of closeness that never returns even for the family and friends who may have waited. The difficulty in expressing your feelings or understanding them can result in immense guilt.

An ex-prisoner can possess intense chronic feelings of bitterness, as may some of their family members, and have strong unresolved feelings of loss. From the very first day, an ex-prisoner may feel embarrassed in difficulties coping with ordinary practical tasks. Shopping in a supermarket or even crossing the street can feel like a trip to the twilight zone. Depending on how long they were caged, they may not know how to operate a bank machine, a remote control, or even a cell phone. They may feel shame, which prevents them from asking for help. Contrary to the frugal life prisoners are forced to live, upon release they may have little sense of the value of money and may not be able to budget properly, quickly spending themselves recklessly into debt.

In prison, one learns to deal with emotional pressures and stresses by blocking them out, avoiding communication, and isolating oneself. These learned traits could continue after release. Some will even have moments when they wish they were back inside. There likely won't be anyone they can relate to, and telling their problems and fears to a PO may only help get their parole revoked. They will see their POs as a representation of the oppression they felt in prison. With the widespread trauma or devastation of prison life or the long-term distress of parole, most prisoners have difficulty using the experience to enrich their lives. Many upon release will get flashes of exhilaration but have less of an appetite to be hardworking law-abiding citizens. Most will be weakened by the experience of prison, and even if they never break the law again, they will not be fully functional or ever reach their full potential in life.

As government institutions continue to grow, new models with old philosophical roots will not create a just society nor restore justice. For many released prisoners, the habitual return to crime after each release is like the compulsive gambler trying to recoup his losses the only way he knows how. Their new freedom will be like a pocketful of change to be spent fast, and that "big score" will be the payoff for all the pain and lost time in prison.

Abolition

Quakers, who ironically established one of the very first jails in America, the Walnut Street Jail in Philadelphia, are now part of a movement to abolish all prisons. Others who join in this cause are known as penal abolitionists. They are increasingly aware of the weaknesses and unaccountability of the criminal justice system not only in Canada but also around the world. The criminal justice system does a great job of undermining Western civilization, while abolitionists work to repair and strengthen the fabric of humanity and the community. Offenders are products of the community, even if they are sent far away out of sight.

Abolitionists see the need to address the counterproductivity of penal culture, and their ideas cannot be dismissed out of hand. Many abolitionists identify the mass media as a barrier to social change and struggle to find more community-based educational forms to chronicle the pitfalls of criminal justice, or injustice as some would argue. Recent developments of how the justice system deals with people in its charge and their subsequent incarceration, treatment, and eventual release suggest that we must advance alternative education to the public. As a society, we must put valid and credible theories of democracy, humanity, and tolerance into practice. Even by the reorganizing the present system and its practices we would have fewer people in prisons. People would be released back to society truly rehabilitated and less angry at the authorities that imprisoned them in the first place.

The concept of abolition is centuries old, dating back to efforts to abolish such practices as slavery and child labour, both of which are also forms of imprisonment. In reality, the practice of abolition is deeply rooted in our nature, yet some dismiss the end of incarceration as naive and idealistic. Of course, there are legitimate challenges to the implementation of the abolition of prisons and punishment. How does a society shift away from the established criminal justice system?

Abolitionists argue that more formal healing approaches to social harms would work from the bottom up—from the community, through the community, and up to the government. First Nations communities, for example, have been using healing circles for years. The community must feel comfortable with the proposed changes and be reassured that specific individuals chosen for alternative forms of sentencing pose no harm to that community. Communities are not at present ready and willing to make massive changes to an established system right immediately and all at once, as they lack knowledge on the failures of the criminal justice system and are unaware of the advantages of an abolitionist model. Community education is integral to the promotion of the penal abolitionist movement, a step towards humanitarian alternatives to rehabilitative criminal justice practices.

The development of a non-authoritarian non-punitive model conceptualizes communication and respect in the community, regardless of social status. We must develop and nurture dignity and the exercising of responsibility in all individuals who, in our current authoritarian punitive form of criminal justice, might possibly face incarceration. The gradual abolition of the current system would relieve the pressures that increase daily for those incarcerated. With the current cost-cutting regressive legislation, detention and remand centres are more unstable and overcrowded than ever, and they remain understaffed in many areas. These changing conditions often inhibit the delivery of programs and necessary services as well as discourage many volunteers who might be prisoners' best and only advocates in the outside community.

Stories featuring the police, crime, courts, punishment, sentences, jails, and justice appear regularly in the media. Subjects addressed by the media tend to be negative, as the focus is on tragedies, whether they're the result of human actions or uncontrollable natural forces. Rarely does the media present positive feel-good stories. Instead, we hear about random acts of violence, political scandals, theft, fraud, and various types of property damage. The general reaction both through the media and from the public is to demand punishment for the perpetrators. Rarely do they look further into the incidents and the total impact on all concerned. Alternatives to the sort of "justice" presently in effect rarely make headlines and generally receive little press. We have divided our society into "good" versus "bad," into "us" versus "them," and punishment, often in the form of incarceration, is the expected simplistic solution to many problems. If it's out sight, it's out of mind.

Jails house many problems, including mentally ill people who should not be in a place that's often bursting at the seams. Correctional investigator Howard Sapers in his 2005 annual report stated the number of inmates with "significant mental health needs" has doubled over the past decade but treatment services have declined. In all, about 12 percent of male and 21 percent of female federal inmates (more in provincial) are seriously mentally ill.[lxxiv] Penny Marrett, chief executive officer of the Canadian Mental Health Association, also said prisons "have become warehouses for the mentally ill due to funding cuts and closures in the community psychiatric facilities."[lxxv] In prison, people suffering from mental illness are easy targets, as they are vulnerable and exploited by both other prisoners and staff.

Punishment is a response to crime and not a solution. An aggressive approach to alternative forms of sentencing and punishment would automatically reduce prison populations across Canada. Instead of serving, say, a thirty-day jail term, more people could be fined, be subject to arbitration, or be required to serve 300 hours of community work. Being sentenced to help at a food bank, assist in a senior's home, or help clean up a park are constructive methods for rehabilitation. Not only does this save tax dollars instead of wasting them, it helps lawbreakers participate in their community instead of their being ostracized at a distant location.

Prisoners may be allowed to serve short sentences with a temporary absence provision allowing them to work each day on the outside while returning to jail at the end of the workday. They may be allowed to work during the week and serve intermittent sentences that require them to spend their weekends in jail. Such sentences are available but often ignored. There are presently too few house arrest, restitution, and community service sentences. Retributivists will argue that this approach steals jobs away from others and has little deterrence value, but jobs such as these are not above minimum wage or in great demand. Lawbreakers would still be paying for their mistakes while saving instead of wasting tax dollars.

What most of the public knows about prison and the justice system is what they want to believe. They want to believe it's not cruel and unusual punishment, or at least not too cruel. The public wants to believe they are compassionate and that the system is no longer barbaric and inhumane. However, estrangement prevails among all beings and flourishes in the prison setting. It swells in the cage of the cellar-beast, where life is separated from life and moves against itself through aggression, hatred, fear, and despair. And as anyone knows, despair destroys all joy and courage. Even if a prisoner is released and does not commit another crime, it doesn't necessarily mean they will be a well-functioning fully productive member of society.

What people glean from the police, politicians, or the media isn't a very accurate or detailed portrayal of existence inside the belly of the beast. The grey existence of being accused and found guilty of a crime and then locked in a cage fosters a personality fit for darkness. What better way can the system continue to portray to the public that it's just and true than by locking up and silencing the very people who would claim otherwise? Many of those who claim to protect Canadians—cops, guards, POs—now earn $80,000 to $100,000 a year or more. With half of Canadians earning only

$30,000 a year or less, one should consider where all their tax money is being sent and what harsh and longer terms do to people on the receiving end of justice.

A large percentage of prisoners were abandoned or neglected as children by both their parents and their community. As adults, they are abandoned again, carted off to prison and forgotten by the public and most, if not all, of their family and friends. We live in the most wasteful throwaway generation in history, and the planet is finally telling us this. The government adores consumerism because it generates tax revenue. We can only wonder if the skyrocketing cost of fuel will curb our consumption, drastically cutting the excess tax dollars that fuel the voracious justice/corrections machine. Cities and especially smaller towns must learn to take back what the corporations and larger governments have taken away. If more people from the community cared enough to attempt to reclaim their lost members, to help them reintegrate back into society, half the prisons would very quickly be emptied. More important, prisoners would feel a sense of belonging, and recidivism would plummet. As Robert Nisbet writes in *History of the Idea of Progress*, "without roots, human beings are condemned to a form of isolation in time that easily becomes self-destructive."

It has been proven that excessive punishment doesn't change poor behaviour; rather, it builds deep-seated resentment. The public doesn't care that prisons are cesspools of contamination, but when a prisoner is released and commits a serious crime, the public demands to know why they were released. Few ever ask what caused the person to become such a bad criminal. The simplest answer is that cold punitive prisons help create, as well as build and breed, both sociopaths and psychopaths.

Appendix A
Websites/Organizations/ Prison Addresses across Canada

Federal Government Websites

Department of Justice Canada	www.canada.justice.gc.ca
Correctional Service of Canada	www.csc-scc.gc.ca
Parole Board of Canada	www.pbc-clcc.gc.ca
Public Safety Canada	www.publicsafety.gc.ca
Supreme Court of Canada	www.scc-csc.gc.ca

Provincial and Territorial Government Websites

Alberta

Alberta Government	www.alberta.ca
Justice and Solicitor General	www.justice.alberta.ca

British Columbia

British Columbia Government	www.gov.bc.ca
Ministry of Justice	www.gov.bc.ca/justice/
Ministry of Justice Corrections	www.pssg.gov.bc.ca/corrections

Nunavut

Government of Nunavut	www.gov.nu.ca
Department of Justice	www.justice.gov.nu.ca

Northwest Territories

Government of the Northwest Territories	www.gov.nt.ca
Department of Justice	www.justice.gov.nt.ca

Prince Edward Island

Government of Prince Edward Island	www.gov.pe.ca
Dept. of Environment, Labour and Justice	www.gov.pe.ca/jps/

Saskatchewan

Government of Saskatchewan	www.gov.sk.ca
Justice and Attorney General	www.justice.gov.sk.ca

Yukon

Government of Yukon	www.gov.yk.ca
Department of Justice	www.justice.gov.yk.ca

Manitoba

Government of Manitoba	www.gov.mb.ca
Manitoba Justice	www.gov.mb.ca/justice

New Brunswick

Government of New Brunswick	www.gnb.ca
Justice and Attorney General	www.gov.nb.ca/justice

Newfoundland and Labrador

Government of Newfoundland and Labrador	www.gov.nl.ca
Department of Justice	www.justice.gov.nl.ca

Nova Scotia

Government of Nova Scotia	www.novascotia.ca
Department of Justice	www.gov.ns.ca/just

Ontario

Government of Ontario www.ontario.ca

Ministry of Community Safety and Correctional Services www.mcscs.jus.gov.on.ca

Quebec

Quebec Government www.gouv.qc.ca

Quebec Sécurité Publique (Public Security) www.msp.gouv.qc.ca

Resources and Links

4Strugglemag

4strugglemag.org

P.O. Box 97048, RPO Roncesvalles Ave., Toronto, ON, M6R 3B3

AIDWYC: The Association in Defence of the Wrongfully Convicted

www.aidwyc.org

111 Peter Street, Suite 408, Toronto, ON, M5V 2H1

Atlantic Halfway House Association (AHHA)

halfwayhouses.ca/en/region/ahha/

Stacey Dort, 45 Alderney Drive, Suite 900,

Dartmouth, Nova Scotia, B2Y 2N6

British Columbia – Yukon Halfway House Association (BCYHHA)

halfwayhouses.ca/en/region/bcyhha/

Attention: Nathan L. Rock, c/o 763 Kingsway,

Vancouver, BC, V5V 3C2

Canadian Families and Corrections Network
www.cfcn-rcafd.org
P.O. Box 35040, Kingston, ON, K7L 5S5

CFRC Prison Radio
www.cfrc.ca
(CFRC 101.9 FM in Kingston,
every Wednesday from 7 to 8 p.m. EST)
CPR c/o CFRC, Lower Carruthers Hall,
Queen's University, Kingston, ON, K7L 3N6

Church Counsel on Justice and Corrections
www.ccjc.ca
200 Isabella Street, Suite 303, Ottawa, ON, K1S 1V7

Freeing the Human Spirit
www.freeingspirit.com
P.O. Box 65142, 358 Danforth Avenue, Toronto, ON, M4K 3Z2

Innocence Project
www.osgoode.yorku.ca/innocence-project
Osgoode Hall Innocence Project, Osgoode Hall Law School,
York University, 4700 Keele Street, Toronto, ON, M3J 1P3

Journal of Prisoners on Prisons
www.jpp.org
c/o Justin Piché, Assistant Professor,
Department of Sociology, Memorial University,
St. John's, NL, A1C 5S7

Ontario Halfway House Association (OHHA)
ohhaonline.ca
224 Cornwallis Court, Oshawa, ON, L1H 8E8

Open Door Books
opendoorbooks.wordpress.com
c/o QPIRG Concordia University, Attn: Research Requests,
1455 de Maisonneuve West, Montreal, QC, H3G 1M8

Out of Bounds (prisoner magazine)
6000 William Head Road, Victoria, BC, V9C 0B5

PASAN Cell Count (prisoner magazine)
www.pasan.org
Prisoners' HIV/AIDS Support Action Network (PASAN)
314 Jarvis Street #100, Toronto, ON, M5B 2C5

PEN Canada
www.pencanada.ca
24 Ryerson Avenue, Suite 301, Toronto, ON, M5T 2P3

Prairie Region Halfway House Association (PRHHA)
prhha.net
P.O. Box 46007, Inglewood RPO, Calgary, AB, T2G 5H7

Prison Arts Foundation
25 West Street, Brantford, ON, N3T 3E5

Quakers Fostering Justice program
quakerservica.ca/our-work/justice/
Canadian Friends Service Committee (Quakers),
60 Lowther Avenue, Toronto, ON, M5R 1C7

Stark Raven Media Collective
www.prisonjustice.ca
(CFRO 102.7 FM in Vancouver,
www.coopradio.org

first Monday of each month from 7 to 8 p.m. PST)
c/o Co-op Radio, 110-360 Columbia Street,
Vancouver, BC, Coast Salish Territory, V6A 4J1

Interesting Web Sources

Alternative Libraries	www.alternativelibraries.org
Amnesty International	www.amnesty.org
Canadian Association of Elizabeth Fry Societies	www.elizabethfry.ca
Centre for Social Justice	www.socialjustice.org
Democracy Now!	www.democracynow.org
International Centre for Prison Studies (ICPS)	www.prisonstudies.org
John Howard Society of Canada	www.johnhoward.ca
MindFreedom	www.mindfreedom.org
Penal Reform International	www.penalreform.org
Prison Legal News	www.prisonlegalnews.org
St. Leonard's Society of Canada	www.stleonards.ca
The Voice of the Imprisoned	www.prisoners.com

Federal Institutions by Region

Atlantic Region (NB, NL, NS, PE)

Atlantic Institution (maximum)
(506) 623-4000
13175 Route 8, P.O. Box 102, Renous, NB, E9E 2E1

Dorchester Penitentiary (medium)
(506) 379-2471
4902 Main Street, Dorchester, NB, E4K 2Y9

Nova Institution for Women (multilevel)
(902) 897-1750
180 James Street, Truro, NS, B2N 6R8

Shepody Healing Centre (multilevel)
(506) 379-4271
4902 Main Street, Dorchester, NB, E4K 2Y9

Springhill Institution (medium)
(902) 597-8651
330 McGee Street, P.O. Box 2140, Springhill, NS, B0M 1X0

Westmorland Institution (minimum)
(506) 379-4595
4902A Main Street, Dorchester, NB, E4K 2Y9

Quebec Region

Archambault Institution (medium)
(450) 478-5960
242 Montée Gagnon, Sainte-Anne-des-Plaines, QC, J0N 1H0

Cowansville Institution (medium)
(450) 263-3073
400 Fordyce Avenue, Cowansville, QC, J2K 3G6

Donnacona Institution (maximum)
(418) 285-2455
1537 Highway 138, Donnacona, QC, G3M 1C9

Drummond Institution (medium)
(819) 477-5112
2025 Jean-de-Brébeuf Boulevard, Drummondville, QC, J2B 7Z6

Federal Training Centre (minimum)
(450) 661-7786
6099 Lévesque Boulevard East, Laval, QC, H7C 1P1

Joliette Institution (women's multilevel)
(450) 752-5257
400 Marsolais Street, Joliette, QC, J6E 8V4

La Macaza Institution (medium)
(819) 275-2315
321 Chemin de l'Aéroport, La Macaza, QC, J0T 1R0

Leclerc Institution (medium)
(450) 664-1320
400 Monteé Saint-François, Laval, QC, H7C 1S7

Montée Saint-François Institution (minimum)
(450) 661-9620
600 Montée Saint-François, Laval, QC, H7C 1S5

Port-Cartier Institution (maximum)
(418) 766-7070
Chemin de l'Aéroport, P.O. Box 7070, Port-Cartier, QC, G5B 2W2

Regional Mental Health Centre (multilevel)
(450) 478-5960
242 Monteé Gagnon, Sainte-Anne-des-Planes, QC, J0N 1H0

Regional Reception Centre (multilevel)
(450) 478-5977
246 Monteé Gagnon, Sainte-Anne-des-Planes, QC, J0N 1H0

Sainte-Anne-des-Plaines Institution (minimum)
(450) 478-5933
244 Montée Gagnon, Sainte-Anne-des-Plaines, QC, J0N 1H0

Ontario Region
Bath Institution (medium)
(613) 351-8346
5775 Bath Road, P.O. Box 1500, Bath, ON, K0H 1G0

Beaver Creek Institution (minimum)
(705) 687-6641
P.O. Box 1240, Gravenhurst, ON, P1P 1W9

Collins Bay Institution (medium)
(613) 545-8598
1455 Bath Road, P.O. Box 190, Kingston, ON, K7L 4V9

Fenbrook Institution (medium)
(705) 687-1895
2000 Beaver Creek Drive, P.O. Box 5000,
Gravenhurst, ON P1P 1Y2

Frontenac Institution (minimum)
(613) 536-6000
1455 Bath Road, P.O. Box 7500, Kingston, ON, K7L 5E6

Grand Valley Institution for Women (multilevel)
(519) 894-2011
1575 Homer Watson Boulevard, Kitchener, ON, N2P 2C5

Joyceville Institution (medium)
(613) 536-6400
Highway 15, P.O. Box 880, Kingston, ON, K7L 4X9

Kingston Penitentiary (maximum)
(613) 545-8460
560 King Street West, P.O. Box 22, Kingston, ON, K7L 4V7

Millhaven Institution (maximum)
(613) 351-8000
Highway 33, P.O. Box 280, Bath, ON, K0H 1G0

Pittsburgh Institution (minimum)
(613) 536-4046
Highway 15, No. 3766, P.O. Box 4510, Kingston, ON, K7L 5E5

Regional Treatment Centre (maximum)
(613) 536-6901
560 King Street West, P.O. Box 22, Kingston, ON, K7L 4V7

Warkworth Institution (medium)
(705) 924-2210
County Road #29, P.O. Box 760, Campbellford, ON, K0L 1L0

Prairie Region (AB, SK, MB)
Bowden Institution and Annex (medium/minimum)
(403) 227-3391
Highway #2, P.O. Box 6000, Innisfail, AB, T4G 1V1

Drumheller Institution and Annex (medium/minimum)
(403) 823-5101
Highway #9, P.O. Box 3000, Drumheller, AB, T0J 0Y0

Edmonton Institution (maximum)
(780) 472-6052
21611 Meridian Street, P.O. Box 2290, Edmonton, AB, T5J 3H7

Edmonton Institution for Women (multilevel)
(780) 495-3657
11151 – 178th Street, Edmonton, AB, T5S 2H9

Grand Cache Institution (medium/minimum)
(780) 827-4200
Hoppe Avenue, Bag 4000, Grand Cache, AB, T0E 0Y0

Grierson Centre (minimum)
(780) 495-2157
9530 – 101st Avenue (Basement), Edmonton, AB, T5H 0B3

Okimaw Ohci Healing Lodge (women's medium/minimum)
(306) 662-4700
P.O. Box 1929, Maple Creek, SK, S0N 1N0

Pê Sâkâstêw Centre (minimum)
(780) 585-4104
Highway #2A, P.O. Box 1500, Hobbema, AB, T0C 1N0

Regional Psychiatric Centre (multilevel)
(306) 975-5400
2520 Central Avenue North, P.O. Box 9243,
Saskatoon, SK, S7K 3X5

Riverbend Institution (minimum)
(306) 765-8200
15th Street West, P.O. Box 850, Prince Albert, SK, S6V 5S4

Rockwood Institution (minimum)
(204) 344-5111
Highway #7, P.O. Box 72, Stony Mountain, MB, R0C 3A0

Saskatchewan Penitentiary (medium/maximum)
(306) 765-8000
15th Street West, P.O. Box 160, Prince Albert, SK, S6V 5R6

Stony Mountain Institution (medium)
(204) 344-5111
Highway #7, P.O. Box 4500, Winnipeg, MB, R3C 3W8

Willow Cree Healing Lodge (minimum)
(306) 467-1200
P.O. Box 520, Duck Lake, SK, S0K 1J0

Pacific Region (BC)
Ferndale Institution (minimum)
(604) 820-5720
33737 Dewdney Trunk Road, P.O. Box 50, Mission, BC, V2V 4L8

Fraser Valley Institution for Women (multilevel)
(604) 851-6000
33344 King Road, Abbotsford, BC, V2S 6J5

Kent Institution (maximum)
(604) 796-2121
4732 Cemetery Road, P.O. Box 1500, Agassiz, BC, V0M 1A0

Kwikwèxwelhp Healing Village (minimum)
(604) 796-1650
Harrison Mills, BC, V0M 1L0

Matsqui Institution (medium)
(604) 859-4841
33344 King Road, P.O. Box 2500, Abbotsford, BC, V2S 4P3

Mission Institution (medium)
(604) 826-1231
8751 Stave Lake Street, P.O. Box 60, Mission, BC, V2V 4L8

Mountain Institution (medium)
(604) 796-2231
4732 Cemetery Road, P.O. Box 1600, Agassiz, BC, V0M 1A0

Pacific Institution/Regional Treatment Centre (multilevel)
(604) 870-7770
33344 King Road, P.O. Box 3000, Abbotsford, BC, V2S 4P4

William Head Institution (minimum)
6000 William Head Road, Victoria, BC, V9C 0B5
(250) 391-7000

Provincial Institutions
Alberta
Calgary Correctional Centre
(403) 662-3660
11808 – 85 Street NW, Calgary, AB, T3R 1J3

Calgary Remand Centre
(403) 695-2100
12200 – 85 Street NW, Calgary, AB, T3R 1J3

Edmonton Remand Centre
(780) 427-1600
9660 – 104 Avenue, Edmonton, AB, T5H 4B5

Fort Saskatchewan Correctional Centre
(780) 992-5900
7802 – 101 Street, Fort Saskatchewan, AB, T8L 2P3

Kainai Community Correctional Centre
(403) 737-2555
P.O. Box 530, Stand Off, AB, T0L 1Y0

Lethbridge Correctional Centre
(403) 388-3000
P.O. Bag 3001, Old Coaldale Road, Lethbridge, AB, T1J 3Z3

Medicine Hat Remand Centre
(403) 529-2111
874 – 2 Street SE, Medicine Hat, AB, T1A 8H2

Peace River Correctional Centre
(780) 624-5480
P.O. Bag 900 – 40, Peace River, AB, T8S 1T4

Red Deer Remand Centre
(403) 340-3200
4720 – 49 Street, Red Deer, AB, T4N 1T7

British Columbia
Alouette Correctional Centre for Women
(604) 476-2660
24800 Alouette Road, Maple Ridge, BC, V4R 1R8
Mail: P.O. Box 1000, Maple Ridge, BC, V2X 7G4

Ford Mountain Correctional Centre
(604) 824-5350
57657 Chilliwack Lake Road, Chilliwack, BC, V4Z 1A7
(604) 824-5373 (visits)
Mail: P.O. Box 1500, Maple Ridge, BC, V2X 7G3

Fraser Regional Correctional Centre
(604) 462-9313
13777 – 256th Street, Maple Ridge, BC, V4R 1C9
(604) 462-8865 (visits)
Mail: P.O. Box 1500, Maple Ridge, BC, V2X 7G3

Fraser Sentence Management Unit
(604) 462-5156
13777 – 256th Street, Maple Ridge, BC, V4R 1C9
Mail: P.O. Box 1500, Maple Ridge, BC, V2X 7G3

Kamloops Regional Correctional Centre
(250) 571-2200
2250 West Trans Canada Highway, Kamloops, BC, V2C 5M9
Mail: P.O. Box 820, Kamloops, BC, V2C 5M9

Nanaimo Correctional Centre
(250) 756-3300
3945 Biggs Road, Nanaimo, BC, V9R 5N3
(250) 729-7721 (visits)
Mail: Bag 4000, Nanaimo, BC, V9R 5N3

North Fraser Pretrial Centre
(604) 468-3500
1451 Kingsway Avenue, Port Coquitlam, BC, V3C 1S2
(604) 468-3566 (visits)

Prince George Regional Correctional Centre
(250) 960-3001
795 Highway 16 East, Prince George, BC, V2L 5J9
(250) 564-0465 (visits)
Mail: P.O. Box 4300, Prince George, BC, V2L 5J9

Surrey Pretrial Services Centre
(604) 599-4110
14323 – 57th Avenue, Surrey, BC, V3X 1B1
(604) 572-2103 (visits)

Vancouver Island Regional Correctional Centre
(250) 953-4400
4216 Wilkinson Road, Victoria, BC, V8Z 5B2
(250) 953-4433 (visits)
Mail: P.O. Box 9224, Stn Prov Govt, Victoria, BC, V8W 9J1

Manitoba
Brandon Correctional Centre
(204) 725-3532
375 Veterans Way, Brandon, MB, R3C 0B1

Daupin Correctional Centre
(204) 622-2083
114 River Avenue West, Dauphin, MB, R7N 0J7

Headingley Correctional Centre
(204) 837-1351
6030 Portage Avenue, Headingley, MB, R4H 1E8

Milner Ridge Correctional Centre
(204) 268-4011
P.O. Box 460, Beausejour, MB, R0E 0C0

The Pas Correctional Centre
(204) 627-8450
P.O. Box 659, The Pas, MB, R9A 1K7

Winnipeg Remand Centre
(204) 945-3540
141 Kennedy Street, Winnipeg, MB, R3C 4N5

Women's Correctional Centre
(204) 948-8803
31 Routledge Avenue, Headingley, MB, R4H 0A9

New Brunswick
Dalhousie Regional Correction Centre
(506) 684-7517
265 Miller Boulevard, Dalhousie, NB, E8C 2A2

Madawaska Regional Correction Centre
(506) 737-4510
15 Fournier Street, Saint-Hilaire, NB, E3V 4W5

Moncton Detention Centre
(506) 856-2311
125 Assomption Boulevard, Moncton, NB, E1C 1A2
Mail: P.O. Box 5001, Moncton, NB, E1C 8R3

Saint John Regional Correctional Centre
(506) 658-5400
930 Old Black River Road, Saint John, NB, E2J 4T3

Southeast Regional Correctional Centre
(506) 453-3992
435 Lino Road, Shediac, NB, E4P 0H6

Newfoundland and Labrador

Bishop's Falls Correctional Centre
(709) 258-6966
P.O. Box 880, Bishop's Falls, NL, A0H 1C0

Corner Brook Lockup
(709) 637-4139
P.O. Box 2006, Corner Brook, NL, A2H 6J8

Her Majesty's Penitentiary
(709) 729-1200
P.O. Box 5459, St. John's, NL, A1C 5W4

Labrador Correctional Centre
(709) 896-3327
P.O. Box 1240, Happy Valley – Goose Bay, NL, A0P 1E0

Newfoundland & Labrador Correctional Centre for Women
(709) 466-3101
P.O. Box 1030, Clarenville, NL, A0E 1J0

St. John's Lockup
(709) 729-3873
c/o Her Majesty's Penitentiary, P.O. Box 5459,
St. John's, NL, A1C 5W4

West Coast Correctional Centre
(709) 643-5601
P.O. Box 660, Stephenville, NL, A2N 3B5

Northwest Territories

Fort Smith Correctional Complex: Female Unit
(867) 872-6562
47 Pickerel Street, Box 5, Fort Smith, NT, X0E 0P0

Fort Smith Correctional Complex: Male Unit
(867) 872-6558
Box 388, 97 McDougal Road, Fort Smith, NT, X0E 0P0

North Slave Correctional Centre
(867) 669-8605
71 Kam Lake Road, Box 278, Yellowknife, NT, X1A 2N2

South Mackenzie Correctional Centre
(867) 874-2774
34 Studney Drive, Hay River, NT, X0E 0R6

Nova Scotia
Antigonish Correctional Facility
(902) 863-2527
68 Court Street, Antigonish, NS, B2G 1Z8

Cape Breton Correctional Facility
(902) 563-2114
136 Gardiner Road, Sydney, NS, B1M 1A1

Central Nova Scotia Correctional Facility
(902) 460-5800
90 Gloria McClusky Avenue, Dartmouth, NS, B3B 2B9

Cumberland Correctional Facility
(902) 667-2320
1 Lawrence Street, Amherst, NS, B4H 3G4

Northeast Nova Scotia Correctional Facility
Coalburn, NS (pending as of November 2010)

Southwest Nova Scotia Correctional Facility
(902) 742-4211
227 Forest Street, Yarmouth, NS, B5A 4A8

Nunavut
Baffin Correctional Centre
(867) 979-8103
P.O. Box 368, Iqaluit, NU, X0A 0H0

Ontario
Correctional Centres
Algoma Treatment and Remand Centre
(705) 946-0995
800 Great Northern Road, Sault Ste. Marie, ON, P6A 5K7

Central East Correctional Centre (superjail)
(705) 328-6000
541 Hwy 36, Box 4500, Lindsay, ON, K9V 6H2

Central North Correctional Centre (superjail)
(705) 549-9470
1501 Fuller Avenue, Penetanguishene, ON, L9M 2H4

Maplehurst Correctional Complex (superjail)
(905) 878-8141
661 Martin Street, Box 10, Milton, ON, L9T 2Y3

Monteith Correctional Complex
(705) 232-4092
Junction Hwys 11 & 577, Box 90, Monteith, ON, P0K 1P0

Ontario Correctional Institute
(905) 457-7050
109 McLaughlin Road South, Brampton, ON, L6Y 2C8

St. Lawrence Valley Correctional and Treatment Centre
(613) 345-1461
1804 Hwy 2 East, Brockville, ON, K6V 5T1

Thunder Bay Correctional Centre
(807) 475-8401
Hwy 61 South, Box 1900, Thunder Bay, ON, P7C 4Y4

Vanier Centre for Women
(905) 876-8300
655 Martin Street, Box 1040, Milton, ON, L9T 5E6

Detention Centres

Elgin-Middlesex Detention Centre
(519) 686-1922
711 Exeter Road, London, ON, N6E 1L3

Hamilton-Wentworth Detention Centre
(905) 523-8800
165 Barton Street East, Hamilton, ON, L8L 2W6

Niagara Detention Centre
(905) 227-6321
Highway 58, 1355 Uppers Lane, Box 1050, Thorold, ON, L2V 4A6

Ottawa-Carlton Detention Centre
(613) 824-6080
2244 Innes Road, Ottawa, ON, K1B 4C4

Quinte Detention Centre
(613) 354-9701
89 Richmond Boulevard, Napanee, ON, K7R 3S1

South West Detention Centre
Windsor, ON (to replace Windsor Jail in 2014)

Toronto Intermittent Centre
(416) 354-4030
(To become a part of the Toronto South Detention Centre)
160 Horner Avenue, Toronto, ON, M8Z 4X8

Toronto East Detention Centre
(416) 750-3513
55 Civic Road, Scarborough, ON, M1L 2K9

Toronto South Detention Centre
(To replace Toronto Jail in 2013)
160 Horner Avenue, Toronto, ON, M8Z 4X8

Toronto West Detention Centre
(416) 675-1806
111 Disco Road, Box 4950, Rexdale, ON, M9W 5L6

Jails

Brantford Jail
(519) 752-6578
105 Market Street, Brantford, ON, N3T 6A9

Brockville Jail
(613) 341-2870
10 Wall Street, Brockville, ON, K6V 4R9

Chatham Jail
(519) 352-0150
17 Seventh Street, Chatham, ON, N7M 4J9

Fort Frances Jail
(807) 274-7708
310 Nelson Street, Fort Frances, ON, P9A 1B1

Kenora Jail
(807) 468-2871
1430 River Street, Kenora, ON, P9N 1K5

North Bay Jail
(705) 472-8115
2550 Trout Lake Road, North Bay, ON, P1B 7S7

Sarnia Jail
(519) 337-3261
700 Christina Street North, Sarnia, ON, N7V 3C2

Stratford Jail
(519) 271-2180
30 St. Andrews Street, Stratford, ON, N5A 1A3

Sudbury Jail
(705) 564-4150
181 Elm Street West, Sudbury, ON, P3C 1T8

Thunder Bay Jail
(807) 345-7364
285 MacDougall Street, Thunder Bay, ON, P7A 2K6

Toronto (Don) Jail
(416) 325-8600
550 Gerrard Street East, Toronto, ON, M4M 1X6

Windsor Jail
(519) 973-1324
378 Brock Street, Box 7038, Windsor, ON, N9C 3Y6

Prince Edward Island
Provincial Correctional Centre
(902) 368-4590
508 Sleepy Hollow Road, RR #10, Charlottetown, PE, C1E 1Z4

Prince Correctional Centre
(902) 888-8208
108 Central Street, Summerside, PE, C1N 3L4

Quebec
Amos Detention Centre
(819) 444-5222
851 3e Rue Ouest, Amos, QC, J9T 2T4

Baie-Comeau Detention Centre
(418) 294-8646
73 Avenue Mance, Baie-Comeau, QC G4Z 1N1

Chicoutimi Detention Centre
(418) 698-3838
273 Rue Price Est, Chicoutimi, QC, G7H 4T9

Havre-Aubert
(418) 937-2550
C.P. 25, Îles de la Madeleine, QC, G0B 1J0

Hull Detention Centre
(819) 772-3065
75 Rue Saint-François, Gatineau (Hull), QC, J9A 1B4

Maison Tanguay (Female Facility)
(514) 337-9450
555 Boulevard Henri Bourassa Ouest, Montreal, QC, H3L 1P3

Montreal Detention Centre
(514) 336-7700
800 Boulevard Gouin Ouest, Montreal, QC, H3L 1K7

New Carlisle Detention Centre
(418) 752-6637
87 Rue Principale, C.P. 9, New Carlisle, QC, G0C 1Z0

Quebec Detention Centre
(418) 622-7100
500 Rue de la Faune, C.P. 7130, Quebec City, QC, G1G 5E4

Quebec Detention Centre (Female Facility)
(418) 622-7125
500 Rue de la Faune, C.P. 7130, Quebec City, QC, G1G 5E4

Rimouski Detention Centre
(418) 727-3547
200 Rue des Négociants, C.P. 490, Rimouski, QC, G5L 7C5

Rivière-des-Prairies Detention Centre
(514) 494-3930
11 900, rue Armand-Chaput, Rivière-des-Prairies, QC H1C 1S7

Roberval Detention Centre
(418) 275-0207
756 Boulevard St-Joseph, Roberval, Que G8H 2L5

Saint-Jérôme Detention Centre
(450) 436-8144
40 Montée Meunier, C.P. 513, Saint-Jérôme, QC, J7Z 5V3

Sept-Îles Detention Centre
(418) 968-8632
425 Boulevard Laure, Sept-Îles, QC, G4R 1X6

Sherbrooke Detention Centre
(819) 820-3100
1055 Rue Talbot, Sherbrooke, QC, J1G 2P3

Sorel Detention Centre
(450) 742-0471
75 Boulevard Poliquin, C.P. 529, Sorel-Tracy, QC, J3P 5N9

Trois-Rivières Detention Centre
(819) 372-1311
7600 Boulevard Parent, Trois-Rivières, QC, G9A 5E1

Saskatchewan
Battleford Community Correctional Centre
(306) 446-7800
P.O. Box 996, North Battleford, SK, S9A 3E6

Buffalo Narrows Community Correctional Centre
(306) 235-1756
P.O. Box 340, Buffalo Narrows, SK, S0M 0J0

Pine Grove Correctional Centre (Female Facility)
(306) 953-3100
P.O. Box 3002, 1700 – 7th Avenue Northeast, Prince Albert, SK, S6V 6G1

Prince Albert Provincial Correctional Centre

(306) 953-3000

P.O. Box 3003, Prince Albert, SK, S6V 6G1

Regina Provincial Correctional Centre

(306) 924-9000

P.O. Box 617, Regina, SK, S4P 3A6

Saskatoon Provincial Correctional Centre

(306) 956-8800

910 – 60th Street East, Saskatoon, SK, S7K 2H6

Spiritual Healing Lodge

(306) 953-2498

c/o Prince Albert Correctional Centre, P.O. Box 3003,
Prince Albert, SK, S6V 6G1

3021 – 1st Avenue West, Wahpeton Reserve 94B, Box 2350,
Prince Albert, SK, S6V 6Z1

Yukon

Whitehorse Correctional Centre

(867) 455-2900

25 College Drive, Whitehorse, YT, Y1A 5B6

Appendix B

Halfway Houses, Community-Based Residential Facilities, etc., across Canada

Pacific Region

Abbotsford

Kinghaven Treatment Centre
31250 King Road, Abbotsford, BC, V2T 6C2
Larry Saidman (604) 864-0039

Peardonville House Treatment Centre – Kinghaven (females)
825 Peardonville Road, Abbotsford, BC, V2X 4L8
Wendy Rowat (604) 856-3966

Tims Manor
32160 Tims Avenue, Abbotsford, BC, V2T 2H4
(604) 755-0467

Campbell River

John Howard Society of North Island –
Campbell River Community Programs
#201 – 140A 10th Avenue, Campbell River, BC, V9W 4E3
Steve Ayers, Manager (250) 286-0611

Chilliwack
Chilliwack Community Correctional Centre
45914 Rowat Avenue, Chilliwack, BC, V2H 1J3
(604) 702-4280

Kamloops
Fairview House (CBRF) (females)
133, 135, 137, and 139 Fairview Avenue, Kamloops, BC, V2B 1E7
Grant Wolkosky (250) 434-1700

Georgian Court (CBRF) (males and females)
406 Fortune Drive, Kamloops, BC, V2B 2J3
Grant Wolkosky (250) 434-1700

Light House
1605 East Trans Canada Highway, Kamloops, BC, V2C 3Z5
Grant Wolkosky (250) 434-1700

Linkage House (CBRF)
380 and 382 Monmouth Place, Kamloops, BC, V2E 1N7
Grant Wolkosky (250) 434-1700

John Howard Society Thompson Region
#100 – 529 Seymour Street, Kamloops, BC, V2C 0A1
(250) 434-1700

Victory Inn
1420 Halston Avenue, Kamloops, BC, V2B 8R2
Grant Wolkosky (250) 434-1700

Kelowna
Bernard Residence
1353 Bernard Avenue, Kelowna, BC, V1Y 6R5
Bob Ens, House Manager (250) 717-5613

John Howard Society of the Central and South Okanagan
1440 St. Paul St, Kelowna, BC, V1Y 2E6
(250) 763-1331

Robinson/Chandler Place
1822-1862 Chandler Street, Kelowana, BC, V1Y 3Z1
(250) 862-8363 (Robinson)
Bob Ens, House Manager
(250) 717-3589 (Chandler)

Kelowna House CRF – Okanagan Halfway House Society
1033 Harvey Avenue, Kelowna, BC, V1Y 6E4
Brian Laffan, House Manager (250) 860-5820

Lantzville
Tsow-Tun Lelum Society (males and females)
P.O. Box 370, 699 Capilano Road, Lantzville, BC, V0R 2H0
Yvonne Rigsby-Jones, Director (250) 390-3123

Maple Ridge
Maple Ridge Treatment Centre
22269 Callaghan Avenue, Maple Ridge, BC, V2X 2E2
(604) 467-4371

Mission
Salvation Army Paetzold Centre (formerly Valley of Miracles)
14100 Stave Lake Road, Mission, BC, V2V 4J5
(604) 826-6681

Nanaimo
Nanaimo Region John Howard Society
#200, 1585 Bowen Road, Nanaimo, BC, V9S 1G4
Barbara Rumney, Executive Director (250) 754-1266

Salvation Army New Hope Centre
19 Nicol Street, Nanaimo, BC, V9R 4S6
Rob Anderson (250) 714-1142

Surfside Recovery House
2368 Rosstown Road, Nanaimo, BC, V9T 3R7
Dee Edgar (250) 758-5611

New Westminster
Columbia Place – Elizabeth Fry Society (females)
402 East Columbia Street, New Westminster, BC, V3L 3X1
Marni Ziegler (604) 540-1985

Genesis House – Westcoast Genesis Society
219 Carnarvon Street, New Westminster, BC, V3L 1B7
Andrew Boyd, Executive Director (604) 515-2950

Maria Keary Cottage CRF – Westcoast Genesis Society
305 Carnarvon Street, New Westminster, BC, V3L 1B9
Andrew Boyd, Executive Director (604) 515-2950

Prince George
John Howard Society of British Columbia – Northern Programs
154 Quebec Street, Prince George, BC, V2L 1W2
George Harding, Executive Director (250) 561-7343

Kenneth Creek Camp – c/o PG Activator Society
Mail: 770 2nd Avenue, Prince George, BC, V2L 3A3
Sid Madhok, Facilities Director (250) 960-8324

Ketso Yoh – Prince George Native Friendship Centre
160 Quebec Street, Prince George, BC, V2L 1W2
(250) 563-1982

Phoenix Transition Society (females)
1770 – 11th Avenue, Prince George, BC, V2L 3S8
Sharon Hurd (250) 563-7305

Prince George Activator Society
770 2nd Avenue, Prince George, BC, V2L 3A3
Dave Trepanier, Executive Director (250) 563-5019

St. Patrick's House Society
1735 Yew Street, Prince George, BC, V2L 2X3
Marilyn Rayner, Executive Director (250) 564-5530

Surrey
Ambro House – Phoenix Drug and Alcohol Recovery Society
10373 133A Street, Surrey, BC, V3T 4A1
Linda Fumano, House Supervisor (604) 582-2682

Cwenengitel Aboriginal Society
13632 110A Avenue, Surrey, BC, V3R 2B1 (604) 588-5561
Arthur Smith (604) 588-5910

Hobden House
12817 104th Avenue, Surrey, BC, V3T 1T3
Pat Gilbert (604) 585-4493

Path to Freedom Drug and Alcohol Treatment Centre
19030 – #10 Hwy – 56th Avenue, Surrey, BC, V3S 8E5
Hardev Randhawa, Director and Counsellor (604) 576-6466

Vancouver
Circle of Eagles Lodge Society
1470 East Broadway, Vancouver, BC, V5N 1V6
Gerald Adams, Executive Director (604) 874-9610

Circle of Eagles Lodge Society – Anderson Lodge (females)
2716 Clark Drive, Vancouver, BC, V5N 3H6
Velma Albert, House Manager (604) 874-1246

Dick Bell Irving House – BC Borstal Association
554 West 21st Avenue, Vancouver, BC, V5Z 1Y6
John Cote, House Director (604) 877-2295

Guy Richmond Place – John Howard Society
863 East 12th Avenue, Vancouver, BC, V5T 2J3
Tony Kennedy (604) 876-4611

John Howard Society of the Lower Mainland of BC
763 Kingsway, Vancouver, BC, V5V 3C2 (604) 872-5651

St. Leonard's Society of North Vancouver
312 Bewicke Avenue, Vancouver, BC, V7M 3B7
Mike Horne, Executive Director (604) 980-3684

Salvation Army Belkin House (males and females)
555 Homer Street, Vancouver, BC, V6B 1K8
Jim Coggles, Executive Director (604) 681-3405

Salvation Army Harbour Light Centre
119 East Cordova Street, Vancouver, BC, V6A 1K8
Wayne Oster, Executive Director (604) 646-6800

Victoria

Bill Mudge Residence
138 Dallas Road, Victoria, BC, V8V 1A3
Alan Turnbull, Executive Director (250) 381-7949

John Howard Society of Victoria
2675 Bridge Street, Victoria, BC, V8T 4Y4
(250) 386-3428

Manchester House – John Howard Society
540 Manchester Road, Victoria, BC, V8T 2N8
Kathy Roy, CRF Director (250) 384-1340

Salvation Army CRF/ARC
525 Johnson Street, Victoria, BC, V8W 1M2 (250) 384-3396
Sandra M. Cochlan, CRF Director #230 or local #231

Vernon
John Howard Society of the North Okanagan/
Kootenay Region of BC
2307 43rd Street, Vernon, BC, V1T 6K7
Barbara Levesque, Executive Director (250) 542-4041

Whitehorse
Salvation Army Adult Resource Centre
91678 Alaska Highway, Whitehorse, YT, Y1A 3Y8
Robert Sessford (867) 667-2741

Prairie Region
Alberta
Calgary
Alberta Seventh Step Society
1824 27th Avenue Southwest, Calgary, AB, T2T 1H1
Patti Fisher (403) 245-6661

Aventa Addiction Treatment Foundation for Women
610 25 Avenue Southwest, Calgary, AB T2S 0L6
Mara Thorvaldson (403) 245-9050

Bedford House CRF – John Howard Society (males and females)
615 13 Avenue Southeast, Calgary, AB, T2G 1C4
Lacey Leibel (403) 232-6388

Berkana House (females)
11419 8th Street Southwest, Calgary, AB, T2W 2N4
Brenda Ingham (403) 640-8911

Fresh Start Recovery Centre
411 41 Avenue Northeast, Calgary, AB, T2E 2N4
Stacey Petersen, Executive Director (403) 387-6266

Roberts House –
Canadian Mental Health Association (males and females)
2621 15 Street Southwest, Calgary, AB, T2T 3Z8
Leslie Hill (403) 297-1737

Salvation Army Centre of Hope (males and females)
420 9th Avenue Southeast, Calgary, AB, T2G 0R9
Ron Jean-Baptiste (403) 410-1140

Edmonton
101 Street Apartments – John Howard Society
11908 101 Street, Edmonton, AB, T5G 2B9
Clarissa Johnson (780) 471-4525

Cunningham Place (Section 81)
9330 104 Avenue, Edmonton, AB
Sheila Coutoreille (780) 990-1120

Elpida House East – Catholic Social Services
10638 102 Street, Edmonton, AB, T5H 2T5
Ed Fox (780) 479-2464

Elpida House for Women – Catholic Social Services
13035 83 Street, Edmonton, AB, T5E 2W5
Violetta Patora (780) 473-7011

Elpida House West – Catholic Social Services
15520 96 Avenue, Edmonton, AB, T5P 0C3
Ed Fox (780) 484-0274

Independence Apartments – John Howard Society
10637 106 Street, Edmonton, AB, T5H 2X7
Jill Hubbard, Manager (780) 421-7355

Stan Daniels Healing Centre (Section 81)
9516 101 Avenue, Edmonton, AB, T5H 0B3
Sheila Courtorielle (780) 495-3748

Lethbridge
Parkside Home
712 1st Avenue South, Lethbridge, AB, T1J 0A7
Rod S. Smith (403) 320-1103

Southern Alcare Manor (males and females)
520 7 Street South, Lethbridge, AB, T1J 2H1
Holly Lemieux or Ron Fromm (403) 328-0955

Red Deer
Horizon House CBRF (males and females)
4916 50 Street, Red Deer, AB, T4N 1X7
Michelle St. John (403) 343-1770

Manitoba

Brandon

Meredith Place – YWCA (males and females)
148 11th Street, Brandon, Manitoba, R7A 4J4
Pat Babiak (204) 571-3680

O-chi-chak-ko-sipi Healing Lodge
Box 81, Crane River, MB, R0L 0M0
Everett Contois, Executive Director (204) 732-2025

Winnipeg

Behavioural Health Foundation (males and females)
Box 250, 35 Avenue de la Digue, Winnipeg, MB, R3V 1L6
Jean Doucha, Executive Director (204) 269-3430

Regina House CRF
160 Mayfair Avenue, Winnipeg, MB, R3L 0A1
Robert M. Chartrand, Executive Director (204) 284-8323

Salvation Army Community and Residential Services (males and females)
180 Henry Avenue, Winnipeg, MB, R3B 0J8
Ivor Grant (204) 946-9401

Tamarack Recovery Centre (males and females)
60 Balmoral Street, Winnipeg, MB, R3C 1X4
Lisa Cowan, Executive Director (204) 772-9836

United Church Halfway Homes (males and females)
P.O. Box 274 RPO Coydon, Winnipeg, MB, R3M 3S7
Sally Walker (204) 471-4281

Northwest Territories

Yellowknife

Salvation Army Yellowknife Resource Centre
4925 45 Street, Yellowknife, NT, X1A 2P9
Brian Birch (867) 920-4673

Saskatchewan

Prince Albert

Métis Addictions Council of Saskatchewan
328 19th Street East, Prince Albert, SK, S6V 1J7
Laura Lee Hatch, Extension Program Coordinator
(306) 953-8250

Prince Albert Grand Council Healing Lodge
Box 2350, Prince Albert, SK, S6V 6Z1
Norma Green, Director (306) 953-2498

YMCA Prince Albert (females)
1895 Central Avenue B West, Prince Albert, SK, S6V 4W8
Donna Brooks or Linda Staff (306) 763-8571

Regina

Salvation Army Waterson Centre
1845 Osler Street, Regina, S4P 1W1
Amanda Carlson (306) 569-6088

YWCA Regina (females)
1940 McIntyre Street, Regina, SK, S4P 2R3
Louise Burns-Murray (306) 525-2141

Saskatoon

Elizabeth Fry Society of Saskatchewan
600 – 245 3rd Avenue South, Saskatoon, SK, S7K 1M4
(306) 933-6181
Angeline Gabrielle Battiste, Executive Director (306) 668-0604

Meewasinota Aboriginal Healing Centre (males and females)
265 Avenue B South, Saskatoon, SK, S7M 1M3
Scot Evacheski, Executive Director (306) 651-3405

Salvation Army New Frontiers – Men's Hostel
339 Avenue C South, Saskatoon, SK, S7M 1N5
Major Malba Holliday, Executive Director (306) 244-6280

Ontario Region

Barrie

Joyce Kope House – Elizabeth Fry Society (females)
102 Maple Avenue, Barrie, ON, L4N 1S4
Terri Soukup (705) 725-0613

Windermere Gardens
55 Peel Street, Barrie, ON, L4M 3K9
Jeff (705) 726-1100

Brampton

St. Leonard's House – Peel
P.O. Box 2607, 1105 Queen Street East, Brampton, ON, L6T 5M6
Richard Brown, Executive Director (905) 457-3611

Ellen House – Elizabeth Fry Society (females)
30 Ellen Street, Brampton, ON L6V 1J6
Pam Cassista, House Director (905) 451-7282

Brantford

St. Leonard's Community Services – Buffalo Street
19 Buffalo Street, P.O. Box 638, Brantford, ON, N3T 5P9
Bill Jones, Program Manager (519) 753-4600

Dundas

Salvation Army Ellen Osler Home (females)
34 Hatt Street, Dundas, ON, L9H 2E8
Jo-Anne Davis, Executive Director (905) 627-1632

Guelph

Stonehenge Therapeutic Community (males and females)
60 Westwood Road, Guelph, ON, N1H 7X3
Heather Kerr, Executive Director (519) 837-1470

Hamilton

Emerald Street Residence – St. Leonard's Society
24 Emerald Street South, Hamilton, ON, L8N 2V2
John Clinton, Executive Director (905) 529-8494

Robert Street Residence – St. Leonard's Society
73 Robert Street, Hamilton, ON, L8L 2P2
John Clinton, Executive Director (905) 572-1150

Salvation Army Booth Centre
94 York Boulevard, Hamilton, ON, L8R 3L4
Vaden Vincent (905) 527-1444

Kingston

Detweiler House – Elizabeth Fry Society (females)
129 Charles Street, Kingston, ON, K7L 1V8
Trish Crawford, Executive Director (613) 544-1744

Salvation Army Harbour Light
562 Princess Street, Kingston, ON, K7L 1C7
Ian McAlister (613) 546-2333

Kitchener

Salvation Army New Directions
657 King Street East, Kitchener, ON, N2G 2M4
Denis Skipper (519) 744-4666

London

Cody Centre – St. Leonard's Society
108 King Edward Avenue, London, ON, N5Z 3T1
Heather Callender, Executive Director (519) 668-2701

Gallagher Centre – St. Leonard's Society
266 Egerton Street, London, ON, N5Z 2G7
Heather Callender, Executive Director (519) 451-7707

Maison Louise Arbour (females)
658 Little Grey Street, London, ON, N5Z 5E9
Heather Callender, Executive Director (519) 850-1975

North Bay

Four Elms Residence – Crisis Centre North Bay
(males and females)
1675 Cassells Street, North Bay, ON
Mail: P.O. Box 1407, North Bay, ON, P1B 8K6
Doug Davidson (705) 474-1031

North Bay Recovery Home
393 Oak Street West, North Bay, ON, P1B 2T2
Peter Hull (705) 472-2873

Oshawa

Cornerstone Community Association Durham
133 Simcoe Street South, Oshawa, ON, L1H 4G8
Polly Peyman, Program Director (905) 433-0254

Orillia

Seven South Street Treatment Centre
7 South Street, Orillia, ON, L3V 3T1
Phyllis Gordon, Executive Director (705) 325-3566

Ottawa

House of Hope
32 Gilmour Street, Ottawa, ON, K2P 0N3
Tracey Cortes (613) 230-7676

JF Norwood House – Elizabeth Fry Society (females)
211 Bronson Avenue #301, Ottawa, ON, K1R 6H5
Nina Biancardi, Manager of Residential Services
(613) 237-7427 ext. 115

Kirkpatrick House – John Howard Society
591 MacLaren Street, Ottawa, ON, KlR 5K8
Scott Hole, House Director (613) 236-3077

Maison Décision House
37 Irving Avenue, Ottawa, ON, K1Y 1Z2
Louis Bérubé (613) 728-5013

St. Anne Residence – John Howard Society
259 St. Anne Avenue, Ottawa, ON, K1L 7C3
Rob Remus, Director (613) 749-7047

Tom Lamothe Apartment Building – John Howard Society
387 MacLaren Street, Ottawa, ON, K2P 0M7
Tina Matchett-Bianco, Director of Adult Justice Services
(613) 565-1739

Peterborough

Edmison House – St. Leonard's Society
458 Rubidge Street, P.O. Box 1707, Peterborough, ON, K9J 7S4
Darryl Rowe, Executive Director (705) 743-9351

St. Catharines

Salvation Army Community Resource Centre/Booth Centre
184 Church Street, St. Catharines, ON, L2R 3E7
Michael Hennessy (905) 684-7813

Sudbury

Larch House – St. Leonard's Society
238 Larch Street, Sudbury, ON, P3B 1M1
Vince Marconato, Executive Director (705) 674-2887

Salvation Army New Life Centre –
Addiction and Rehabilitation Services
146 Larch Street, Sudbury, ON, P3E 1C2
David Carey (705) 673-1175

Thunder Bay

Salvation Army Booth Centre
545 Cumberland Street North, Thunder Bay, ON, P7A 4S2
Marilyn Dyer (807) 345-7319

Toronto

Elizabeth Fry Society of Toronto (females)
215 Wellesley Street East, Toronto, ON, M4X 1G1
Michelle Coombs, Executive Director (416) 924-3708

Keele Community Correctional Centre
330 Keele Street, 2nd Floor, Toronto, ON, M6P 2K7
(416) 762-8171

Salvation Army Bunton Lodge/W.P. Archibald ARC
422 Sherbourne Street, Toronto, ON, M4X 1K2
Art Rasmusson, Executive Director (416) 964-6316

Salvation Army Maxwell Meighen Centre
135 Sherbourne Street, Toronto, ON, M5A 2R5
Christopher Dickens (416) 366-2733

Crossroads House – St. Leonard's Society
419 Jones Avenue, Toronto, ON, M4J 3G6
Sonya Spenser, Executive Director (416) 469-8312

Windsor
St. Leonard's House – Windsor
491 Victoria Avenue, Windsor, ON, N9A 4N1
Skip Graham, Executive Director (519) 256-1878

Quebec Region
Amos
CRC D'Abitibi-Témiscamingue et du Nord du Québec
121 Principale Street South, P.O. Box 38, Amos, QC, J9T 3A5
Serge Béchard, Director (819) 732-5253

Baie-Comeau
Point de Rencontre
619 de l'Hôpital Street, Baie-Comeau, QC, G5C 3H2
Nicole Porlier (418) 589-7551

Charlesbourg
Expansion-Femmes de Québec (females)
4785 5th Avenue East, Charlesbourg, QC, G1H 3R7
Pierrette Cliché, Director (418) 623-3801

Chicoutimi
CRC La Relève
672 Ste-Geneviève Boulevard, Saguenay, QC, G7G 2E6
Nadia Gagnon, Coordinator (418) 543-6123

Deux-Montagnes
Foyer Marie Beemans (males and females)
51 Grand Moulin Road, Deux-Montagnes, QC, J7R 3C5
Marie Beemans (450) 473-6110

Gatineau
Les CRC de l'Outaouais Inc.
575 Gréber Boulevard, Gatineau, QC, J8T 8G2
Richard Gagnon (819) 568-1131

Granby
Auberge Sous Mon Toit
317 Chapais Street, Granby, QC, J2G 7E7
Alain Massé, Executive Director (450) 378-4269

La Maison Le Joins-Toi
479 Rue Principale, Granby, QC, J2G 2G9
Madeleine Ferland, Director (450) 378-9924

Joliette
CRC Joliette-Lanaudière,
785 Manseau Boulevard, Joliette, QC, J6E 3G1
Raymond Charlebois (450) 752-0556

Lanoraie
Pavillon du Nouveau Point de Vue (males and females)
356 Notre-Dame Street, Lanoraie, QC, J0K 1E0
(450) 887-2392
Yvon Picotte, Executive Director 1-800-267-2392

Laval

Résidence Carpe Diem Inc.
845 Lippman Street, Laval, QC, H7S 1G3
Sylvain Touchette (450) 668-2277

La Maisonnée Paulette Guinois Inc. (males and females)
2255 Bienville Street, Auteuil, Laval, QC, H7H 3C9
Paulette Guinois, Executive Director (450) 628-1011

Longueil

La Maison Le Joins-Toi
6505 Maricourt Boulevard, arr. St-Hubert, Longueil, QC, J3Y 1S8
Madeleine Ferland, Director (450) 445-8000

Montreal

Corporation Maison Charlemagne
2267 Jeanne d'Arc Street, Montreal, QC, H1W 3V8
Bernard Cartier, Executive Director (514) 253-1926

CRC Jeun'aide
4430 Saint-Jacques Street, Montreal, QC, H4C 1K2
André Labelle, Executive Director (514) 932-4857

CRC Madeleine-Carmel
4251 Hochelaga Street, Montreal, QC, H1V 1C1
Bernard Cartier, Executive Director (514) 522-9133

CRC Maison Essor
9419 Lajeunesse Street, Montreal, QC, H2M 1S5
Robert Woodrough (514) 388-4433

Foundation Carrefour Nouveau Monde
6970 15th Avenue, Montreal, QC, H2A 2T7
Daniel Dupot, Executive Director (514) 727-2259

Maison Belfield
5321 Belfield Place, Montreal, QC H3X 1M8
Rabbin Zushe Silberstein (514) 735-9654

Maison L'Issue (Transition Centre-Sud)
1819 Boulevard Rosemont, Montreal, QC, H2G 1S5
Marc Meloche, Executive Director (514) 270-6633

La Maison du Père
550 Boulevard René-Lévesque Est, Montreal, QC, H2L 2L3
Daniel Dumond, Executive Director (514) 845-0168

Maison Saint-Léonard
5262 Notre-Dame Street West, Montreal, QC, H4C 1T5
Michel Gagnon, Director (514) 932-7188

Maison Thérèse-Casgrain (females)
5105 Côte Saint-Antoine, Montreal, QC, H4A 1N8
Ruth Gagnon, Executive Director (514) 489-3887

Maison de transition de Montreal, CHC St-Laurent
6060 Renoir Street, Montreal North, QC, H1G 2N8
François Bérnard, Director (514) 326-8577

Pavillon Prosper Boulanger
11931 Notre-Dame Street East, Montreal East, QC, H1B 2Y4
Sophie Sarda, Assistant Clinical Director (514) 640-5361

Salvation Army Abris D'Espoir (females)
860 Rue Guy, Montreal, QC, H3J 1T4 (514) 934-5615

Salvation Army Centre Booth
880 Rue Guy, Montreal, QC, H3J 1T4 (514) 932-2214

Salvation Army Montclair Residence
4413 Avenue Montclair, Montreal, QC, H4B 2J4
Edith Verstege (514) 481-5638

Salvation Army Service d'Aide à la Famille
1655 Rue Richardson, Montreal, QC, H3K 3J7
Andy Albert (514) 766-2155

Société Emmanuel-Grégoire, CRC Pavillon Emmanuel-Grégoire
11430 Notre-Dame Street East, Montreal East, QC, H1B 2T5
Luc Durocher, Assistant Clinical Director (514) 645-7416

Société Emmanuel-Grégoire, CRC Résidence Emmanuel-Grégoire
2205 Des Ormeaux Street, Montreal, QC, H1B 3B5
Myriam Arsenault, Assistant Clinical Director (514) 354-4742

Prévost
Centre Portage (Adult Substance Abuse Program)
1790 Chemin du Lac Écho, Prévost, QC, J0R 1T0
François Bourdon, Director (450) 224-2944

Quebec City
Aumônerie Communautaire (Foyer Maufils)
560 St-Joseph Street East, Québec, QC, G1K 3B8
Francis Gagnon (418) 527-3700

Maison D'Entraide l'Arc-en-Ciel
346 du Parvis Street, P.O. Box 30010, Québec, QC, G1K 8Y1
Vincent Roy (418) 522-2915

Maison Painchaud
1415 Saint-Pascal Avenue, Québec, QC, G1J 4R1
Christine Lamarche (418) 661-0203

Salvation Army Hôtellerie pour Hommes
14 Cote du Palais, Québec, QC, G1R 4H8
June Carver (418) 692-3956

Salvation Army Service d'Aide à la Famille
1125 Chemin de la Canardiere, Québec, QC, G1J 2C3
Donald Carver (418) 641-0050

Rimouski
Le Répit du Passant
205 St-Cyprien Street, Rimouski, QC, G5L 3J4
Marguerite Pelletier, Director (418) 722-6559

Rivière-du-Loup
CRC Arc-en-Soi Inc.
60 Iberville Street, Rivière-du-Loup, QC, G5R 1H1
Sylvie Legacé, Executive Director (418) 862-3721

Roberval
CRC Roberval
96 Gagné Avenue, Roberval, QC, G8H 1E5
André Bonneau, Executive Director (418) 275-7017

Sainte-Angèle-de-Prémont
Résidence Lafleur Inc.
101 Lac Lambert, Sainte-Angèle-de-Prémont,
Maskinongé County, QC, J0K 1R0
Réjean Bergeron, Director (819) 268-2348

Sainte-Alphonse-Rodriguez
Waseskun Healing Center
501 Boulevard Marguerite d'Youvillle, P.O. Box 1159,
Saint-Alphonse-Rodriguez, QC, J0K 1W0
Stan Cudek, Executive Director (450) 883-2034

Sainte-Augustin-de-Desmaures
Résidence le Portail (females)
1240 route de Fossambault Nord,
Sainte-Augustin-de-Desmaures, QC, G3A 1W8
Pierre Vachon, Director (418) 878-2867

Sainte-Béatrix
Maison de Thérapie L'Entre Temps (females)
1011 Chantal Poulin Street, Sainte-Béatrix, QC, J0K 1Y0
Serge Valiquette, Director (450) 883-8191

Sainte-Pacôme
Centre la Montée (males and females)
127-B Galarneau Street, Saint-Pacôme, QC, G0L 3X0
Réjeanne Hudon (418) 852-2866

Sainte-Jérôme
Manoir Rose-Alyne (senior males)
972 Boulevard de la Salette, Sainte-Jérôme, QC, J5L 2K1
Johanne Gravel or Philipp Williams (450) 569-2222

Sherbrooke
CRC Maison la Traverse
219 Montréal Street, Sherbrooke, QC, J1H 1E4
Gaétan Cloutier, Executive Director (819) 564-8198

Service d'aide Bruno Dandenault CRC Centre l'Étape
605 Cégep Street, Sherbrooke, QC, J1E 2K1
Gaétan Cloutier, Executive Director (819) 564-5043

Trois-Rivières
La Maison Carignan (males and females)
7515 Parent Boulevard, Trois-Rivières, QC, G9A 5E1
Yvon Carignan, Executive Director (819) 373-9435

Maison Radisson
962 Rue Sainte-Geneviève, P.O. Box 1075,
Trois-Rivières, QC, G9A 5K4
Daniel Bellemare (819) 379-3598 ext. 221

Vallée Jonction
CRC Beauce (a division of Réhabilitation de Beauce)
294 Bisson Street, Vallée Jonction, QC, G0S 3J0
Michèle Michaud, Executive Director (418) 253-6764

Atlantic Region
New Brunswick
Fredericton
Island View House CRC
65 Brunswick Street, Fredericton, NB, E3B 1G5
Ross Randall, House Director (506) 444-5611

Moncton
Cannell House CRF – Atlantic Human Services
122 Church Street, Moncton, NB, E1C 4Z6
Brian MacLeod, Program Manager (506) 857-4206

Salvation Army Greenfield House (males and females)
64 Gordon Street, P.O. Box 1121, Moncton, NB, E1C 8P6
Cpt. Sherrie Williams (506) 858-9486

Saint John
Coverdale Centre for Women
148 Waterloo Street, Saint John, NB, E2L 3R1
Betty MacDonald (506) 634-1649

Hart House – John Howard Society CBRF
120 Carleton Street, Saint John, NB, E2L 2Z7
Ron Hines (506) 643-2013

Newfoundland and Labrador

Labrador

Labrador Friendship Centre (males and females)
49 Grenfell Street, P.O. Box 767, Station B,
Happy Valley-Goose Bay, Labrador, A0P 1E0
Jennifer Hefler-Elson, Executive Director (709) 896-8302

St. John's

Emmanuel House (males and females)
83 Cochrane Street, St. John's, NL, A1C 3L7
Jocelyn Greene, Executive (709) 754-2072

Salvation Army New Hope Community Centre –
Addiction and Rehabilitation Services
18 Springdale Street, St. John's, NL, A1E 2R1
Katie Bungay (709) 739-0290

Howard House – John Howard Society
7 Garrison Hill, St. John's, A1C 3Y7
Rod Harris (709) 722-1849

Stephenville

West Bridge House – John Howard Society (males and females)
92 West Street, Stephenville, NL, A2N 1E4
Audrey Gracie, House Manager (709) 643-2903

Nova Scotia

Dartmouth

Salvation Army Railton House
318 Windmill Road, Dartmouth, NS, B3A 1H5
Bob DeMont (902) 465-2690

Frenchvale

Talbot House
1777 Frenchvale Road, Frenchvale, NS, B2A 4E2
Paul J. Abbass (902) 794-2852

Halifax

Adsum House for Women & Children
2421 Brunswick Street, Halifax, NS, B3K 2Z4
Sheri Lecker, Executive Director (902) 423-5049

The Margurite Centre (females)
3178 St. Margaret's Bay Road, P.O. Box 1, Lakeside, NS, B3T 1M6
Beverly Hickman Southcott (902) 876-0006

Nehiley House (females)
3170 Romans Avenue, Halifax, NS, B2L 3W9
Stacey Dort, Director of Community Corrections (902) 454-5532

Salvation Army Centre of Hope
2044 Gottingen Street, Halifax, NS, B3K 3A9
Ross Bungay (902) 422-2363

Sir Sandford Fleming House – St. Leonard's Society
2549 Brunswick Street, Halifax, NS, B3K 2Z5
Michelle MacRae, House Director (902) 423-1219

Sydney

Howard House of Cape Breton (males and females)
P.O. Box 384, 262 Bentinck Street, Sydney, NS, B1P 6H2
Jeanette Thompson, Executive Director (902) 562-2306

Elizabeth Fry Satellite Apartment
14C Levatte Crescent, Sydney, NS, B1N 3K3
Darlene MacEachern, Executive Director (902) 539-6165

Truro

Lavers House – Dismas Society
454 Queen Street, Truro, NS, B2N 2C6
Charlene Buote, Executive Director (902) 893-7226

Prince Edward Island

Charlottetown

Addiction Services – Queens Region Detox (males and females)
P.O. Box 2000, Charlottetown, PE, C1A 7N8
Kay Trainor, Manager (902) 368-4047

Addiction Services – Queens Region Rehab (males and females)
P.O. Box 2000, Charlottetown, PE, C1A 7N8
Dan Malone (902) 368-4288

Lacey House (females)
283 Fitzroy Street, Charlottetown, PE, C1A 1S8
Mary Clark, House Supervisor (902) 368-4083

Mt. Herbert Provincial Addictions Treatment Facility
(males and females)
P.O. Box 2000, Charlottetown, PE, C1A 7N8
Darren O'Handley (902) 368-4120

Talbot House
205 Kent Street, Charlottetown, PE, C1A 1P1
Irene Shankel-Birch (902) 368-4297

Summerside

St. Eleanor's House
571 South Drive, Summerside, PE, C1N 3Z5
Evelyn Weeks (902) 888-8386

Jail Terms and Slang

10.9 – grade ten educational level needed for many institutional jobs
532 – a form for transferring jail funds
810 – a court application that puts one-year conditions on a released prisoner

A&D – admitting and discharge
adjudicate – to resolve an institutional charge
APR – accelerated parole review; the earliest parole for non-violent first-time offenders, abolished in 2011
AWCP – assistant warden correctional programs
AWMS – assistant warden management services
AWOL – absent without official leave

back your play – to support another prisoner's story or actions
B.I.F.A. – Black Inmates and Friends Assembly
Bay, The – Collins Bay Institution, Kingston, Ontario
bird – idiot
bit – sentence given
bitch, the – life sentence for habitual offenders; referred to as having been DOed
block rep – prisoner spokesperson elected by others on their block
blues – previous colour of clothes in provincial prisons
boss – a guard

bounce – to tell or force a prisoner to leave a range or cellblock

box thief – a prisoner who steals from other prisoners

brew – homemade beer

bridge/bubble bandit – a prisoner who loiters around the guards' bridge

Brook, The – Millbrook Correctional Centre located near Peterborough, Ontario, which closed in 2003

brown eye – anus

bucket – local jail

bug – an irritable or tiresome prisoner who bugs others (*see also* dunker)

bug juice – medication

bug out – to snap or lose it

bulks – lists to sign for goods and charity drives

bullpen – a holding area for prisoners at court or A&D area

bulls – guards

bumbaclot – black slang meaning "a tampon," i.e., a worthless thing

burp a brew – releasing pressure from a distilling brew

buttyboy – black slang meaning "buttboy," i.e., a homosexual

CC – correctional centre (prison)

CCC – community correctional centre (high-security halfway house)

CCRA – Corrections and Conditional Release Act; allegedly governs the federal correctional system from incarceration to parole expiry

CDs – Commissioners Directives; a set of prison rules and procedures compiled by the Commissioner of Corrections

CO – Classification/Correctional Officer

CPIC – Canadian Police Information Centre; a criminal databank maintained by the RCMP

CRF – community residential facility; also called a CCC

CSIS – Canadian Security Intelligence Service

camp – the lowest security federal facility, often without a fence; also referred to as a Club Fed

can – a local jail; *also* a can of tobacco

cell studies – school work done in one's cell

chain – prisoners chained together for transfer

champ – a dependable, trustworthy, solid person who gets things done for others

check-in – a prisoner who checks into protective custody (PC)

cheese eater – an informant; also called a rat

chicken hawk – someone who preys sexually on young males

choke off – to strangle

chonie bars – chocolate bars

Christmas drive/package – a yearly purchase of limited goods from an outside grocer

clique – a small exclusive group of people

Club Fed – *see* camp

CMT – case management team

CO II – correctional officer level two

con – a convict; *also* to convince someone to do or believe something

contraband – forbidden, banned, prohibited, smuggled, or illegal items

cooler – solitary confinement

coop – jail, or specifically the pigeon coop for protective custody (PC)

copper – a guard

cop to it – to confess to or take the blame for something

CORCAN – The Correctional Service of Canada's prison factory program, where beds, clothing, tables, and other government products are made. Located in some federal pens.

correctional plan – a written report done by a parole officer (PO), compiled from data interpreted from tests and prisoner interviews upon arrival at a federal reception prison. It predicts chances of reoffending and recommends institutional programs to reduce chances of reoffending.

cornhole – anus

count-up – counting of prisoners done twice or more daily

crack(ed) – to talk, as in "don't crack to him"; *also* to confess under duress

crank – heroin

cut someone's grass – to get in on someone else's good fortune without their approval

CX – a correctional officer

DC – detention centre (prison)

DO – detention order; *also* dangerous offender

dead time – time spent in jail waiting for court

detainment act/hearing – legislation forcing prisoners deemed high-risk to serve their entire sentence

deuce-less – the maximum provincial sentence of two years less one day

diddler – a child molester; *also* in England, a professional forger or "scribbler"

digger – solitary confinement

dime drop – "someone dropped a dime into a phone to rat"; *also* a ten-year sentence

dis – to act with disrespect, as in "don't dis me"

do a smash – to shoot heroin

do him – to assault or kill another person

Don, The – the old Don Jail in Toronto, Ontario; also called "the dungeon"

down below – the penitentiary; often called "down under," which is mistaken for slang meaning Australia

drift – a term used to tell someone to beat it, but it can also be used jokingly

drives – sales of assorted items, e.g., chips, magazines, food and other goods, to raise money for groups
drum – a cell or cage
ducket – an institutional charge
dump truck – a crappy lawyer
dunker – a homemade electric prong for boiling water. Also called a bug.

ETA – escorted temporary absence
East, The – The Toronto East Detention Centre in Toronto, Ontario

FPS # – fingerprint service number
faint hope clause – recently revised and fainter than ever (*see also* judicial review)
falldown – idiot
federal – the national government as opposed to provincial
fence clearance – Given to trusties allowed outside the wall. No longer allowed except at camp.
fish – first-time arrivals
fishing line – a piece of string used as a fishing line by prisoners to pass messages and small items from cell to cell
fit – a hypodermic needle
furback – a rat

GATU – Guelph Assessment and Treatment Unit
GP – general population
GVI – Grand Valley Institute for federal women, located in Kitchener, Ontario
gated – *see* 810
gearbox – an idiot; *also* a homosexual
ghost chain (train) – a constant transfer mode used by jails and police to uproot prisoners from their ties to the community while awaiting a court date; also known as “diesel therapy” in

the U.S.

gladiator school – Collins Bay Institution in Kingston, Ontario; *also* any place with higher incidences of violence

go-boy – an escapee

good time – an early release from system during the final third of a sentence, earned for good behaviour; no longer applies to federal time

goof – the most insulting name to be called in prison; *also* an invitation to fight

goon squad – a group of guards, especially the riot squad

Goose, The – the prison transfer bus; once blue and called the Blue Goose

greens – federal prison clothing required to be worn during work hours; white for kitchen work

grievance official – a paper complaint by a prisoner against the institution

gun/tat gun – a tattoo gun/machine

gunning someone off – staring

habeas corpus – a writ to bring a person to court or release from unlawful imprisonment

hack – a guard

hammerhawk – a person who stares at prisoners in the shower or while they are dressing

hard time – difficult time in prison, especially in maximum security

Haven, The – Millhaven Institution, a maximum-security prison in Bath near Kingston, Ontario

heatbag – a prisoner drawing unwanted attention

heavy – a prisoner who is or thinks they are a big shot

heavy load – a prisoner who constantly asks for help or items

hideout – a prisoner who checks into protective custody (PC)

holdout – a prisoner who won't surrender goodies

hole – solitary confinement/segregation
hook up – to connect one person to another
hoop it – to stash drugs in one's anus
hound – a rape hound
house – a cell
house of shame (or pain) – prison

IPSO – institutional preventive security officer
ISO – information security officer
ITU – inmate transition unit
IWF – inmate welfare fund; it takes several dollars from each prisoners pay for cable TV and to purchase items needed by the entire population, such as fridges, kettles, toasters, etc.
ink work – tattoo work
inmate committee – a group of prisoners voted in annually by other prisoners to settle matters
institutionalized – prisoners who become comfortable and dependant on the system
institutionally gay – prisoners who, often jokingly, justify homosexuality by claiming it's all right when trapped in custody
ion scanner – a machine that scans visitors IDs for traces of drugs; the machine is often faulty, resulting in visitors being denied
it's a go – an insult that is a call to fight
it's a good go – an easy place to do time

JP – justice of the peace
jackrabbit parole – an escape
jailbait – an underage girl
jail merchant – a prisoner who obtains free institutional goods and sells them to other prisoners
jam – guts
jazz – heroin
Jerkworth – Warkworth Institution located outside Campbellford,

Ontario

Joe grind – a person who hits on another's woman

jointman – a prisoner whose only interest is in working for himself and the Man

J-unit – Millhaven Institution's maximum-security unit

judicial review – allows prisoners serving life to apply for an earlier parole after fifteen years; also known as the "faint hope clause"

jug-up – mealtime

juice – interest paid on loans or debts; *also* steroids

KP – Kingston Penitentiary located in Kingston, Ontario; Canada's oldest pen

keeper – warden

key-up – a call for a guard, usually to open a door

kid – a young immature prisoner; *also* a younger prisoner who hangs with an older prisoner and who may participate in homosexual acts; can be used insultingly or humorously

kiddie bit – a very short sentence

kife – something detested such as bad food

kite – a message on paper sent to another prisoner or to a guard

LOAP – loss of all privileges

LTSO – long-term supervision order

life on the installment plan – a prisoner who keeps returning to prison is referred to as doing life on the installment plan

load – a load of prisoners being shipped

lockdown – locking (doors) of the entire institution

lockup – count-up or nighttime when prisoners are locked up

loon – an idiot

louie – a lieutenant

lug – to mule something

MAU – Millhaven Assessment Unit
Man, The – a guard
mandatory parole/release – automatic parole after two thirds of a sentence, now called "statutory release"
mandatory sentencing – a growing list of select crimes with mandatory sentences that a judge cannot alter
max – maximum security
meth – methadone; *also* methamphetamine
misconduct – an institutional charge; also called a "ducat" in the U.S.
midnight special – old American slang meaning a pardon
Mission Statement – CSC propaganda
mouse – any small makeshift object tied to the end of a fishing line to help propel it
mouthpiece – a lawyer; *also* a mouthy person
mule – someone used to transport drugs or other items
muscled – forced to give up something or to submit to something

nailed – caught
NG or NFG – no good or no fucking good
no inmate contact – a prisoner not allowed contact with other prisoners
no parts – no guts
number four – heroin

OMS – Offender Management System (computer data files)
on charge – a prisoner facing disciplinary charges
on the cuff – on credit
OP – off privileges

P4W – prison for women
PC – protective custody
PFVs – private family visits

PO – parole officer

package thief – anyone who steals a drug package

paperwork – official documentation of a prisoner's offence or other data

patch – a payment or a trade of something such as information, guns, money, or stolen property to deal away a charge, debt, etc.

pay levels – six pay levels are available in the federal system

Pen Squad – a special squad of provincial police that investigates alleged crimes occurring in Ontario federal prisons

permit – an official document given to prisoners to show proof of ownership of property or allowed possession of tools, etc.

phone bug/hog – a prisoner who use phones excessively

pigeon – a rat; *also* a metal detector

pillow-biter – a homosexual, i.e., bites a pillow to stifle the sound

piped – being attacked with a pipe

pipeline – the prison grapevine

popped – busted

Prisoners' Justice Day – August 10th marks a day of fasting and work refusal to remember fallen prisoners

puffer – a person who enjoys giving oral sex

pull-up – to get one's act together

pumpkin suit – a provincial orange jumpsuit

punk – derogatory U.S. slang equal to "bitch" or Canada's slang word "goof"

punked-off – being ignored or disrespected by another

pussyclot – black slang meaning "a tampon," i.e., a useless dirty thing

quarterman – prisoner who serves others locked up on a range

quiet time – time alone in a cell or segregation; it can also mean time alone in a trailer in federal

ROPE Squad – the Repeat Offender Parole Enforcement Squad is used by the police as surveillance or to hunt down parolees and suspects

RTC – regional treatment centre

range rep – a prisoner elected by prisoners to represent a cellblock or range

ran to the Man – informed guards

reception – the A&D area of a jail; one in each province receives all federal prisoners

rec-up – called by guards, usually after dinner, to announce the yard/gym is open

redbag(ged) – a property bag used to ship a prisoner's possessions; to be redbagged means to be shipped out

rehash – a reusable postal stamp

revoked – having parole revoked

residency hearing – a meeting of CSC officials to tell a prisoner they will not be released at two-thirds but instead placed in a halfway house or CRC/CRF

rig – drug-injecting paraphernalia

rock star – a crack addict

rolled or rolled over – ratted

rossclot – black slang meaning "a tampon," i.e., a useless thing

rounder – a person who knows their way around prison or the underworld

SHU – Special Handling Unit, Canada's highest security prison located at Ste-Anne-des-Plaines Institution in Quebec

SRD – statutory release date occurring at two-thirds of a full sentence

sally port – the entrance to an institution, usually to the A&D area

Schedule 1 and 2 – Schedule 1 refers to indictable offences (Criminal Code); Schedule 2 refers to indictable offences under the Narcotic Control Act; non-schedule offences are ones not contained in Schedule 1 or 2 of the Corrections and Conditional Release Act (CCRA)

screw – a guard

seg – segregation/solitary confinement

server – prisoners who serve food

shaking it rough – a prisoner having a very difficult time

shank – a homemade knife

shine – homemade alcohol

shipped out – transferred to another location

shiv – *see* shank

shoot up – to inject drugs

shooter – a prisoner who is or acts like a big shot or tries to be involved in everything

short-timer – a prisoner with a short sentence or who is very close to being released

showerhawk – a homosexual who glances in showers

SIS – Supervisor, Institutional Services; those responsible for providing basic needs such as food, clothing, canteen services, etc.

six up – a term used to warn another prisoner of approaching guards

skiddler – a pedophile

skin beef – a sex charge

skinner – a rapist or skin hound

skittles – candy used to entice children for sex

slash-up – a person who slashes their wrists

sluff – ignore

smash-up – a prisoner who gets upset and smashes everything

social events – events in an institution where outside people visit

solid – a dependable person who won't squeal

special handling – prisoners who are extremely violent or need special attention

spit meth – when prisoners on the meth program swallow in front of a nurse and then moments later try to spit it back up unseen

stand-up count – a count taken regularly where prisoners are required to stand

stand-up guy – a solid person

star – the black equivalent of saying "man," i.e., "Hey, man" or "Yeah, man"

stat – statutory release

still – a boiling apparatus for making homemade brew into shine

stooge – an idiot

stoolie – a rat

stores – *see* SIS

story up – an expression announcing that someone is about to tell a fictional story

street-charged – an institutional offence taken to outside authorities

striker – a strip of carbon for striking a match; *also* a hitman for biker gangs; *also*, in the U.S., a three-strike offender

string-up – a suicide

suitcase – *see* hoop it

supercoop – protective custody (PC)

supercop – a cop or guard who overdoes their job

superjail – a large maximum-security provincial institution

supermax – a super-maximum-security prison

sweet kid – a younger prisoner who hangs out with an older one

TAP – temporary absence pass

TD unit – temporary detention unit, usually regional for parole violators

taken down – busted

taking it dry – not responding to direct insults from another prisoner

top left – a saying often followed with a gesture of placing the right hand or fist over the heart to express truth or loyalty

tossing salad – a homosexual act using salad dressing to kiss ass

tossing a cell – when guards tear apart a cell during a search
trailer visits – see PFVs
truckers – mules
trusties – prisoners trusted by guards with slightly more freedom
turnkey – old slang meaning "guards"
turtles – guards dressed in riot gear
two-for-one/three-for-one – time given by a judge for dead time already served (abolished in 2011); *also* canteen items acquired on credit to be paid back two for one

UTA – unescorted temporary absence; official permission to leave
unit – a living unit; *also* pop, chips, chocolate bar, etc.
unlawfully at large – a parolee on the run
up it – a request to surrender something

V&C – the visiting and correspondence area
Valley of the Dolls – Grand Valley Institute (GVI) or any prison for women (P4W)
Ville, The – Joyceville Institution north of Kingston, Ontario
voire dire – a legal term referring to a trial within a trial to determine admissibility of evidence

Wally World – Warkworth Institution near Campbellford, Ontario
warrant expiry date – the last day of an entire sentence, now extended by an 810 or an LTSO
waterhead – an idiot
weekender – a prisoner sentenced to weekends in a local jail
West, The – Toronto West Detention Centre in Toronto, Ontario
white shirt – guards who are management as opposed to regular guards
wigger – a white person trying to act like a black person
wolf – a sex hound or rapist
work-up – called by guards at work time

yard-up – called by guards when the yard is opened

zeen – black slang meaning "okay" or "you understand"

zip – a gun; *also* peashooter, homemade one-shot gun

References Used in the Foreword

Ballinger, Anette. 2003. Researching and Redefining State Crime in *Unmasking the Crimes of the Powerful.* S. Tombs and D. Whyte, eds. New York: Peter Lang Publishing: 219-238.

Bunker, Edward. 2000. *Education of a Felon.* New York: St. Martin's Griffin.

Carlson, L. Wayne. 2001. *Breakfast with the Devil.* Toronto: Insomniac Press.

Caron, Roger. 1978. *Go Boy! Memoirs of a Life Behind Bars.* Toronto: McGraw-Hill Ryerson.

Charrière, Henri. 1970. *Papillon.* June P. Wilson and Walter Michaels, trans. New York: Morrow.

Chessman, Caryl. 1954. *Cell 2455, Death Row.* Westport, CT: Greenwood Press.

Clemmer, Donald. 1940. *The Prison Community.* New York: Holt, Rinehart & Winston.

Dailey, Lige Jr. 2001. Reentry: Prospects for Postrelease Success in *Prison Masculinities.* D. Sabo, T. Kupers, and W. London, eds. Philadelphia: Temple University Press: 255-264.

Davis, Nanette J. 1975. *Sociological Constructions of Deviance.* Dubuque, IA: Wm. C. Brown Co. Publishers.

Dostoyevsky, Fyodor. 1914. *Crime and Punishment.* London: W. Heinemann.

Dreyfus, Alfred. 1901. *Five Years of My Life.* James Mortimer, trans. London: Newnes.

Folsom Prison Convicts. 1976. *The Hardened Criminal.* Millbrae,

CA: Celestial Arts.

Frazier, Mansfield B. 1995. *From Behind the Wall: Commentary on Crime, Punishment, Race, and the Underclass by a Prison Inmate.* New York: Paragon House.

Gaucher, Robert. 1991. Organizing Inside: Prison Justice Day (August 10th) – A Non-Violent Response to Penal Repression. *Journal of Prisoners on Prisons* (Autumn) 3, Nos. 1-2: 93-110.

Genet, Jean. 1964. *The Thief's Journal.* New York: Grove.

Gonnerman, Jennifer. 2004. *Life on the Outside: The Prison Odyssey of Elaine Bartlett.* New York: Farrar, Straus & Giroux: 368.

Hanks, Eva Evelyn. 2000. *Test of Faith.* Toronto: Canadian Scholars' Press.

Harding, Sandra. 1987. Conclusion: Epistemological Questions in *Feminism and Methodology.* Bloomington, IN: Indiana University Press: 181-190.

Harding, Sandra. 1998. Borderlands Epistemologies in *Is Science Multicultural? Postcolonialisms, Feminisms, and Epistemologies.* Bloomington, IN: Indiana University Press.

Harris, Jean. 1988. *They Always Call Us Ladies.* New York: Charles Scribner's Sons.

Hassine, Victor. 1995. Runaway Prison or Mr. Smith goes to Harrisburg in *Journal of Prisoners on Prisons* 6, No.1: 5-10.

Irwin, John. 1970. *The Felon.* Englewood Cliffs, NJ: Prentice-Hall.

Irwin, John. 2005. *The Warehouse Prison: Disposal of the New Dangerous Class.* Los Angeles: Roxbury Publishing.

Jackson, Bruce. 1972. *In the Life: Versions of the Criminal Experience.* New York: Holt, Rinehart & Winston.

Jacobs, James B. 1977. *Stateville: The Penitentiary in Mass Society.* Chicago: University of Chicago Press.

Kirby, Sandra, and Kate McKenna. 1989. *Experience Research Social Change: Methods from the Margins.* Toronto: Garamond Press.

Lerner, Jimmy A. 2002. *You Got Nothing Coming: Notes from a Prison Fish.* New York: Broadway Books.

MacLean, Brian D. 1991. Master Status, Stigma, Termination and Beyond in *Journal of Prisoners on Prisons* (Autumn) 3, Nos. 1-2: 111-118.

Melnitzer, Julius. 1995. *Maximum, Minimum, Medium: A Journey Through Canadian Prisons.* Toronto: Key Porter Books.

Olsen, Jack. 2001. *Last Man Standing: The Tragedy and Triumph of Geronimo Pratt.* New York: Anchor Books.

Rinser, Luise. 1987. *A Woman's Prison Journal: Germany, 1944.* New York: Schocken Books: 151.

Rodriguez, Luis J. 1993. *Always Running: La Vida Loca, Gang Days in L.A.* Willimantic, CT: Curbstone Press.

Ross, Jeffrey Ian, and Stephen C. Richards. 2003. *Convict Criminology.* Belmont, CA: Wadsworth.

Shaw, Clifford R. 1930. *The Jack-Roller: A Delinquent Boy's Own Story.* Chicago: University of Chicago Press.

Shelden, Randall G. 2001. *Controlling the Dangerous Classes.* Boston: Allyn & Bacon.

Solzhenitsyn, Aleksandr I. 1974. *The Gulag Archipelago.* New York: Harper and Row.

Solzhenitsyn, Aleksandr I. 1975. *The Gulag Archipelago, Two.* New York: Harper and Row.

Solzhenitsyn, Aleksandr I. 1976. *The Gulag Archipelago, Three.* New York: Harper and Row.

Sutherland, Edwin H. 1937. *The Professional Thief.* Chicago: University of Chicago Press.

Sykes, Gresham M. 1958. *The Society of Captives.* Princeton, NJ: Princeton University Press.

Taylor, Jon Marc. 1995. The Resurrection of the Dangerous Classes in *The Journal of Prisoners on Prison* 6, No. 2: 7-16.

Thomas, Jim. 1993. *Doing Critical Ethnography.* Newbury Park, CA: Sage Publications, Qualitative Research Methods No. 26.

Further Reading

Adelberg, Ellen, and Claudia Currie, eds. 1991. *Too Few to Count: Canadian Women in Conflict with the Law.* Vancouver: Press Gang Publishers.

Anderson, Gail S. 2006. *Biological Influences on Criminal Behaviour.* Boca Raton, Florida: CRC Press.

Caron, Roger. 1978. *Go-Boy!: Memoirs of a Life Behind Bars.* Whitby, ON: McGraw-Hill Ryerson.

Caron, Roger. 1985. *Bingo!: The Horrifying Eyewitness Account of a Prison Riot.* Toronto: Methuen.

Cayley, David. 1998. *The Expanding Prison: The Crisis in Crime and Punishment and the Search for Alternatives.* Toronto: House of Anansi Press.

Culhane, Claire. 1979. *Barred from Prison: A Personal Account.* Vancouver: Pulp Press.

Culhane, Claire. 1984. *Still Barred from Prison: Social Injustice in Canada.* Montreal: Black Rose Books.

Culhane, Claire. 1991. *No Longer Barred from Prison: Social Injustice in Canada.* Montreal: Black Rose Books.

Dineen, Dr. Tana. 2000. *Manufacturing Victims: What the Psychology Industry Is Doing to People.* Third edition. Robert Davies Multimedia.

Dubé, Richard. 2002. *The Haven: A True Story of Life in the Hole.* Toronto: HarperCollins Canada.

Faith, Karlene. 1993. *Unruly Women: The Politics of Confinement.*

Vancouver: Press Gang Publishers.

Gabor, Thomas. 1994. *Everyone Does It!: Crime by the Public.* Toronto: U of T Press.

Garland, David. 2001. *The Culture of Control: Crime and Social Order in Contemporary Society.* Chicago: U of Chicago Press.

Gosselin, Luc. 1982. *Prisons in Canada.* Montreal: Black Rose Books.

Green, Ross Gordon. 1998. *Justice in Aboriginal Communities: Sentencing Alternatives.* Saskatoon: Purich Publishing.

Hennessy, Peter H. 1999. *Canada's Big House: The Dark History of Kingston Penitentiary.* Toronto: Dundurn Press

Jackson, Michael. 2002. *Justice behind the Walls: Human Rights in Canadian Prisons.* Vancouver: Douglas & McIntyre.

John Howard Society of Canada. 2005. *Prison Voices.* Kingston, ON: John Howard Society of Canada.

Kershaw, Anne, with Mary Lasovich. 1991. *Rock-A-Bye Baby: A Death Behind Bars.* Toronto: McClelland & Stewart.

Marron, Kevin. 1996. *The Slammer: The Crisis in Canada's Prison System.* Toronto: Doubleday Canada.

McNeil, Gérard, and Sharon Vance. 1978. *Cruel and Usual.* Ottawa: Deneau and Greenberg.

Melnitzer, Julius. 1995. *Maximum, Medium, Medium: A Journey Though Canadian Prisons.* Toronto: Key Porter.

Morris, Ruth. 1989. *Crumbling Walls: Why Prisons Fail.* Oakville, ON: Mosaic Press.

Morris, Ruth. 1995. *Penal Abolition: The Practical Choice.* Toronto: Canadian Scholars' Press.

Murphy, P.J., Loyd Johnsen, and Jennifer Murphy. 2002. *Paroled for Life: Interviews with Parolees Serving Life Sentences.* Vancouver: New Star Books.

Oliver, Peter. 1998. *"Terror to Evil-Doers": Prisons and Punishment in Nineteenth-Century Ontario.* Toronto: U of T Press.

Solomon, Arthur. 1994. *Eating Bitterness: A Vision Beyond Prison*

Walls. Toronto: New Canada Press.

Stern, Vivien. 2006. *Creating Criminals: Prisons and People in a Market Society.* Blackpoint, NS: Fernwood Publishing.

Tadman, Peter. 2001. *Fallen Angel: Inside Canada's Toughest Women's Prison.* Calgary: Detselig Enterprises.

Waldram, James. 1997. *The Way of the Pipe: Aboriginal Spirituality and Symbolic Healing in Canadian Prisons*. Toronto: U of T Press.

Weaver, John C. 1995. *Crimes, Constables, and Courts: Order and Transgression in a Canadian City, 1816–1970.* Montreal: McGill-Queen's U Press.

Yates, J. Michael. 1993. *Line Screw: My Twelve Riotous Years Working Behind Bars in Some of Canada's Toughest Jails.* Toronto: McClelland & Stewart.

Young, Alan N. 2003. *Justice Defiled: Perverts, Potheads, Serial Killers & Lawyers.* Toronto: Key Porter.

Endnotes

i "Learning and memory," Beth Azar and Bridget Murray, in *Close Up on Psychology: Supplemental Readings from the* APA Monitor on Psychology, Jill Reich, Elizabeth Q. Bulatao, Gary R. VandenBos, and Rhea K. Farberman (eds.) (American Psychological Association, 1997).

ii *Sexual Personae: Art and Decadence from Nefertiti to Emily Dickinson*, Camille Paglia (Yale University Press, 1990): 166.

iii "Pardon me – a guide to the federal pardon program," *CBC News*, January 24, 2004: http://www.cbc.ca/news/background/crime/fed-pardon-program.html, accessed June 25, 2012; "Statistics for national DNA Data Bank," Royal Canadian Mounted Police, May 31, 2012: http://www.rcmp-grc.gc.ca/nddb-bndg/stats-eng.htm, accessed June 25, 2012.

iv Carolyn M. Shafer and Marilyn Frye, "Rape and Respect" in *Feminism and Philosophy*, Vetterling-Braggin et al., eds. (Littlefield, Adams & Co., 1977).

v "Doing 'Dead Time': Custody before trial," John Howard Society of Ontario, Fact Sheet #17, January 2002.

vi "Police officers, by province and territory," Statistics Canada, December 12, 2011: http://www.statcan.gc.ca/tables-tableaux/sum-som/l01/cst01/legal05a-eng.htm, accessed June 25, 2012; Federation of Law Societies of Canada, http://www.flsc.ca/en/canadas-law-societies/, accessed June 25, 2012.

vii "Legal aid spending up 4%, says StatsCan," Gail J. Cohen, Legal Feeds: The Blog of *Canadian Lawyer & Law Times*, April 20, 2011: http://www.canadian lawyermag.com/legalfeeds/Legal-aid-spending-up-4-says-StatsCan.html, accessed June 25, 2012.

viii "Legal aid lawyers get pay raise," Tracey Tyler, *Toronto Star*, April 1, 2003; "Ontario AG, lawyers agree to legal-aid talks," Shannon Kari, *National Post*, December 3, 2009: A8.

ix "HIV & HCV Crisis in Federal Prisons, According to New CSC Report," *Cell Count #58*, Summer 2010: 7.

x *The Silent System: An Enquiry into Prisoners Who Suicide*, B. E. Burtch and R. V. Ericson (Toronto Centre for Criminology, 1979): 7.

xi *Brain Gym Handbook*, Paul E. and Gail Dennision (Educational Kinesiology Foundation, 1989).

xii "The Psychological Effects of 60 Days in Administrative Segregation," Ivan Zinger and Cherami Wichmann, Research Branch (Correctional Service of Canada, March 1999): 65.

xiii *Oscar: An Inquiry into the Nature of Sanity*, Peter J. Wilson (Random House, 1974).

xiv "A One-Day Snapshot of Inmates in Canada's Adult Correctional Facilities," David Robinson, Frank J. Porporino, and William A. Millson, *Juristat*, Vol. 18, No. 8, Statistics Canada, Cat. No. 85-002-XIE: 4-5.

xv Freeing the Human Spirit newsletter, Spring 2010: 6.

xvi "Justice Spending in Canada, 2000/01," Andrea Taylor-Butts, *Juristat*, Vol. 22, No. 11.

xvii "Adult correctional services," *The Daily*, Statistics Canada, October 26, 2010: http://www.statcan.gc.ca/daily-quotidien/101026/dq101026b-eng.htm, accessed June 25, 2012.

xviii *Justice Defiled: Perverts, Potheads, Serial Killers & Lawyers,* Alan N. Young (Key Porter, 2003).

xix "Traditional and new perspectives for understanding and researching gender and aggression," Kelly Taylor, FORUM on Corrections Research, Vol. 19, No. 1, September 2007.

xx "How Quickly They Forget!" Harold Levy, *AIDWYC Journal* (No. 3), April 2003: 17.

xxi "Corrections and Conditional Release in Canada – A General Primer 2010," Public Safety Canada: http://www.publicsafety.gc.ca/res/cor/rep/2010-03-nt-bkgr-eng.aspx, accessed June 25, 2012.

xxii "Police-reported crime statistics in Canada, 2010: Highlights," *Juristat*, Statistics Canada, Cat. No. 85-002-X.

xxiii "Adult criminal court statistics," *The Daily*, Statistics Canada, July 28, 2010: http://www.statcan.gc.ca/daily-quotidien/100728/dq100728b-eng.htm, accessed February 23, 2012.

xxiv "30% of criminal cases never make trial," Shannon Kari, *National Post*, February 21, 2009: A12.

xxv "Adult criminal court statistics," *The Daily*, Statistics Canada, July 28, 2010: http://www.statcan.gc.ca/daily-quotidien/100728/dq100728b-eng.htm, accessed February 23, 2012.

xxvi "Adult Criminal Court Statistics, 2003/04" Mikhail Thomas, *Juristat*, Vol. 24, No. 12, Statistics Canada, Cat. No. 85-002-XPE.

xxvii "Adult Criminal Court Statistics, 1997-98," Candace Brookbank and Bob Kingsley, *Juristat*, Vol. 24 No. 12, Statistics Canada, Cat. No. 85-002.

xxviii "Adult criminal court statistics, 2008/2009," Jennifer Thomas, *Juristat*, Statistics Canada, Summer 2010: http://www.statcan.gc.ca/pub/85-002-x/2010002/article/11293-eng.htm, accessed February 23, 2012.

xxix "1 in 3 Ontario criminal verdicts overturned," Tracey Tyler, *Toronto Star*, July 6, 2010: A13.

xxx "Adult criminal court statistics, 2008/2009," Jennifer Thomas, *Juristat*, Statistics Canada, Summer 2010: http://www.statcan.gc.ca/pub/85-002-x/2010002/article/11293-eng.htm, accessed February 23, 2012.

xxxi "Adult correctional services," *The Daily*, Statistics Canada, October 26, 2010: http://www.statcan.gc.ca/daily-quotidien/101026/dq101026b-eng.htm, accessed January 24, 2012.

xxxii "Adult correctional services, average counts of offenders in provincial, territorial and federal programs, Table 251-0004," CANSIM, Statistics Canada, January 30, 2012: http://www.statcan.gc.ca/tables-tableaux/sum-som/l01/cst01/legal31a-eng.htm, accessed February 23, 2012.

xxxiii "Adult Criminal Court Statistics, 2003/04" Mikhail Thomas, *Juristat*, Vol. 24, No. 12, Statistics Canada, Cat. No. 85-002-XPE.

xxxiv "The Benevolent Paternalism of Japanese Criminal Justice," Daniel H. Foote, *California Law Review*, Vol. 80, No. 2, March 1992: note 29 at 318.

xxxv "Adult Criminal Court Statistics, 2003/04" Mikhail Thomas, *Juristat*, Vol. 24, No. 12, Statistics Canada, Cat. No. 85-002-XPE.

xxxvi "The Justice Data Factfinder," Richard Du Wors, *Juristat*, Vol. 17, No. 13, Statistics Canada, Cat. No. 85-002-XPE.

xxxvii "Police-reported crime statistics," *The Daily*, Statistics Canada, July 20, 2010: http://www.statcan.gc.ca/daily-quotidien/100720/dq100720a-eng.htm, accessed January 24, 2012.

xxxviii *The Perpetual Prisoner Machine: How America Profits from Crime*, Joel Dyer (Basic Books, 2000): 145-146.

xxxix "Frequently asked questions about the release of offenders," Public Safety Canada, May, 8, 2012: http://www.publicsafety.gc.ca/prg/cor/tls/faq-eng.aspx, accessed June 25, 2012.

xl "A review and estimate of time spent in prison by offenders sentenced for murder," Mark Nafekh, Jillian Flight, Research Branch, Correctional Service of Canada, November 2002: http://www.csc-scc.gc.ca/text/rsrch/briefs/b27/b27-eng.shtml, accessed June 25, 2012.

xli "Fair and Effective Sentencing: A Canadian Approach to Sentencing Policy," Department of Justice Canada, October 2005.

xlii "Frequently asked questions about the release of offenders," Public Safety Canada, May, 8, 2012: http://www.publicsafety.gc.ca/prg/cor/tls/faq-eng.aspx, accessed June 25, 2012.

xliii "The Statistical Information on Recidivism – Revised 1 (SIR-R1) Scale: A Psychometric," Mark Nafekh and Laurence L. Motiuk, Research Branch, Correctional Service of Canada, November 2002: http://www.csc-scc.gc.ca/text/rsrch/reports/r126/r126-eng.shtml, accessed June 25, 2012.

xliv "Report on Plans and Priorities," Correctional Service of Canada, 2008-2009: http://www.tbs-sct.gc.ca/rpp/2008-2009/inst/pen/pen-eng.pdf, accessed June 25, 2012.

xlv "Taser Guns Introduced into Federal Prisons," *Cell Count #45*, Spring 2007: 6.

xlvi *Tasers Backgrounder*, Amnesty International Canada: http://www.amnesty.ca/themes/tasers_backgrounder.php, accessed June 25, 2012.

xlvii "How We Get Labelled," John Cloud, *Time*, January 20, 2003: 70-73.

xlviii "Antisocial personality disorder," *Diagnostic and Statistical Manual of Mental Disorders*, fourth edition (American Psychiatric Association, 2000): 645-650.

xlix "Diagnosis of antisocial personality disorder in two prison populations," R. D. Hare, *American Journal of Psychiatry* 140, 1983: 887-890.

l "Prison Tattoo Project Axed Too Soon, MD Says," *Cell Count #45*, Spring 2007: 7.

li "A One-Day Snapshot of Inmates in Canada's Adult Correctional Facilities," *Juristat*, Vol. 18, No. 8, Statistics Canada, Cat. No. 85-002-XIE.

lii *Manufacturing Victims: What the Psychology Industry Is Doing to People*, Dr. Tana Dineen (Robert Davies Pub, 1996): 162.

liii "The Changing Face of Ontario Corrections: An Assessment," John Howard Society of Ontario, Fact Sheet #15, August 2000.

liv "Incarcerated mothers and their children: Maintaining family ties," Barbara Bloom (American Correctional Association, 1993).

lv "Single mothers by choice: what social science says about the new trend," Jennifer Roback Morse, Institute of Marriage and Family Canada, March 1,

2007: http://www.imfcanada.org/issues/single-mothers-choice, accessed July 19, 2012.

lvi "Rights? What Rights?" Ian Smith, *Cell Count #57*, Spring 2010: 5.

lvii "SFU study confirms statistics can't precisely predict who will reoffend" [press release], Simon Fraser University Public Affairs and Media Relations, retrieved from: http://www.sfu.ca/archive-pamr/media_releases/media_releases_archive/media_release07030701.html, accessed July 19, 2012.

lviii In 2011, the National Parole Board officially changed its name to Parole Board Canada.

lix "Adult correctional services, average counts of offenders, by province, territory, and federal programs," Statistics Canada: http://www.statcan.gc.ca/tables-tableaux/sum-som/l01/cst01/legal31b-eng.htm, accessed July 19, 2012; "Adult Provincial Prisons in Ontario: The current picture and trends," John Howard Society of Ontario, Fact Sheet #12, December 1998: 3.

lx "PBC QuickStats," Parole Board of Canada, April 6, 2011: http://pbc-clcc.gc.ca/infocntr/factsh/parole_stats-eng.shtml, accessed June 25, 2012.

lxi "Highlights: 2007-2008 Parole Board of Canada: (PBC) Performance Monitoring Report," Parole Board of Canada: http://pbc-clcc.gc.ca/infocntr/factsh/hghlghts/highlights_2007-2008-eng.shtml, accessed June 25, 2012.

lxii "Performance Monitoring Report 2009-2010," Performance Measurement Division, National Parole Board: http://pbc-clcc.gc.ca/rprts/pmr/pmr_2009_2010/4-eng.shtml, accessed June 25, 2012.

lxiii "Provincial Parole in Ontario: The case for renewal," John Howard Society of Ontario, Fact Sheet #20, May 2004: 3.

lxiv "The Changing Face of Ontario Corrections: An Assessment," John Howard Society of Ontario, Fact Sheet #15, August 2000: 4.

lxv "The Changing Face of Ontario Corrections: An Assessment," John Howard Society of Ontario, Fact Sheet #15, August 2000: 3.

lxvi "Submission to the Legislative Assembly of Ontario Standing Committee on Public Accounts regarding *Special Report on the Accountability and Value for Money (2000)*," John Howard Society of Ontario, February 22, 2001: 2.

lxvii "Provincial Parole in Ontario: The case for renewal," John Howard Society of Ontario, Fact Sheet #20, May 2004: 3.

lxviii "Demographic Overview of Aboriginal Peoples in Canada and Aboriginal Offenders in Federal Corrections," Correctional Service of Canada: http://www.csc-scc.gc.ca/text/prgrm/abinit/know/10-eng.shtml, accessed June

25, 2012.

lxix "Basic Facts About the Correctional Service of Canada," Correctional Service of Canada, 2005: 18.

lxx "A One-Day Snapshot of Inmates in Canada's Adult Correctional Facilities," David Robinson, Frank J. Porporino, William A. Millson, *Juristat*, Vol. 18, No. 8, Statistics Canada, Cat. No. 85-002-XIE: 13.

lxxi "Orientation and activities of the parole officer," R. Dembo, *Criminology: An Interdisciplinary Journal,* 10(2), 1972: 193-215.

lxxii "Adult Correctional Services in Canada, 2008/2009," Donna Calverley, *Juristat*, Statistics Canada, Fall 2010: http://www.statcan.gc.ca/pub/85-002-x/2010003/article/11353-eng.htm, accessed June 25, 2012.

lxxiii "A One-Day Snapshot of Inmates in Canada's Adult Correctional Facilities," David Robinson, Frank J. Porporino, and William A. Millson, *Juristat*, Vol. 18, No. 8, Statistics Canada, Cat. No. 85-002-XIE: 8.

lxxiv "Mental Health and Drug and Alcohol Addiction in the Federal Correctional System," Report of the Standing Committee on Public Safety and National Security, Kevin Sorenson MP, House of Commons Canada, December 2010: 1.

lxxv "Number of prisoners with mental illness on upswing: report," CBC.ca, November 4, 2005: http://www.cbc.ca/news/canada/story/2005/11/04/MentalPrisoners_051104.html, accessed June 25, 2012.